The Challenge of Effective Speaking
Second Edition

The Challenge
of Effective Speaking
Second Edition

Rudolph F. Verderber
University of Cincinnati

Wadsworth Publishing Company, Inc.
Belmont, California

ISBN–0–534–00233–1

L. C. Cat. Card No. 72–91086

Printed in the United States of America

1 2 3 4 5 6 7 8 9 10—77 76 75 74 73

Preface

The goal of this the second edition of *The Challenge of Effective Speaking* is essentially the same as it was in the first: to provide a clear explanation of speech principles in a form that enables the student to study and to apply them systematically. Any speech textbook presupposes that effective speaking can be learned and that the principles can be applied to public speaking, discussion, and everyday informal communication. Where this book differs from most is in its assumption that learning takes place best and most effectively when specific principles are presented in units and are applied in assignments that stress those principles. Thus, Fundamental Principles are discussed as background for preparing a first speech assignment. Each of the remaining chapters then focuses on such skills as explaining processes, describing, defining, incorporating research, inventing lines of development, reasoning, and motivating; and in nearly every case, each contains an assignment, a student outline, and a student speech illustrating the assignment.

The test of any textbook is how well it works in practice. An evaluation of the use of the first edition of *Challenge* showed its strength in achieving its objectives—it also revealed areas that needed to be improved to maximize its value as a teaching instrument. I believe this second addition has strengthened nearly every aspect of the book without changing the basic structure, intent, or methodology.

Part One, Orientation, has been expanded to include a new opening chapter, Effective Speaking and the Communication Process. This new chapter defines communication, discusses the variables of the process, and considers effective speaking as communication. The original introductory chapter on Listening to Speeches has been revised and is now Chapter 2.

Part Two, Fundamental Principles, has been considerably revised in order to present the principles more clearly and more comprehensively. The nine exercises included within the unit now lead to the preparation and delivery of a first speech—the assignment for the speech serves as a culmination or synthesis of the steps of preparation and delivery.

Part Three, Putting Fundamentals into Practice, gives the chapters on Adapting to Audiences and Using Visual Aids a special significance. Although they could be considered as a part of the fundamentals unit, they are discussed in a separate unit to encourage their use either in specially prepared speech assignments or in conjunction with specific informative or persuasive speeches.

The units on informative and persuasive speaking have been limited to the speech assignments that best explain and illustrate basic informative and persuasive speaking skills. In nearly every chapter additional supporting material has been introduced. The chapters on Definition, Description, Reasons, Refutation, and Discussion show many minor changes. A chapter on Explaining Processes has been added; the two chapters introducing these units and two of the key chapters of the text, Expository Speaking and A Speech of Motivation, have been completely rewritten. Throughout the text, several new speeches have been substituted for those used in the first edition.

For this edition special thanks are due all the students who have evaluated materials in the first edition and who have contributed speeches and outlines appearing in the text. Likewise I owe a debt of gratitude to the following: the many instructors who commented specifically and helpfully about their experience in using the first edition; my colleagues—faculty and graduate students alike—who read portions of the revised text; Gary Miller, West Valley College, and James E. Sayer, Northern Arizona University, who read the complete manuscript for this edition and offered excellent suggestions; and, of course, my wife, Mary Jo, for her continued patience and understanding.

R. F. V.

Contents

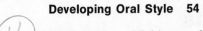
Three   Putting Fundamentals into Practice

Four   Informative Speaking

Five   Persuasive Speaking

Six   Small Group Discussion

Appendix   Four Contemporary Speeches

Orientation

One

Effective Speaking and the Communication Process

1

Although we are born with an innate need to communicate, our ability to communicate effectively is learned. Unfortunately, our informal method of learning based upon models we know and tested through trial and error is rather haphazard. The all too often heard comment "We're having a communication problem" indicates the difficulty of good communication and the frequency of what has come to be called "communication breakdowns." To begin our study of how to become more effective speakers—how to function more effectively in face-to-face, one-to-one or one-to-many situations—we need to examine the communication process.

An analysis of more than fifty different definitions leads us to suggest this working definition: *Communication is the process of sending and receiving messages. A source stimulates meaning in the mind of a receiver by means of a message conveyed by symbols; the receiver responds either mentally or physically to the message.* As we study this definition, we become aware that the communication process involves at least six variables: *source, message, channel, receiver, feedback,* and *noise.* Let's consider each of these six as they apply to communication in general and to effective speaking in particular.

The Source

The source is the *originator* of the communication message. The source is usually an individual; however, it may be a group of people such as a committee, a company, or even a nation. As the author of this book, I am the source of the communication you are reading. In speeches you prepare and deliver, you will be the source. In this book we will discuss how the source affects the informational or persuasive value of the message he intends to communicate.

The Message

The message is the *idea* or *feeling* that the source communicates. Messages are most frequently conveyed either verbally or nonverbally. In this textbook, the words printed in phrases and in sentences form a verbal message to you the reader. Although my primary means of communicating with you is verbal, the typeface, spacing, paper, and other physical characteristics of this book convey a nonverbal message. From them, you make conscious or unconscious judgments about the readability, about the aesthetic value of the book, and perhaps about how much you will read. For your speeches, your mind will select words to convey your message; however, your facial expressions, your gestures, your tone of voice, and your attitude—all nonverbal cues—will accompany your words and will affect your message.

In effective speaking, the verbal and the nonverbal symbols should coordinate to reinforce an *intended* message. When the verbal and nonverbal symbols are at odds, communication is inhibited. The source may consciously intend to send one message, but unintentionally he may send another. For instance, when you say to someone "How are you doing?" and he responds "Fine," your interpretation of the message received is different depending upon whether "fine" is accompanied by a smile or by a scowl. If it is accompanied by a smile, the standard meaning of "fine"—being in good health or in good spirits—is reinforced. If it is accompanied by a scowl, you must decide whether the scowl is accidental or a true indication of his feeling. In such situations, the saying "actions speak louder than words" may well apply. Julius Fast's bestseller *Body Language* has made millions of us more aware of the importance of nonverbal behavior as a possible indication of our true feelings. In our study of speaking, we will be concerned with selecting appropriate verbal and nonverbal symbols that act in concert to convey the message intended.

Good intentional communication requires message preparation. Although some people look upon message preparation as something that relates only to formal speaking, it should be noted that the process is much the same whether the message is to be sent in conversation on the spur of the moment or in a formal speech involving considerable preparation time. For instance, supposing someone said "How do you get to the post office from here?" Even though you would be expected to answer nearly instantaneously, your mind would still take time to prepare an answer. In fact, if the route were complicated you might even reply, "Let me think . . . ," to give yourself a few more seconds to prepare your answer. So whether you must speak virtually instantaneously or whether you have considerable time, your mind must still consider idea selection and development, message organization, and the verbal and nonverbal symbols that will convey the message. At first, putting carefully prepared statements together coherently so that they meet all the tests of effective communication will take time and will appear to be quite difficult. Later, as you improve with practice, you will find yourself speaking more effectively, even when message preparation time is nearly instantaneous. Nearly all of Part 2, Fundamental Principles, is devoted to message preparation. The remainder of the book deals with the preparation of particular kinds of informative and persuasive messages.

The Channel

The channel is the *means* of conveyance of the symbols. Words are delivered from one person to another by air waves; facial expressions are delivered by light waves. Usually the more channels that can be utilized to carry a message, the more likely the successful communication of that message. Although our everyday interpersonal communication is carried intentionally and unintentionally by any of the sensory channels—a fragrant scent and a firm handshake are both forms of communication—effective speaking is basically two channel.

The Receiver

The receiver is the *destination* of the message. Like the source, it may be an individual or a group of individuals. The process of the receiver's translating the sound waves and the light waves into meaning is called "decoding." When a message is decoded by a receiver, some theorists would say that communication is complete. Although such an assessment is technically correct, a receiver will have some mental or physical response to a message, and it is the nature of the response that enables us to determine whether communication—understanding the message—really took place. In any event, your classmates will be the receivers, the decoders, of the messages you send in your classroom speeches. Because an understanding of the nature of the potential receiver is so important to effective speaking, Chapter 7 is devoted entirely to understanding and adapting to your receivers.

Feedback

Whether communication really takes place is determined by the nature of the verbal and nonverbal *response* of the receiver. This response, called feedback, tells the source whether his message was heard, seen, or understood. If feedback indicates that the communication was not received, or was received incorrectly, or was misinterpreted, the source can send the message again, perhaps in a different way.

Different kinds of communication situations provide for different amounts of feedback. A zero feedback situation is said to exist when it is virtually impossible for the sender to be aware of a receiver's response. Suppose that right now I stated in this book: "Stop what you are doing and draw an equilateral triangle resting on one of its sides." I would have no way of knowing whether you understood what I was talking about, whether you actually drew the triangle, or, if you drew it, whether you drew it correctly. As the source of that message—as well as the other messages in this textbook—I cannot know for sure whether I am really communicating. The lack of direct feedback is one of the weaknesses of any of the forms of mass communication. The source has little or no immediate opportunity to test the impact of his message. Suppose, however, that instead of being the author of a book I am your instructor in a class of fifty students. Now suppose that I asked you to draw an equilateral triangle resting on one of its sides. Even if you said nothing, my presence would enable me to monitor your nonverbal feedback directly. If you drew the triangle, I could see it; if you refused, I would know; in some cases I could see exactly what you were drawing. Now suppose that in this classroom, as I asked you to draw the triangle, you were free to ask me any direct questions and I was free and willing to respond. The free flow of interacting communication that would take place represents the highest level of feedback.

How important is feedback to effective communication? Levitt and

Mueller[1] conducted an experiment similar to the one described above. They reported that communication improved markedly as the situation moved from zero feedback to complete interaction. In our communication, whether conversation or public speaking, we want to stimulate as much feedback as the situation will allow. In various places in this book we will be concerned with monitoring feedback and responding to it. Although many of your speaking assignments will not allow direct verbal feedback during the regular speaking time, you should learn to maximize the value of the nonverbal feedback you do get.

Noise

An analysis of the communication process is incomplete without consideration of the final variable, noise. Communication deals with stimulating meaning. Yet our capabilities for interpreting, understanding, or responding to symbols is often inhibited by the amount of noise accompanying the communication. Here we define noise as both the *external* factors in the channels and the *internal* perceptions and experiences that affect communication. Much of your success as a communicator will depend on how you avoid, lessen, or deal with noise. For instance, if, while I am giving the verbal instructions for drawing a triangle, a jack hammer is going full blast outside the window of our classroom, you wouldn't hear the message because of the physical noise; and communication couldn't take place until the noise was eliminated. If, while giving the directions, I exhibit certain annoying mannerisms or speak with a severe speech impediment, these noise factors could intrude enough so that communication couldn't take place unless the source lessened the noise or the receiver determined not to let the noise bother him. In each of these cases, actual physical noise would be clogging the channels of communication.

More often the "noise" that provides a barrier to communication is not physical but semantic noise that grows from our perceptions and experiences—and semantic noises may cause us to misinterpret or misunderstand without our even knowing it. For instance, suppose I asked you to meet me at the green house. You may perceive a green house as a place where plants are grown under glass; if I perceived a greenhouse as a house painted green, we might never meet. Suppose in

---

[1] H. J. Leavitt and Ronald A. H. Mueller, "Some Effects of Feedback on Communication," *Human Relations*, Vol. 4 (1951), p. 403.

my speech I talked of the benefits of democracy in insuring personal freedom. If I and all of my listeners had the same middle-class experiences, then communication would probably take place. But if some of the listeners were extremely poor, or had been forced to live in a ghetto, or had experienced some social injustice, the concept of "democracy insuring personal freedom" might well sound like hypocrisy. Communication cannot take place if semantic noise causes the source and the receiver to perceive the symbols of communication differently. Because we view language in terms of our own experiences, the semantic noise factor may be the most important barrier to the communication process and the most difficult one to deal with. Especially in Chapter 5, Style, we will discuss the use of language to convey ideas and feelings clearly, vividly, emphatically, and appropriately.

Now, to summarize, let's relate a simple communicative act and trace these six variables in operation. Upon leaving the classroom after a test, Joe slouches his shoulders, frowns, and says in a sullen tone of voice, "That was a miserable test." Mary, equally forlorn, replies in much the same tone, "You can say that again." Joe, the source of the message, conveys his message in verbal and nonverbal symbols. The language "that was a miserable test" is the verbal representation of his thoughts; his sullen tone, slouching posture, and frown are the nonverbal representation of his miserable feeling. In this case, the nonverbal symbols support and reinforce the words. The words and the tone of Joe's voice are carried by air waves; the facial expression and bodily action are carried by light waves to Mary, the prospective receiver. Mary's nervous system records the sound and light waves; she then interprets (decodes) the verbal and nonverbal symbols that sent the message. As a result of her interpretation of the message, Mary responds with a message that is conveyed by the words "You can say that again," and by a facial expression, tone of voice, and posture similar to Joe's. Joe interprets the feedback as a sign of understanding of and sympathy with his message. In this example, there were no barriers to the satisfactory completion of the communication.

The variables of source, message, receiver, channel, feedback, and noise are used to analyze the nature of any communication act whether it is accidental or intentional. As we have discussed these variables we have tried to show how each of them may be considered in the context of effective speaking. We have noted that, first, effective speaking is message oriented; it deals with transmission of information. Second, the meaning of the message is source selected; a speaker intends to get some point across with his communication, and he makes an effort to prepare the message so that it will communicate that point. Third, effective speaking is basically verbal and nonverbal.

The ultimate value of effective speaking arises from the fact that we live in a society that requires comprehensive and accurate information to function. Our role in that society is furthered by our ability to prepare and to send messages effectively, by our sensitivity to the barriers of effective communication, and by our understanding of the importance of meaningful listening. How we meet these goals is the concern of the rest of this book.

Listening to Speeches

2

Because response and monitoring response are so important to the communication process, this second chapter of our orientation unit focuses on the instrument of response—listening.

In contrast to the five to ten speeches you will be giving in this class, you can expect to hear somewhere between one hundred and two hundred—probably more than you will hear during the next several years outside the classroom. Through careful analysis of these speeches you will see a wide selection of methods and techniques in operation—methods and techniques you may consider for your speeches. By identifying the accomplishments and the mistakes of others, you may be able to utilize workable methods and avoid their mistakes in your speeches.

In addition, through good listening you can provide the important analysis that will help others in class evaluate their effectiveness. To become effective speakers, people need honest, accurate appraisal. Although your instructor will discuss the speeches in terms of speech-making standards, it will be up to you as part of a sympathetic but critical audience to describe the effect the speech had on you.

As a bonus, your careful listening will enable you to learn about more subjects in this course than in any other course you are taking. Remember, much of what your classmates say will be new information or will give new insights. You will find that your speech class is truly a liberal arts course, and you will want to make the most of your opportunity to learn. To maximize your value as a critical listener, let's consider how you can improve your listening and what criteria of critical listening you need to apply in your evaluation of speeches.

How You Can Improve Your Listening

Perhaps you believe you are already a good listener. Unfortunately, most college students are not. Studies indicate that listening proficiency among college students is only about 50 percent—with a short period of delay between time of utterance and testing, average listening efficiency drops to near 25 percent. Dr. Ralph Nichols, a leading authority on listening, has conducted numerous studies and has reported the research of others for the last 20 years. All his work points to the same sad figures: 25 percent to 50 percent efficiency.[1] These percentages are especially important when we realize that roughly half our daily communication time is spent listening. Paul Rankin's original study of time spent communicating (a study completed more than 40 years ago) showed 45 percent listening, 9 percent writing, 16 percent reading and 30 percent speaking.[2] Ralph Nichols reports a variety of recent studies to substantiate these findings.[3] Now these figures refer to *listening*, not to hearing. What's the difference? Hearing is your ability to record the sound vibrations that are transmitted; listening means making sense out of what we hear.

Since listening and speaking are by far the two most important communication tools, we should try to improve them as much as we try to improve our reading and writing. Assuming that your listening efficiency is about average, what can you do about it? An average listener can almost double his listening efficiency in a few months if he wants to. In fact, by following a few simple steps, you can improve your listening immediately.

Get Ready to Listen

The first step to improved listening is to get yourself ready to listen. Good listening takes time, effort, and energy; and to be perfectly frank, most of us just aren't willing to work at it. What is characteristic of being ready to work at listening? An outward sign is whether you look as if you are listening. Poor listeners often slouch in their chairs. Their eyes wander from place to place. They appear to be

[1] Ralph Nichols and Leonard A. Stevens, *Are You Listening?* New York: McGraw-Hill Book Co., 1957, pp. 5–6.

[2] Paul Tory Rankin, "The Measurement of the Ability to Understand Spoken Language," doctoral dissertation, University of Michigan, 1926, University Microfilm, 1952, Publ. No. 4352; cited by Ralph G. Nichols and Leonard A. Stevens, *Are You Listening?* (New York: McGraw-Hill Book Co., 1957), p. 6.

[3] Nichols, pp. 6–10.

bored by what is going on. In contrast, good listeners sit upright—
sometimes almost on the edge of their chairs. They rivet their eyes on
the speaker. These physical signs of attention are indicative of mental
alertness.

At first look these recommendations may seem shallow or over-
drawn. But test these ideas for yourself. When I discuss listening in
class, I precede short comprehension tests by saying "For the next five
minutes, I want you to listen as hard as you can. Then I'm going to
give a test on what you heard." What happens when the class realizes
it has an investment in what will take place? Eyes come forward,
people straighten up, and extraneous noises—coughing, clearing
throats, rustling—drops to near zero.

By sitting upright and looking at the speaker you may be able to
resist distractions and keep from thinking about lunch, about your
date for that evening, about a test you have the next hour, or about
how you feel. Even though you may not be able to listen at peak
efficiency for long periods—attention lags of a split second just do
occur whether we want them to or not, you can help keep distracting
thoughts from capturing your attention and you can improve your
listening—if you maintain a listening posture.

Listen Actively

The second step you can take immediately is to be-
come an active listener. Effective communication involves feedback;
the source sends a message and the receiver responds to that message.
Research on learning psychology indicates that a listener learns better
and faster and makes sounder judgments about what he hears when
he is mentally and physically active—when he is involved. Let's explore the thinking behind such a generalization. A speaker utters
about 140 to 180 words per minute. We think at between 300 and 600
words per minute. Whether we are listening effectively or not depends
a lot on what we are doing during that time difference. Some listeners
do nothing; others think about eating, sleeping, a test the next
hour, and other things that eventually capture all of their attention.
The active listener uses his extra time to weigh and consider what the
speaker has said. He may attempt to repeat key ideas, to ask questions
related to the topic, or to test the accuracy of the speaker's assertions.
When the speaker says, "The first major election reform bill was
passed in England in 1832" the active listener might mentally repeat
"reform bill," "England, 1832." When the speaker says, "Napoleon's
battle plans were masterpieces of strategy," the active listener might
ask himself, "What were the characteristics of his strategy?" When

the speaker says, "An activity that provides exercise of almost every muscle is swimming," the active listener might inwardly question the point examining the supporting material the speaker offers. Each of these forms of involvement helps the listener to master the ideas.

Active listening can also mean taking notes. Whereas the poor listener fidgets, doodles, or looks about the room, the good listener often makes notes on what the speaker is saying. Perhaps he writes down words or phrases denoting key ideas; perhaps he writes the most important ideas in complete sentences. The physical activity reinforces the mental activity. If, as the speaker says, "The first artificial orbiting satellite was launched by Russia in 1957," we write that down, the act of writing, coordinated with thinking the country and the year, will provide both a better chance of mental recall and the written record to refer to later.

Withhold Evaluation

A third step to improved listening is to keep an open mind and to withhold evaluation of what we hear until comprehension is complete. This recommendation involves both the control of arbitrary judgments about a subject and control of emotional responses to content. It is a human reaction to listen attentively only to what we like or what we want to hear. Yet, such an attitude is self-limiting and self-defeating. Let's remind ourselves of why we listen in the first place—to learn and to gather data for evaluation. Neither of these goals is possible if we refuse to listen to anything outside our immediate interests. For instance, if a classroom speaker indicates he will talk about the history of unions, you may say you're neither interested in history in general nor in unions in particular. But if during the first sentence or two of the speech you find yourself saying "I don't think I am going to be interested in this topic," you should remind yourself that judgment must follow and not precede the presentation of information. Poor listeners make value judgments about the content after the first few words; good listeners approach what they are listening to objectively.

But even when we show a willingness to listen to a topic, content elements may so affect us emotionally that we no longer "hear" what the speaker has to say. Ralph Nichols talks about words that "serve as red flags to some listeners." He goes on to list such words as "mother-in-law," "pervert," "income tax," and "evolution."[4] Perhaps

---

[4] Ralph G. Nichols, "Do We Know How to Listen? Practical Helps in a Modern Age," *Speech Teacher*, Vol. 10 (March 1961), p. 123.

these words evoke no emotional response from you, but what if a speaker says "liberal," "racist," "bureaucracy," "CIA," "Southeast Asia," "policemen," or "ghetto"? Would any of these words—or development of them—turn you off? Often, poor listeners (and occasionally even good listeners) are given an emotional jolt by a speaker invading an area of personal sensitivity. At this point all we can do is to be wary. When the speaker trips the switch to your emotional reaction—let a warning light go on before you go off. Instead of quitting or getting ready to fight, work that much harder at being objective. Can you do it? If so, you'll improve your listening!

But in our efforts to make some changes in our behavior, we should try not to take on the characteristics of three types of listeners described by Dominick Barbara in his book *The Art of Listening*.[5] He describes them as those who listen with a modest ear—compulsive nodders who shake their heads in agreement when they are not listening at all; those who listen with a rebellious ear—chatterboxes who are thinking of their next reply rather than listening to what is taking place; and those who listen with a deaf ear—those who close their ears to unpleasantness.

Since it is easier to pay attention to a speech if it is well presented, the principles in this book are directed to our making speeches so clear and interesting that good and poor listeners alike will pay attention. Nevertheless, some of the speeches we hear, in or out of class, will be less than good. In such instances, we will have to work to make the most of the experience. Since attitudes affect our perception of information, the more we allow our emotions to intrude into the listening process, the more distorted will be our recollection of what was said.

Listening for Ideas and Meaning: Separating Intent from Content

When have we really listened? Some of us mistakenly think we have listened when we can feed back the words themselves or the details that were communicated. Actually neither of these acts is necessarily characteristic of good listening. Good listeners listen for ideas more than for details. Earlier we suggested notetaking as a means of listening actively. But notetaking does not involve outlining every-

---

[5] Dominick A. Barbara, *The Art of Listening*. Springfield, Ill.: Charles C Thomas, 1958.

thing a speaker said. Good notetaking refers to getting down key ideas. If all our effort is used to master each detail as it comes up, we are unable to relate detail to principle or for that matter to differentiate the important from the unimportant. Fortunately, listening for ideas is one of the easiest parts of listening to learn. The information we will discuss in Chapter 4 that deals with organizational patterns will contribute to our ability to separate ideas from details.

Of equal importance is our ability to separate speaker intent from speaker content. We all know that when a person says, "Isn't this a beautiful day" when it's raining like mad, that the speaker is being sarcastic. In this case we realize that intent of the message differs from the content, the ordinary meaning of the words. But much of our listening poses less obvious problems. On an interpersonal level friends will often say things that don't really express what they mean or how they feel. When a roommate says, "Go ahead, I don't mind," to our request to borrow something, his statement may or may not really be reflecting his attitude. Although the contradiction between content and intent is probably less frequent in public speaking than in interpersonal communication, such differences still exist; a good listener, therefore, virtually absorbs all the speaker's meaning by being sensitive to tone of voice, facial expression, and bodily action as well as to the words themselves. Sincerity, depth of conviction, confidence, true understanding, and many subtle implications may well be revealed regardless of the words used.

Criteria for Evaluation

Let's review what we hope to gain from listening to speeches: (1) we hope to gain information about the topics, (2) we wish to make an evaluation of a speaker's ability, and (3) we wish to weigh and consider a speaker's method to help determine what elements we should adopt and what elements we should avoid. Improving general listening efficiency will help us meet the first of these goals. The other two require a critical capacity that presupposes some standard criteria we can apply. How we proceed correlates with the principles to be discussed in the next four chapters. For all speeches, in addition to listening to the substance, you should also listen to how the speaker develops his specific purpose, how the speaker organizes his material, how the speaker words his ideas, and how the speaker delivers the speech. Thus, with each speech given in class, you should make a complete analysis of content and method.

The following questions are applicable to all kinds of speeches. Most of them review the material covered in the next part (Chapters 3–6). Your answers will enable you to prepare a complete profile of what you have heard. When you have applied these questions, you should have a sound basis for speech criticism and an awareness of the criteria for effective speaking.

Evaluation Questionnaire

Content:

Topic:

Was the topic a good one for this class?

Did the speaker seem to have sufficient knowledge of and interest in the topic?

Specific purpose:

Was the specific purpose clear? meaningful?

Developmental materials:

Was the development clear? interesting?

Did the development really explain or support key ideas?

Ethical Considerations:

Did the speaker present the facts without distorting them or exaggerating their importance?

Did the speaker give his source for strategically important or damaging material?

Did the speaker communicate rationally without either using emotionally charged language that has no relationship to fact or attacking personalities and engaging in name calling?

Did the speaker place audience considerations ahead of his own self-interest?

Organization

Introduction:

Did the introduction gain attention?

Did the introduction lead into the body of the speech?

Body:

Were the main points clear, substantive ideas?

Were the main points limited in number and scope?

Was there an identifiable order to the main points?

Conclusion:

Did the conclusion tie the speech together?

Did the conclusion leave the speech on a high note?

Style:

Was the speech delivered in an oral style?

Was the language clear?

Was the language vivid?

Was the language emphatic?
Was the language appropriate?

Delivery:

Did the speaker have a positive attitude?
Did the speaker look at his audience?
Was the delivery spontaneous?
Did the speaker show sufficient variety and emphasis?
Was articulation satisfactory?
Did the speaker show sufficient poise and have a good posture?

Fundamental Principles

Two

Selecting Topics and Finding Material

3

Principle 1   Effective speaking begins with good content.

What am I going to talk about? Where will I find my material? These are probably the first two questions you ask when you begin to think about preparing a speech. By using a little common sense and by proceeding systematically, you will find that deciding what you will talk about and determining what you will say will be much easier than what you might expect. Let's consider the essentials of good content: selecting topics, determining purposes, and finding material.

Selecting a Topic

In daily conversation you don't usually consider the selection of a topic as a conscious effort—often it may seem that you just start talking. What then determines your subject matter? In conversation you talk about subjects that concern you—that interest you. Did you just see a good movie? Are you distressed over the showing of your football team? Are you concerned about City Council's position on dealing with crime? Do you have a big test coming up tomorrow? If so, it is likely that these are the things you will be talking about today at lunch, while you are walking to class, in a bull session after dinner, or with your date. And what is true of conversation is also true of public speaking: George Meany talks about the problems of labor; Betty Friedan talks about women in society; Roy Wilkins talks about Black progress, goals, and commitments; Paul Samuelson talks about economic trends; William Buckley, Jr., talks about conservative principles; Billy Graham talks about his view of God. In public speaking as in conversation, people talk about the things they are concerned with and interested in.

Where beginning and even professional speakers sometimes have trouble is in translating their concerns and interests into specific topics. So what you need now is a good specific *modus operandi*— a workable method to follow. If good topics don't often occur to you, my advice is to go through a process known as "brainstorming," which is an uncritical, nonevaluative attempt at verbalizing responses to given stimuli. You know the old word-association process: When you think the word "snow," associatively you may think of "sled," "cold," "shoveling," and "snowman." Likewise, when you suggest a word or idea related to your major areas of interest, you can often associate twenty, thirty, or even fifty other related ideas and concepts. The procedure allows you to get a multitude of related ideas about your concerns and interests down on paper.

How do you start? One way is to take a sheet of paper and divide it into three columns. Label column 1 "Major" or "Vocation"; label column 2 "Hobby" or "Activity"; and label column 3 "Current Events" or "Social problems." Work on one column at a time. If you begin with column 3, "Hobby," you might write "chess." Then you would jot down everything that comes to mind, such as "master," "Bobby Fisher," "openings," "carving chess men." Work for at least five minutes on a column. Then begin with a second column. Although you may not finish in one sitting, don't begin an evaluation until you have noted at least twenty items in each column.

Suppose your prospective vocation is "elementary education." A five- to ten-minute session might yield the following word associations:

teachers	discipline	desks	math	supervisors
classroom	creativity	tests	science	principals
children	materials	quizzes	music	school nurse
books	financing	spelling	art	visiting teacher
learning	bulletin boards	language	friends	assemblies
interest	schedules	reading	problems	grouping
motivation	lesson plans	health	phys ed	programmed texts

After you believe you have exhausted your personal resources, look over your list and check the three or four items that "ring a bell," that best capture your concerns and interests. Now the point of this exercise is to enable you to take advantage of a basic psychological principle—it is easier to answer a multiple-choice question than it is to answer the same question without the choices. Thus, whereas you may be stumped if you saddle yourself with the question "What should I talk about for my speech?" you may find it easy to make a choice from among the twenty or more topics you yourself have listed. For instance, if you are interested in elementary education, you may find it much easier to decide that you like "programmed texts," "reading," or "motivation" from the list than it would be to come up with one of these topics cold.

You may find, however, that the words or phrases you select are still too general to give you direction. If so, start a new list with one of the general topics. For instance, a few additional minutes of brainstorming on "programmed texts" might yield: "writing programs," "principles underlying programs," "use of programmed texts," "effectiveness of programmed learning." From this list you might be inclined to select "principles underlying the construction of programmed texts." If you make a selection of this kind from each of the three columns, you may realize that you have three good topics to choose from for your first speeches.

Exercise 1

---

1. Divide a sheet of paper into three columns labeled "Vocation" or "Major," "Hobby" or "Activity," and "Current Event" or "Social Problem"; complete a list of twenty to forty items in each column.

2. Select three items from each list.

3. If any of these seem too broad, continue the brainstorming process until you have limited the topic sufficiently.

4. In order of preference, indicate the three topics that are most interesting or most important to *you*.

Determining Your Specific Purpose

Your topic states the general subject area, and if you have worked carefully, it should limit the scope of the material you wish to cover as well. The topic selection process is completed by deciding what you plan to do with that topic in your speech. Although you may want to delay your final decision until you have further explored the material, let's consider the concept of specific purpose now.

A specific purpose is a single statement that summarizes exactly what you want to do with the speech or exactly what response you want from your audience as a result of the speech. Although some people prefer the terms "governing idea," "central idea," "theme statement," or "proposition," they all mean about the same thing: distilling the goal of the speech into a single specific statement. In this text it is suggested that the specific purpose be stated as an infinitive phrase: the infinitive indicates the intent of the speaker and the rest of the phrase contains the thesis statement. From the subject area of "elementary education" on the brainstorming sheet shown earlier, we could select the topic "principles underlying programs." A specific purpose based upon that topic could be phrased: "To explain three major principles underlying construction of programmed texts." Notice that this purpose states exactly what the speaker hopes to achieve with his topic. From the subject area "health," we could select the topic "programs of disease research." "To motivate the audience to support the Easter Seals campaign" is a specific purpose based on the topic—a purpose that clearly states the response the speaker wants as a result of the speech. With any one topic a number of specific purposes are possible. You want to arrive at one clear statement that embodies a single purpose.

Let's examine two examples that illustrate the process of wording acceptable purpose statements:

Subject area: football

Topic: screen pass

Specific purpose:

"How to throw a screen pass." (No direction)

"How a screen pass develops." (Better)

"The steps required for execution of a screen pass." (Better)

"To show the four steps required for successful execution of a screen pass." (Acceptable)

"To explain that a successful screen pass depends upon the deception created by the players, the positioning of key players to form the 'screen,' the timing of the receiver, and the blocking after the pass is completed." (A more complete statement of the same idea; a statement that probably could not be made until after material was gathered.)

Subject area: punishment of criminals

Topic: capital punishment

Specific purpose:

"We should do something about capital punishment." (No direction)

"Why capital punishment is bad." (Better)

"To prove that capital punishment should be abolished." (Acceptable)

"To prove that because it does not deter crime and because it is not just, capital punishment should be abolished." (A more complete statement that probably could not be made until after material was gathered.)

After you have written a number of purpose statements, you will note that almost all of them can be loosely classified under the headings of purposes stated (1) to entertain an audience, (2) to inform an audience, or (3) to persuade an audience. Because speech is a complex act that may serve a multipurpose function, we never want to hold slavishly to any rigid guidelines that these categories might suggest. They are useful only in showing that in any communicative act one overriding purpose is likely to predominate. For instance, Johnny Carson's opening monologue may have some informative elements and may even contain some intended or unintended persuasive message, yet his major goal is to entertain his viewers. Your history professor's discussion of the events leading up to the Great War may use elements of entertainment to gain and to hold your attention, and the implication of the discussion of those events may have persuasive overtones, yet the primary goal is to explain those events in a way that will enable the class to understand them. Proctor and Gamble may seek to amuse you with their commercials and they may well include some elements of information in their presentation, but there can be no question that their goal is to persuade you to buy their soap.

Because one common way of assigning speeches is by purpose, the assignments discussed later in this textbook are made by purpose: Part 4, informative speeches, and Part 5, persuasive speeches.

Why is it so important to have a clearly stated specific purpose so early in speech preparation? First, the specific purpose helps to limit your research. If you know you want to talk about "the causes of juvenile delinquency," you can limit your reading to causes, at a saving of many hours of preparation time. Second, a good specific purpose will assist you in the organization of your ideas, and you will see how this is true in the next chapter. And third, the phrasing of a good specific purpose will put your topic in a form that will enable you to apply the necessary tests.

When you believe that your topic is clearly phrased in specific purpose form, you should test it by asking these five questions:

1. *Am I really interested in the topic?* Although you began your selection of the topic on the basis of interest, you should make sure that you have not drifted into an area that no longer reflects that interest.

2. *Does my purpose meet the assignment?* Whether the assignment is made by purpose (to inform or to persuade), or by type of speech (expository or descriptive), or by subject (book analysis or current event) your specific purpose should reflect the nature of that assignment.

3. *Can I cover the topic in the time alloted?* "Three major causes of the Great War" can be discussed in five minutes; "a history of the Great War" cannot. Your time limits for classroom speeches will be relatively short; although you want your topics to have depth, avoid trying to cover too broad an area.

4. *Is this topic one that will provide new information, new insights, or reason for a change of opinion for my audience?* Usually, there is no sense taking time to talk about a subject the audience already understands or believes in. "How to hold a tennis racket" would be a waste of time for a group of tennis players; "a comparison of wooden and aluminum rackets by their ability to generate power and spin" would be much better. Likewise, "to persuade you to go to college" would be a waste of time for college students; "to persuade you to take a course in economics" would be much better. When you have decided that your audience already knows much of what you are going to say, or already believes in or is doing what you wish, you should work for a different specific purpose within the same subject area. An audience is making a time investment; it is up to you to make that time worthwhile. Likewise, try to stay away from the superficial, the banal, and the frivolous: "how to tie shoe laces" and "my first day at camp" are just not good topics. If you have worked on your brainstorming lists, superficiality should be no problem. Because audience consideration is so important to the entire speechmaking process, a complete discussion of audience analysis and adaptation is the subject of Chapter 7.

5. *Are my motives for speaking legitimate?* Examination of the speech purpose is the starting point for ethical consideration. If you find yourself using the assignment as a platform for airing personal views regardless of audience reaction, you should take time to question your motives. Likewise if your only purpose is personal gain, you should reexamine your goals.

Exercise 2

1. For each of the three topics you selected in Exercise 1, phrase one or more specific purposes.

2. Evaluate each in terms of the five tests above.

Finding Material—Where to Look

What you say about the topic you have selected is going to determine much of your effectiveness as a speaker. Knowing where to look for material is a starting point for finding the best possible information on your topic. Most speakers find that the best way to look for material is to start from within their own experiences and work outward to other sources. Let's explore what you can expect to find from exploring your own knowledge, observation, interviewing, and reading.

Your Own Knowledge

What do you know? At times you may have questioned the extent and the accuracy of your knowledge; yet, when you test yourself, you discover that you really know quite a lot, especially about your major interests. For instance, athletes have special knowledge about their sports, coin collectors about coins, detective-fiction buffs about detective fiction, do-it-yourself advocates about house and garden, musicians about music and instruments, farmers about animals or crops and equipment, and camp counselors about camping. As a result of the special knowledge, you should be your first, if not your best, source of information for the topics you have selected. After all, firsthand knowledge of a subject enables the speaker to develop unique, imaginative, original speeches. Regardless of what topic you have selected, take the time to analyze and record your knowledge before you go to any other source.

Of course, you must not accept every item you know or remember without testing its accuracy. Our minds play tricks on us, and you may well find that some "fact" you are sure of is not really a fact at all. Nevertheless, you should not be discouraged from using your prior knowledge. Verifying a fact is far easier than discovering material in the first place.

Observation

Take advantage of one of your best resources, your power of observation. Many people are poor observers because they just don't apply their critical powers. Why are policemen better observers than most eye-witness reporters? Because they have been trained to use their powers. You, too, can be a better observer if you will only try. Get in the habit of seeing and not just looking. Pay attention to everything about you. The development of nearly any topic you select can profit from the utilization of materials gained by observation. Are you planning to give a speech on how newspapers are printed? Before you finish your preparation, go down to your local newspaper printing plant and take a tour. The material drawn from your observation will provide excellent additions to your speech. Are you planning to evaluate the role of City Council in governing the city? Attend a couple of City Council meetings. Do you want to talk about the urban renewal of your downtown area? Go downtown and look around. Remember, through observation, you can add a personal dimension to your speech that will make it more imaginative and probably more interesting.

Interviewing

The time it takes to set up and conduct an interview usually multiplies itself in speaker benefits. Through the interview you get the ideas and feelings of a person involved firsthand. Although some public officials appear to be too busy to take time to talk with a student, you will be surprised to find that most people in public positions are approachable. The reason? Publicizing what they do and how they do it is an important part of their public relations. Moreover, many officials have a vested interest in keeping their constituents informed. Are you concerned with the way a recent Supreme Court ruling will affect policework in your community? Make an appointment with a local judge, the chief of police, or a precinct captain to get his views on the subject. Are you interested in more information on some aspect of your college? Make an appointment with the head of a division, the chairman of a department, or even a dean, the provost, or the president himself. Make sure, however, that you are trying to see the person who is in the best position to answer your question. The old adage "When you want to know something, go to the top" has its limitations. A better approach is "Discover who has the information you need, and go see him or her."

One of the most important features of interviewing is that you have a good idea of the questions you wish to ask. People are far more likely to grant interviews when you tell them that you have three or four specific questions you would like them to answer. Moreover, the interviewee is likely to be impressed by your careful preparation, and he might be more open with you than you would expect.

A variation of the interview is the survey. When you have a topic in which you need individual comments, you can conduct a poll of students, dorm residents, commuters, or any segment of the group whose views you want. Again, if you prepare a few well-worded questions, you are more likely to get answers. You may well be surprised at how many times the answers to your questions are worth quoting in your speech. Of course, you will want to make sure that you have polled a large enough group and that you have sampled different segments of the larger group before you attempt to draw any significant conclusions from your poll.

Source Material

Experience has shown that the most effective speakers are also effective researchers. Whether your library is large or small, well equipped or poorly equipped, its contents are of little value to you unless you know how to find what you need. This section is intended to acquaint you with the sources that will provide most of the developmental materials you will need for speeches in or out of the classroom.

Card Catalog   The card catalog indexes all your library's holdings by author, title, and subject. Your principal use of the card catalog will be to locate the best books on your topic.

Periodicals and Magazines   Periodicals are publications that appear at fixed periods: weekly, biweekly, monthly, quarterly, or yearly. The materials you get from weekly, biweekly, and monthly magazines are more current than you will find in books. Of course, some magazines are more accurate, more complete, and more useful than others. Since you must know where and how to find articles before you can evaluate them, you should know and use three indexes: *Readers' Guide to Periodical Literature*, *Education Index*, and *Index to Behavioral Sciences and Humanities*.

By far the most valuable source for topics of current interest, *Readers' Guide to Periodical Literature* is an index of articles in some 125 popular American journals. Articles, indexed by topic, come from such magazines as *The Atlantic, Ebony, Business Week, New Yorker, Life, Reader's Digest, Vital Speeches,* and *Yale Review.*

If your purpose sentence is related directly or indirectly to the field of education, including such subject areas as school administration, adult education, film strips, intelligence, morale, tests and scales, Project Head Start, or ungraded schools, *Education Index*, a cumulative subject index to a selected list of some 150 educational periodicals, proceedings, and yearbooks, will lead you to the available sources.

In contrast to *Readers' Guide*, which will lead you to articles in popular journals, the *Index to Behavioral Sciences and Humanities*, a guide to some 150 periodicals, will lead you to articles in such scholarly journals as *American Journal of Sociology*, *Economist*, *Modern Language Quarterly*, and *Philosophical Review*.

Encyclopedias   Not only do encyclopedias give you an excellent overview of many subjects, but also they offer valuable bibliographies. Nevertheless, because the articles could not possibly cover every topic completely, relatively few are very detailed. In addition, because of the time lag, an encyclopedia is seldom of value for the changing facts and details needed for contemporary problems. Most libraries have a recent edition of *Encyclopedia Britannica*, *Encyclopedia Americana*, or *Collier's Encyclopedia*.

Biographical Sources   When you need biographical details, from thumbnail sketches to reasonably complete essays, you can turn to one of the many biographical sources available. In addition to full-length books and encyclopedia entries, you should explore such books as *Who's Who* and *Who's Who in America* (short sketches of British and American subjects respectively) or *Dictionary of National Biography* and *Dictionary of American Biography* (rather complete essays about prominent British and American subjects respectively).

Statistical Sources   When you need facts, details, or statistics about population, records, continents, heads of state, weather, or similar subjects, you should refer to one of the many single-volume sources that report such data. Three of the most noteworthy sources in this category are *World Almanac and Book of Facts* (1868 to date), *Statistical Abstract of the United States* (1878 to date), and *Statesman's Yearbook: Statistical and Historical Annual of the States of the World* (1867 to date).

Newspapers   Despite the relatively poor quality of reporting in many of our daily newspapers, newspaper articles should not be overlooked as sources of facts and interpretations of contemporary problems. Your library probably holds both an index of your nearest major daily and the *New York Times Index*.

Since the holdings of libraries vary so much, a detailed account of other bibliographies, indexes, and special resources is impractical. To locate additional sources, you should consult your reference librarian. He will be able to lead you to special sources and indexes in your interest areas. If, however, you take full advantage of those listed above, you will find an abundance of material for your prospective topics.

Exercise 3

For each of the three purpose sentences you wrote for Exercise 2 compile a partial bibliography, including books, articles, and notations from at least three categories mentioned in the preceding section.

Finding Material—What to Look for

Although tapping your own knowledge, observing, interviewing, and discovering useful library sources will facilitate the research process, these sources will yield speech material only if you know what you are looking for. Rather than unsystematically reading all materials before you, you should attempt to discover items of information that will amplify or prove the points you wish to make. In addition, you should be alert for the most interesting developmental material available. Examples, illustrations, comparisons, statistics, and quotations are some of the forms of material that are most adaptable to speeches. In this section we will define the forms of development and show you how the forms may be used to make your point in speeches.

Examples

A common response to a generalization is "Give me an example." The example, a single instance that represents or illustrates a generalization or an assertion, is perhaps one of the most useful of speech materials. Your intellect allows you to generalize—to draw conclusions from your experiences and observations. Yet your listeners may not have had the benefit of those experiences, and they will not be impressed by the assertions or generalizations alone. The example really serves two functions: (1) it helps to test assertions and generalizations and (2) it helps to illustrate them for others. Examples make reading matter easier to comprehend or more persuasive, and they will serve the same purposes for your listeners.

The examples you find will be of three kinds: *real* examples that indicate actual specifics; *fictitious* examples that allude to instances that are or have been made up to explain the point; and *hypothetical* examples that suggest what would happen in certain circumstances. For instance:

Real: Automobile companies are making some effort to make their cars safer. Disc brakes are being used more frequently. Sharp or extended pieces of chrome on the interior are being eliminated.

Fictitious: Just because a person is slow does not mean that he is or should be considered a loser. Remember the story of the tortoise and the hare: the tortoise who was much slower still won the race.

Hypothetical: Dogs do very poorly on simple tests of intelligence. If a 10-foot section of fence were put between a dog and a bone, he would try to paw through the fence rather than go the 5 feet or so it would take to get around that fence.

Consider how Jayne Baker Spain, Director of Litton Industries, used examples to develop her point that the woman leadership factor is hardly new in her speech entitled "A Woman Could be President":

Consider this: Ours is the same century in which man made not only his first flight—120 feet—but he also landed on the moon just a short time ago. We now accept this feat as matter of fact, yet I believe it is not nearly as matter of fact as a woman becoming president. The woman leadership factor is hardly new. England made her greatest moves under Elizabeth I, and consolidated her greatest empire under Queen Victoria. If there had been no Queen Isabella willing to gamble because she believed a man's conviction, and willing to hock her royal jewels for three pint-size boats, who knows how long it might have been before the known world would have included North and South America. In modern times, with India in terms of geographic spread being the most populous nation on earth, how fortunate it may be that it has a woman for Prime Minister. In a country ruled by men for ages past, cursed with a free running, burgeoning population which must somehow be brought into check, it is high time for a woman Prime Minister who can talk to other women about these problems and what to do about them. And one could hardly ask for a country with more spirit and daring and confidence than Israel headed by Golda Meir —and at a time when it is faced with every form of threat and intimidation, and is being tested as never before.[1]

---

[1] Jayne Baker Spain, "A Woman Could Be President," *Vital Speeches*, April 1, 1971, p. 358. (See also the complete text of this speech in the Appendix.)

Because examples are such excellent aids to clarity and vividness, you should keep a constant lookout for them and employ them frequently.

Illustration, Anecdote, and Narrative

Illustrations are verbal explanations; anecdotes are brief, often amusing stories; and narratives are accounts, tales, or lengthier stories. In essence, each of these means about the same thing, the detailed relating of material, often in story form. Because interest is so important to any kind of communication and because our attention is always focused by a story, illustrations, anecdotes, and narratives are worth looking for. Actually, these forms are very closely related to examples. If you will think of illustrations, anecdotes, and narratives as extended examples or as one or more examples in story form, you will appreciate that relationship. For instance, by adding details, dialogue, or elements of plot, each of the three examples noted above could be made into an illustration. For a two-minute speech, you do not have the time to develop a very detailed illustration, so one or two examples or a very short story would be preferable. In longer speeches, however, the inclusion of at least one longer illustration or anecdote will pay dividends in audience attention. Remember the last time one of your professors said, "That reminds me of a story"? Probably more people listened to the story than to any other part of the lecture.

As an example, notice how E. J. Hanley, Chairman, Allegheny Ludlum Industries, makes his point that the most outrageous increases in wages have taken place with contractors whose completion of jobs is more important than unit cost:

> I heard a story about a lawyer in Philadelphia in whose home there was a leaking faucet. He had a plumber go out to take care of it and got a bill for $30. He called the plumber, asking what he had done. The plumber said he had replaced a washer. The lawyer asked him how much the washer cost and the plumber said approximately 2¢. "Gosh" said the lawyer, "I am surprised you get $30 for an hour's work. I am a lawyer and I don't get that much." The plumber replied, "I didn't either when I was still practicing law."[2]

---

[2] E. J. Hanley, "The Crisis of Costs," *Vital Speeches*, March 1, 1971, p. 300.

Comparison

Since you will need to discuss new ideas in terms that can be understood, you will probably learn what many successful communicators have learned before you: the value of giving meaning to a new idea by comparing it with a familiar concept. Comparison involves showing the similarities between two entities. Although you will be drawing your own later in speech preparation, you should still keep your eye open for comparisons in your research.

Comparisons may be figurative or literal. A figurative comparison expresses one thing in terms normally denoting another. We may speak of a person who is "slow as a turtle." We don't mean that he actually moves as slowly as a turtle, only that he is extremely slow in comparison to other persons. A literal comparison is an actual comparison. We may describe a ball as being about the same size as a tennis ball. In this instance, we mean that both balls are about 2½ inches in diameter.

Comparisons may be cast as metaphors or as similes. A metaphor is a figure of speech in which a word or phrase literally denoting one kind of object or idea is used in place of another. "Advertising is the spark plug that makes our system work" and "Their line is a stone wall" are both metaphors. A simile is a figure of speech in which a thing or idea is likened to another. "He walks like an elephant" and "She smiles like a Cheshire cat" are both similes.

Occasionally a comparison is cast as a contrast which focuses on differences rather than on similarities. "Unlike last year when we did mostly period drama, this year we are producing mostly comedies and musicals," would be a contrast. As you do your research, try to find comparisons that will help you express your ideas more meaningfully and more interestingly.

Statistics

Statistics are numerical facts. Statements such as "seven out of every ten voted in the last election" or "the cost of living rose three tenths of one percent" enable you to pack a great deal of information into a small package. When statistics are well used, they can be most impressive; when they are poorly used, they may be boring and, in some instances, downright deceiving.

Your first and most important concern should be the accuracy of the statistics you find. By taking statistics from only the most reliable sources and by double-checking statistics that are startling against another source will help you to avoid a great deal of difficulty. In addition, record only the most recent statistics. Times change; what was true five or even two years ago may be significantly different today. For instance, in 1971 only 12 out of 435 members of Congress were women. If you wanted to make a point about the number of women in Congress today, you would want the most recent figures.

If you are satisfied that you have found recent, reputable statistics, you will also want to be careful with how you use them. Statistics are most meaningful when they are used for comparative purposes. When Marion Stephenson, Vice President of Administration, NBC Radio Corporation, pointed out that, in 1970, industry offered the nation's supermarkets about 5,200 new products, the statistic did not take on meaning until she added that 5,200 products "is equal to the total number already on their shelves."[3]

In comparisons, we should make sure that we do not present a misleading picture. For instance, if we say that during the last six months Company A doubled its sales while its nearest competitor, Company B, improved by only 40 percent, the implication would be misleading if we did not indicate the size of the base; Company B could have more sales, even though its improvement was only 40 percent.

Although statistics may be an excellent way of supporting material, be careful of overdoing them. A few well-used statistics are far better than a battery of statistics. When you believe you must use a number of statistics, you may find that putting them on a visual aid, perhaps in the form of a chart, will help your audience understand them more readily.

The following passage from a speech on "Cancer" by William Aitken, an attorney from Nebraska, illustrates a good use of some impressive statistics. Notice the clear statement of the statistics, the excellent use of comparison, and the effort to make the statistics vivid:

> In the early 1900's few cancer patients had any hope of cure. In the late 1930's fewer than one in five was being saved (that is, alive after 5 years after first being treated). Ten years later one in four was being saved. Since 1956, the ratio has been one in three. Of every 6 persons who get cancer today, two will be saved and four will die. Numbers 1 and 2 will be saved. Number 3 will die but might have been saved had proper treatment been received in time. Numbers 4, 5, and 6 will die of cancers which cannot yet be controlled and only the results of further research can save these patients. This means that the immediate goal of cancer control in

---

[3] "Marion Stephenson, "Blind People Do Not Fear Snakes," *Vital Speeches*, July 15, 1971, p. 584.

this country is the annual saving of 318,000 lives, or half of those who develop cancer each year.[4]

Quotable Explanations and Opinions

When you find that a writer's explanation or opinion is valuable either for what was said or the way it was said, you may record the material precisely as stated. If you use the material in the speech, you should remember to give credit to your source. Use of any quotation or close paraphrasing that is not documented is plagiarism, an unethical procedure that violates scholarly practice. Many of our most notable quotations are remembered because they have literary merit. Winston Churchill's "I have nothing to offer but blood, toil, tears, and sweat," included in his first speech as Prime Minister in 1940, and John F. Kennedy's "Ask not what your country can do for you—ask what you can do for your country," from his 1961 Inaugural Address, are examples from speeches that are worth remembering and repeating. At other times, you will find that the clear, concise manner in which ideas were stated is worth repeating, even if the words themselves have no literary merit. In your speeches you have an opportunity and a right to use the words of others, as long as you keep quotations to a minimum and give credit where it is due.

Another form of development—visual aids—is important enough to merit special consideration. Chapter 8 will consider the types and uses of visual aids in informative and persuasive speeches.

Finding Material—How to Record

In your research (including observation, interviewing, and prior knowledge as well as printed sources), you may find a variety of examples, illustrations, quotations, statistics, and comparisons that you want to consider for your speech. How should you record these materials so that they will be of greatest value? You will be able to use only a fraction of the material you find. Moreover, you can never be sure of the order in which you will use the materials in the speech. Therefore, you need a method of recording that will allow you to use or select the better materials and to order the materials to

[4] William Aitken, "Cancer: The Problems and Progress," *Vital Speeches,* July 1, 1971, p. 552.

meet your needs. The note card method is probably the best that is available to you. As you find materials, record each item separately on 3 x 5 or 4 x 6 cards. Although it may seem easier to record materials from one source on a single sheet of paper or on a large card, sorting and arranging material is much easier when each item of that material is recorded on a separate card. In addition to recording each item separately, you should indicate the name of the source, the name of the author if one is given, and the page number from which it was taken. You will not necessarily need this material, but should you decide to quote directly or to reexamine a point, you will know where it came from. The following illustrates a useful notecard form:

> Topic: *Invasion of Privacy*
>
>   "A file was started on a man whose sin was to say, on seeing a girl demonstrator hauled away by Philadelphia police, 'Gee, it's a shame to carry away a pretty girl like that.' An agent assumed the remark indicated sympathy for the demonstration."
>
> > "How the U. S. Army Spies on Citizens," *Life*, March 26, 1971, p. 23.

In light of all that has been said so far in this section, you may be wondering how much source material is required for a speech. A rule-of-thumb answer is to have at least two or three times the amount of developmental material that you could use in the speech. If your speech is a three-minute assignment and you can read aloud all the material you have discovered in two or three minutes of material for a three-minute speech, the volume of material is probably sufficient. In addition, you should never use fewer than three sources. One-source speeches often lead to plagiarism; furthermore, a one-source or two-source speech just doesn't give you sufficient breadth of material. The process of selection, putting material together, adding, cutting, and revising will enable you to develop an original approach to your topic. How you go about organizing, developing, and adapting material to your audience will be considered in the next two chapters.

Exercise 4

For one of the specific purposes you plan to use for a speech this term, gather three examples of each kind of developmental material discussed above: example, illustration, comparison, statistics, and quotation. Make sure that you draw your material from at least three and preferably from four or more sources.

Organizing
Speech Materials

4

Principle 2   Effective speaking involves organizing material so that it develops and heightens the speech purpose.

Now that you have enough material to enable you to talk for the required time limit, your next step of preparation is to organize the material meaningfully. Effective speech organization is achieved through a systematic preparation of the body, the introduction, and the conclusion of the speech; and it is tested by means of a speech outline.

Preparing the Body of the Speech

Since the body of the speech contains the essence of the content and since the introduction and the conclusion relate to it directly, the body should be prepared first. Its preparation involves selecting and stating main points and selecting and adapting developmental materials.

Selecting and Stating Main Points

If you think of your prospective speech as a series of ideas, some more important than others, you should begin to understand the principle of subordination that underlies the theory of speech organization. The specific purpose states the goal of the speech; the main points divide the specific purpose into its key parts; and the rest of the body of the speech develops, explains, or proves the main points. Since the main points anchor the structure of the speech and since they are next in importance to the purpose of the speech, they should be carefully selected and phrased.

As a rule, main points are complete sentence statements that best develop the specific purpose. Let's consider the practical application of this rule to speech preparation. For the specific purpose "To explain that three major causes of juvenile delinquency are poverty, broken homes, and lack of discipline," what would be the main points? The answer can be expressed in complete-sentence outline form:

   I. One cause of juvenile delinquency is poverty.

  II. A second cause of juvenile delinquency is broken homes.

 III. A third cause of juvenile delinquency is lack of discipline.

Likewise, the main points for the specific purpose "To prove that the ungraded primary system has many advantages" would be the sentence statements of each of the advantages. Remember, there is nothing mysterious, unusual, peculiar, or tricky about selecting main points. Each of the stated or implied areas of the specific purpose will be one of the main points of the speech.

Actually, the ease with which you can determine your main points may prove to be an excellent test of the soundness of your specific purpose. For if you cannot determine what your main points are, the the specific purpose is probably too vague and should be revised. For instance, what would be the main points for the specific purpose "To talk about airplanes"? Since the phrase "about airplanes" gives no clue to the intended line of development, the main points cannot be determined.

Once you have selected the main points, you need to consider whether you have phrased them in clear, specific complete-sentence form. Vague, meaningless main points will have the same effect on the speech development as a vague purpose. If you don't know exactly what your main points mean, you can't expect your audience to understand them. To illustrate careful phrasing, let's examine three different sets of main points, one composed of labels, a second composed of carelessly phrased sentences, and a third composed of complete, substantive statements:

Purpose: To explain that our clothes tell us a great deal about our society.

Set 1	Set 2	Set 3
I. Casual	I. They are casual.	I. Our clothes indicate our casual look.
II. Youthful	II. They are youthful.	II. Our clothes indicate our emphasis on youthfulness.
III. Similarities	III. There is a similarity between men's and women's.	III. Our clothes indicate the similarity in men's and women's roles.
IV. Little distinction	IV. There is little distinction between rich and poor.	IV. Our clothes indicate the lack of visual distinction between the rich and poor.

The labels in the first column indicate the subject areas only. Although the words "youthful," "casual," "similarities," and "little distinction" relate to the purpose and indicate the subject areas of the main points, the nature of the relationship is unknown. In the second set, the complete-sentence main points are more meaningful than the labels. Nevertheless, the use of "they" and "there" along with the copulative verb "to be" makes the statements vague, indirect, and generally unclear. The speaker might get his point across, but any effectiveness would be a result of speech development rather than a result of clear statement of main points. The third set is considerably better. The main points include each of the classifications; moreover, they explain the relationships of the categories to the purpose sentence. If the audience remembers only the main points of Set 3, they would still know exactly what our clothes tell us about our society.

As you begin to phrase prospective main points, you may find your list growing to five, seven, or even ten that seem to be main ideas. If you will remember that every main point must be developed in some detail and that your goal is to help the audience retain the subject matter of each main point, you will see the impracticality of more than two, three, four, or at most, five main points. More than five is usually a sign that your purpose needs to be limited or that like ideas need to be grouped under a single heading.

Stating main points is also a matter of order. Effective speakers have found that their ideas blend together better, will be more easily phrased, and will be more easily understood if they follow one of the three major speech patterns of time order, space order, or topic order.

Time Order   Time order is a kind of organization in which each of the main points follows a chronological sequence of ideas or events. It tells the audience that there is a particular importance to the sequence as well as to the content of those main points. This kind of order often evolves when you are explaining how to do something, how to make something, how something works, or how something happened. For each of the following examples notice how the order is as important to the fulfillment of the purpose as the substance of the points:

Purpose: To explain the four simple steps involved in antiquing a table.

  I. Clean the table thoroughly.

 II. Paint on the base coat right over the old surface.

III. Apply the antique finish with a stiff brush, sponge, or piece of textured material.

IV. Apply two coats of shellac to harden the finish.

Purpose: To explain the steps involved in the course of office of the Roman citizen.

  I. Before he was eligible for office, a young Roman needed 10 years' military experience.

 II. At age 28, he was eligible for the office of Quaester.

III. The office of Aedile, next in line, could be skipped.

IV. After serving as Aedile, or Quaester, if he skipped Aedile, a Roman could become a Praetor.

 V. Finally, at age 42, the Roman could obtain a Consulship.

Purpose: To indicate the major events leading to the Great War.

  I. Between 1904 and 1910, a series of entangling alliances committed the major nations of Europe to the defense of almost any nation in Europe.

 II. In 1912, several Balkan wars affected relationships among Turkey, Serbia, Greece, and Bulgaria.

III. In 1914, the assasination of Archduke Francis Ferdinand precipitated a series of ultimatums eventuating in Germany's invasion of Belgium.

IV. Once Germany moved, nearly every nation in Europe became involved.

Space Order   Space order is a kind of organization in which each of the main points indicates a spatial relationship. If a speaker's intent is to explain a scene, place, object, or person in terms of its parts, a space order will allow him to put emphasis on the description, function, or arrangement of those parts. Because we remember best when we see a logical order of items, the speaker should proceed from top to bottom, left to right, inside to outside, or any constant direction that will enable the audience to follow visually. For each of the following examples, notice how the order proceeds spatially:

Purpose: To describe the arrangement of the tower dormitory.

   I. The first floor contains the administrative offices, meeting rooms, and student lounges.

   II. The next 15 floors contain 12 four-man rooms each.

   III. The top floor contains two penthouse apartments for the resident counselors.

Purpose: To describe the three layers that comprise the earth's atmosphere.

   I. The troposphere is the inner layer of the atmosphere.

   II. The stratosphere is the middle layer of the atmosphere.

   III. The ionosphere is the succession of layers that constitute the outer regions of the atmosphere.

Purpose: To describe the function of the parts of a golf club.

   I. The grip allows the golfer to hold the club securely.

   II. The shaft provides leverage.

   III. The head affects the nature of the drive.

Topic Order   Topic order is a kind of organization in which each of the main points arbitrarily develops a part of the purpose. Although the points may go from general to specific, least important to most important, or some other logical order, the order is still at the discretion of the speaker and is not a necessary part of the topic. With this kind of order, the content of the topics and not their relationship to each other is of paramount importance. The following illustrate the use of topic order in informative speeches:

Purpose: To indicate that telepathy, clairvoyance, and precognition are three elements of extrasensory perception.

   I. Telepathy refers to the communication of an idea from one person to another without benefit of the normal senses.

   II. Clairvoyance refers to seeing events and objects that take place elsewhere.

   III. Precognition refers to the ability to know what is going to happen before it happens.

Purpose: To explain major duties of the Presidency.

I. The President is the chief of foreign relations.

II. The President is commander-in-chief of the armed forces.

III. The President is the head of his party.

IV. The President is the head of the executive branch.

Purpose: To prove that more stringent controls should be imposed upon government agencies gathering information about U. S. citizens.

I. The use of advanced technology to gain information is a serious invasion of U. S. citizens' rights of privacy.

II. The laws that are supposed to protect our right of privacy are ineffective or inapplicable to the use of advanced technology.

III. More stringent controls would solve the problems.

Selecting and Adapting Developmental Materials

Taken collectively, your main points outline the structure of your speech. Whether your audience understands, believes, or appreciates what you have to say will usually depend upon the nature of your development of those main points. In Chapter 3, you learned that examples, illustrations, statistics, comparisons, and quotations were the materials you should be looking for; now you must select the best of that material, and you must think about whether it relates to the knowledge, interests, and attitudes of your audience.

If you have done adequate research, you will have plenty of material to choose from, so that as your outline evolves, you should be able to develop each main part rather completely with little difficulty. The more interesting and more challenging aspect of speech development is adapting what you have found to your audience. Since an audience responds most favorably when the material relates to its knowledge, interests, and attitudes, you should consider the potential for adaptation of every item of information you plan to use. Because audience adaptation is so important to successful speaking, a separate chapter is devoted to its application to determining the scope of topics and developing ideas. At this stage of preparation, the following three suggestions will guide you in the evaluation and selection of your developmental material for your first speech:

1. If you have a choice between two kinds of material, use audience adaptation as the major criterion for making the selection. If two examples are equally informative and one of them relates more directly to the audience, choose it.

2. If you have a variety of developmental material that supports your point, but none of it relates to your audience, create an adaptation. Remember, comparisons, hypothetical examples, and narratives can be invented by the speaker if he will think creatively.

3. If most of your developmental material is composed of statistics, detailed explanations, or elaborate quotations, make a special effort to find additional material that has built-in audience appeal. Illustrations, anecdotes, narratives, comparisons, and contrasts are inherently more interesting. Their novelty alone will often earn audience attention.

Now, let's see how these three suggestions can be applied to a typical problem of idea development. Suppose you were working on the main point "Japan is a small, densely populated nation." This sentence calls for you to show Japan's area and population. Using material from any reputable almanac, you could say:

Japan is a small, densely populated nation. Her 97 million people are crowded into a land area of 142,000 square miles. The density of her population is 686 persons per square mile.

The essential statistics about population and area have been given. Although the statistics are accurate and the unit is clear, the development is neither as interesting nor as meaningful as it could be. Now compare the following development, which incorporates the suggestions listed above:

Japan is a small, densely populated nation. Her population is 97 million—about one half that of the United States. Even though her population is nearly half that of our nation, her people are crowded into a land area of only 142,000 square miles—roughly the same land area as the single state of California. Just think of the implications of having one half of the population of the United States living in California. To further show the density of population, Japan packs 686 persons into every square mile of land. We in the United States average about 60 persons per square mile. Japan then is about eleven times as crowded as the United States.

This second development was built upon an invented comparison of the unknown, Japan, with the familiar, the United States and California. Even though most Americans don't have the total land area of the United States (let alone California) on the tip of their tongue, they know that the United States covers a great deal of territory and they have a mental picture of the size of California compared to the rest of the nation. It is through such detailed comparisons that the audience is able to visualize just how small and crowded Japan is. In addition to audience adaptation, the speaker can improve idea development using elements of oral style that will be considered in detail in Chapter 5.

If you were trying to explain the size and population of Japan to your class, what kinds of materials would you use to make those ideas meaningful? Suppose a Frenchman was trying to make the same point to a French audience? How could he adapt that content to his audience? When you get in the habit of asking yourself *why* you are developing ideas in a particular way, you will begin using your research material artfully. Remember, speech development is not just putting together ideas and facts you have researched. Not only must you have enough material, but also you must consider how you will adapt the material to your audience.

Preparing the Introduction of the Speech

After the body of the speech is planned, you can think about how you will begin and end your speech. In oral communication, it is especially important to get the audience listening attentively early, before you move into the body of the speech. By motivating them to listen during the first ten or twenty seconds of a short speech or within the first minute or so of a longer one, you can be reasonably assured that they are psychologically prepared to listen to the heart of the speech. Your major goals are to get audience attention and to focus that attention on the subject matter. These two goals are not synonymous. A speaker may get attention by pounding on the stand, by shouting "Listen!" or by telling a very funny joke. The question is whether any of these three approaches will prepare the audience for the body of the speech. If the attention does not relate to the speech topic, it is usually short-lived.

How you go about meeting these goals and how much time you spend is entirely up to you. Much depends upon the length and complexity of the speech, the knowledge and attitudes of your audience, and the nature of the occasion. For some audiences and occasions, the bold statement of the topic is all that is needed to get them interested enough to listen. In other cases, you may have to spend as much as 20 percent or more of your total speaking time preparing them for what you have to say. Speakers have discovered numerous ways for accomplishing their goals. The following are four of the most common:

The Question or Startling Statement

In a short speech, the kind you will be giving for your first few assignments, attention must be obtained and focused on the topic quickly. Although the burden appears to be great, the goal can be accomplished with one or more questions or startling statements along with any explanation that seems appropriate. Consider the following two openings used for short speeches on buying clothes and air pollution:

> Do you know what compels you to buy the clothing you wear? Many pressures are busily at work when we walk into a clothing store. Today I'd like to talk with you about a few of them.

> Look at the glass jar I'm holding. It appears to be empty. It isn't. What it contains is the air we breathe. Be wary—it could kill you. Let's see why.

Quotation

In your research you may well have discovered several quotable statements that are appropriate to your speech. If a particular quotation is especially vivid or thought provoking, you may decide to use it to open your speech. A quotation is best suited to a speech introduction when it is short, concise, and attention getting. The speaker then usually works from the quotation itself to the subject of the speech. Notice how the following short, familiar quotation was used for a speech on cigars:

> It was about 100 years ago that Thomas Marshall said, "What this country needs is a good five-cent cigar." What with one hundred years of inflation, it is rather amazing to find out that today you can buy one for five cents! Let's examine cigar production to see how modern science and technology enable the cigar manufacturer to produce a smokable cigar for as little as five cents.

Anecdote, Narrative, Illustration

Earlier, we talked about how eyes open and ears perk up when someone says, "Did you hear the one about . . . ?" Nearly everyone enjoys a good story. You should be aware, however, that anecdotes, narratives, and illustrations can be the best or the worst ways of beginning a speech, depending upon how they relate to the topic. Some speakers who are so taken with the notion that a story is worth telling may begin with one whether it relates to the topic or not, with the result that the audience enjoys the story and ignores the speech. Since most good stories take time to tell, they are usually more appropriate for speeches of eight to ten minutes or longer. The following illustrates the use of a story to begin a speech on "The Communication Gap":

> A plumber wrote to a government agency, saying he found that hydrochloric acid quickly opened drain pipes. Was this a good thing to use? A scientist at the agency replied that "the efficacy of hydrochloric acid is indisputable, but the corrosive residue is incompatible with metallic permanence." The plumber wrote back, thanking him for assurance that hydrochloric acid was all right. Disturbed by this turn of affairs, the scientist showed the letter to his boss—another scientist—who then wrote to the plumber: "We cannot assume responsibility for the production of toxic and noxious residue with hydrochloric acid and suggest you use an alternative procedure." The plumber wrote back that he agreed, hydrochloric acid worked fine. Greatly disturbed by this misunderstanding, the scientists took their problem to the top boss. He wrote to the plumber: "Don't use hydrochloric acid. It eats hell out of the pipes." I think it's fair to say that this story illustrates a communication gap. All of us are subject to misunderstandings of this kind. Today I'd like to talk with you for a few minutes about four things that we can do to narrow this communication gap with our audiences.

Personal Reference

Since the audience is the object of all communication, a direct reference to the audience or occasion may help achieve your goals. Actually, any good opening has an element of audience adaptation to it. The personal reference is directed solely to that end. Although we have learned to be suspect of insincere use of this method made by individuals who are only after our votes, proper use of the personal reference is particularly effective. The following is a good example of the personal reference opening used by Laurence H. Silberman, Under Secretary, U. S. Department of Labor, before the Conference of the National Foundation of Health, Welfare, and Pension Plans in Honolulu:

> Good morning, members of the National Foundation. As a one-time resident of Hawaii, I still tend to think of it as home. If you think of Hawaii as Heaven—and some people do—then I have one foot in Washington and one foot in heaven. This is not quite the

same as having one foot in heaven and one foot in hell—but sometimes it comes pretty close.

Anyhow, as an old Hawaii hand, I think it's appropriate for me to welcome you here today and to sympathize with you over the fact that, for some of you, your first exposure to the Islands should come in the form of an early morning speech. It's more than a man should be asked to bear. But if we must have a speech, this is the right place to be talking about retirement and pensions. It's a good place to retire—and you'll want a healthy pension if you have the idea of doing it here yourselves.[1]

Although each has been discussed individually, the various types of introductions may be used alone or in combination, depending upon the time you have available and the interest of your audience. The introduction is not going to make your speech an instant success, but an effective introduction will get an audience to look at you and listen to you. That's about as much as you have a right to ask of an audience during the first minute of your speech.

Exercise 5

For any topic that you might use during this term, prepare three separate introductions that would be appropriate for your classroom audience. Which is the better one? Why?

Preparing the Conclusion of the Speech

Inexperienced speakers often end their speeches abruptly after they have completed the body, or they ramble on aimlessly until they find a place that allows them to go sit down. The result of such practices is that the speaker may lose much of the effect he nurtured so carefully during the speech. Like the introduction, even the best conclusion cannot do much for a poor speech; but it can help to heighten the effect of a good speech and, equally important, it can tie the speech together into a compact, concise package for the audience. Look at it this way: you may have talked for five minutes, twenty minutes, or an hour—regardless of the length of time, when

---

[1] Laurence H. Silberman, "Proposed Pension Legislation," *Vital Speeches*, January 15, 1971, p. 197.

you get near the end you have only one last chance to focus upon the main points. Therefore, even though the conclusion is to be a short part of the speech, seldom more than 5 percent, it may have great importance.

By far the easiest way to end a speech is by summarizing the main points. Thus, the shortest appropriate ending for a speech on the causes of juvenile delinquency would be, "In conclusion, the three major causes of juvenile delinquency are poverty, broken homes, and lack of discipline." The virtue of such an ending is that it restates the main points, the ideas that are after all the three main ideas of the speech. Although such a conclusion is appropriate, easy, and generally satisfactory, it isn't very stimulating. A better one would lead up to the summary more interestingly. Notice how the following conclusion improves the overall effect:

> Each of us is concerned with the problem of juvenile delinquency; likewise, each of us realizes that no real dent can be made in the problem until and unless we know the causes. I hope that as a result of what I've said you have a better understanding of the three major causes of juvenile delinquency: poverty, broken homes, and lack of discipline.

Regardless of the purpose of the speech, the summary conclusion is always appropriate. Because the conclusion may be so important to heightening the emotional impact of the speech, even when you are using a summary, you may want to supplement it in some way so that your message is impressed upon the audience. Speakers have found that quotations, illustrations, anecdotes, narratives, and appeals— direct, straightforward requests for audience action—used with a summary or alone may get the desired response.

The following example, a speech conclusion by J. Irwin Miller, Chairman of the Board, Cummins Engine Company, represents a provocative appeal:

> To conclude: the real price tag of the American future is our willingness to grow up and become an adult people. It is a matter of spirit. Are we ready to recognize that all choices are competitive? Money choices are competitive. Even freedoms are competitive. If you want the freedom not to be robbed, you must curtail the freedom to rob. If you want the freedom to buy a house without discrimination, you must abridge the freedom not to sell a house to a black man.
>
> We have to do some national choosing. This is the price of the future. The mature adult understands a world of choice. The adolescent hopes somehow to avoid it.

When a man, in his gut, finally comes to know that there is truly no free lunch, when he then chooses the better—and not the worse —the better for his long term happiness and not his immediate delight: the better for his whole community and nation, and not the appearance of better for his family or his group, and when he decides to pay for these choices by giving up those alternatives on which he places less value, then he has bought and paid for his good fortune.

The statement that he who wished to save his life must lose it was a statement of hard fact and not a pious sermon. A whole nation has never faced up to this fact. It is the price of our future.

Can we afford it?[2]

The conclusion to Douglas MacArthur's famed Address to Congress in 1951 is a classic in the use of emotional impact.

I am closing my 52 years of military service. When I joined the Army even before the turn of the century, it was the fulfillment of all my boyish hopes and dreams. The world has turned over many times since I took the oath on the plain at West Point, and the hopes and dreams have long since vanished. But I still remember the refrain of one of the most popular barrack ballads of that which proclaimed most proudly that—

"Old soldiers never die; they just fade away."

And like the old soldier of that ballad, I now close my military career and just fade away—an old soldier who tried to do his duty as God gave him the light to see that duty.

Good-by.

Exercise 6

For the same topic used in Exercise 5, prepare a short summary conclusion. Is there any way that you can supplement the summary to give the conclusion greater impact?

Evaluating the Speech Structure— The Complete Outline

A speech outline is a short, complete-sentence representation of the speech that is used to test the logic, organization, development, and overall strength of the structure before any practice

---

[2] J. Irwin Miller, "Can We Afford Tomorrow?" *Vital Speeches*, January 1, 1971, p. 192.

takes place. It should contain the purpose, the main points, some of the development, and an indication of a prospective introduction and conclusion. Furthermore, at least the main points of the outline should be written in complete sentences and should use a consistent set of symbols to show idea subordination. So that the outline will be a representation and not a manuscript with letters and numbers, it should seldom contain more than one third[3] the number of words that could be spoken within the time limit. The substance of the outline will be included in every practice—the methods of development, the audience adaptation, and the language will and should vary during each practice and during the speech itself.

The following example illustrates the various rules, parts, and tests of a speech outline. Study it closely and try to make your early outlines conform as nearly as possible to the form of this example. The inside column contains the outline; the outside column contains a detailed analysis:

**Outline for a Speech
(4–6 minutes)**

Outline

Analysis

Specific Purpose: To explain the three major pressures that determine the selection of our clothing.

The specific purpose is not a part of the speech per se. It reminds the speaker of his goal and should be used to test whether everything in the outline is relevant.

Introduction

I. Do you know what compels you to buy the clothing you wear?

II. We are not aware of it at the time, but many pressures are busily at work when we purchase clothing.

The word "introduction" sets this section apart as a separate unit. The content of the introduction is devoted to getting attention and preparing the audience for the speech topic. The introduction may be modified considerably before the speaker is ready to give his speech.

---

[3] Because a lengthy outline can inhibit spontaneity, you should be very careful with your first few outlines to be sure that they are of a suitable length. One way of testing the length of an outline is by computing the total number of words that you could speak during the time limit and then limiting your outline to one third of that total. Since approximate figures are all that are needed, you can assume that your speaking rate is about average—160 words per minute. Thus, for a two- to three-minute speech, which would include roughly 320 to 480 words, the outline should be limited to 110 to 160 words. The outline for an eight- to ten-minute speech, which will contain roughly 1,200 to 1,500 words, should be limited to 400 to 500 words.

The word "body" sets this section apart as a separate unit.

Main point I reflects a topical relationship of main ideas. It is stated as a complete, substantive sentence.

The main point could be developed in many ways. These two subdivisions, shown by consistent symbols (A and B) indicating the equal weight of the points, consider the type and the amount of clothing that will yield physical comfort. Each of the subdivisions of B relate directly to the subject of B, the amount of clothing needed.

Main point II continues the topical relationship. The sentence is a complete, substantive statement paralleling the wording of main point I. Furthermore, notice that each of the main points considers one major idea.

Since main point II considers the determinants of "modesty," the major subdivisions are related to those terms. The degree of subordination is at the discretion of the speaker. Ordinarily, subordination is shown by the following set of symbols: major points—I, II, III, etc.; subdivisions of major points—A, B, C, etc.; subdivisions of subdivisions—1, 2, 3, etc.; further subdivisions—a, b, c, etc. Although greater breakdown can be shown, an outline will rarely be subdivided further. After the first two stages of subordination, words and phrases may be used in place of complete sentences in further subdivisions.

Main point III continues the topical relationship, is parallel to the other two in phrasing,

Body

I. Clothing is selected for physical comfort.

   A. Temperature changes ranging from hot to cold dictate the type of garment that needs to be worn at that particular time.
   B. Weather conditions such as snow or rain decide for us how much or how little clothing is needed for our comfort.
      1. A trench coat seems fitting enough for damp, rainy days.
      2. Then naturally we consider ear muffs for snow and ice in January.
      3. On a hot, muggy day in July, we try to wear as little as we can.

II. Clothing is selected to conform to our attitudes about modesty.

   A. Our dress is in accordance with our Puritan heritage.
   B. Certain religious precepts influence some people as to what is modest and what is not.
   C. Our culture influences our standards of modesty.
      1. In the early 1900s a bare calf was considered indecent.
      2. Today, short skirts and two-piece bathing suits have become standard.

III. Clothing is selected to make us more appealing.

A. Women take great pride, expend energy, and spend money in their clothing decisions.

   1. They dress to please and to attract members of the opposite sex.

   2. They dress to get group approval from their contemporaries.

and is a complete, substantive sentence.

In this case the subdivisions classify on the basis of men's motives and women's motives, as opposed to direct topical development of all the motives that are present. Throughout the outline, notice that each statement is an explanation, definition, or development of the statement to which it is subordinate.

   3. Yet at the same time, they wish to remain distinctive and individualistic.

B. Men also take pride in their appearance when dressed.

   1. They want to look appealing and distinctive.

   2. They put less emphasis on status.

The substance of the outline should be tested by asking the following questions:

1. Is the purpose sentence a clear, concise, statement of intent?

2. Are the main points stated as clear, substantive sentences?

3. Do the main points develop the purpose sentence directly?

4. Does each main point consider only one idea?

5. Are the main points limited to a maximum of five?

6. Do the various subpoints really support the division they are subordinate to?

7. Can each of the points be developed with examples, quotations, comparisons, and other forms of amplification?

Conclusion

I. The next time you are driven to making a clothing decision, ask yourself honestly what has determined your decision.

II. It may be physical comfort, it may be an attitude about modesty, or it may be to make you more appealing.

The word "conclusion" sets this apart as a separate unit.

The content of the conclusion is a form of summary tying the key ideas together. Although there are many types of conclusions, a summary is always acceptable for an informative speech.

Exercise 7

Complete an outline for your first speech assignment. Test the outline to make sure that it conforms to the assignment.

Developing
Oral Style

5

Principle 3 Effective speaking is a product of clear, vivid, emphatic, and appropriate oral style.

Because ideas are communicated for the most part by language, the way those ideas are phrased will determine whether an audience understands or accepts them. As a result, any time spent improving our oral style will pay big dividends. Broadly defined, style is the use of language; and it covers all aspects of word selection, vocabulary, usage, sentence construction, and syntax. However, the purpose of this chapter is not to give a complete review of language but to focus on selected aspects of oral style that makes the greatest difference in effective speaking.

What is oral style? Does it differ from written style? Although speech and writing have many things in common (in fact under some circumstances good speech and good writing are essentially the same), a comparison of your own conversation with your themes, essays, and term papers can show that certain differences do exist. When we set about composing our speeches, we should think of speechmaking as an extension of the conversational process rather than a written essay that will be spoken. Speech is for the ear; writing is for the eye. Every rule governing writing has to do with perception by the eye; but as a speaker, you must affect the ear. Charles James Fox, a great British Parliamentary debater, once remarked: "Does it read well? Then it's not a good speech." What he said contains a great deal of truth.

Oral language must be instantly intelligible. One of the characteristics of conversation that leads to intelligibility is *informality*. Good public speaking should also be informal. Don't be alarmed by or try to avoid familiar words, contractions, short sentences, and simple construction. Of course, informal conversation does not mean sloppiness. Poor grammar, slang, and excessive use of colloquialisms should be avoided in public speaking. Perhaps we should say that speechmaking should contain the same degree of informality as your best conversational style.

Good oral style is also quite *personal*. When you write an essay you may have reason for an impersonal approach to the material. Because a speech is for the audience in front of you, anything you can do to help the audience realize that your words are meant for each of them and not some other undefined group of individuals will be to your advantage. Although you may be encouraged to avoid personal pronouns in theme writing, you should use them in speeches. Get used to talking in terms of "us," "we," "our," "your," and the like. As you read the speeches in the Appendix, notice the great number of personal pronouns used by all of the speakers.

Third, don't be alarmed by the slightly *repetitive* nature of your conversation. Because a speaker must be instantly intelligible, he may have to express the same idea two, three, or even four different ways until he is sure that the audience has the point. You will note that the more impromptu your speaking the more repetitive your words and ideas will tend to be. Moreover, if you are not really prepared to speak your style may be excessively repetitive. Repetition of "uh," "you know," and parts of sentences indiscriminately should be avoided. As you practice your speeches orally, you will begin to eliminate the worst aspects of redundancy, so that excessive repetition should be no real problem in your speeches. Recognizing that oral style serves a different function from written style, let's consider the essentials of oral style you will want to develop.

Clarity

Clarity is achieved by using language that can be understood by an audience as it is spoken. Suppose a speaker, describing a near accident, said, "The big thing almost got me." The audience would have only a vague idea of what happened—the communication would not be very clear. Suppose he said, "As I was crossing the street, I was almost run over by a big Cadillac that was turning the corner." Phrased this way, the idea is much clearer. Suppose, however, he said, "Yesterday about 3:00 P.M., I was almost run over by a large red Cadillac sedan, license AB34456, turning right at the corner of Center and Main, while I was approximately two fifths of the way across the street." In this case, the clarity would be obscured by the excessive detail. Clarity, then, consists of saying specifically, concretely, and accurately all that needs to be said in order to communicate the idea and no more. Let's consider each of these aspects of clarity separately, and then let's draw them together with a specific example from a contemporary speech.

Accuracy

Accuracy of style refers to the ability to make the word represent the idea so well that the receiver (the audience) gets the same message as the source (the speaker) is sending. Basically, accuracy has to do with word selection. Have you ever found yourself in the situation where a person says something like "He's a grouch"? And when you reply, "I never thought of him as grouchy," the person says, "I didn't really mean grouchy, I meant he loses his temper so quickly." Words are an imperfect way of communicating an idea intact from one mind to another. The process is made even more difficult by the shades of meaning that so many words represent. Take the simple verb "said." Notice the changes in meaning when a person uses such words as "stated," "averred," "growled," "indicated," "intoned," "suggested," "pleaded," "shouted," "purred," "answered," or "asked." Successful communication requires an understanding of words, not only what they mean in general but also how they relate to each other.

When the elder William Pitt, regarded by some as one of England's greatest speakers, was a teenager he gained an understanding and an appreciation of the language by reading Bailey's dictionary, a famous work of the day, *twice*. Even today, dictionary reading is not a bad way to sharpen your understanding of words. An interesting method of practice is to play "synonyms." Think of a word, then list as many words as you can that mean about the same thing. When you have completed your list, refer to a book of synonyms, like Roget's *Thesaurus*, to see which words you have omitted; then try to determine the shades of difference among the words. Refer to a dictionary for help—it is useful to look up words even when you're sure you know their meaning. You may be surprised to find how many times a subtle meaning of a familiar word escapes you. Now the goal of this exercise is not to get you to select the rarest word to project an idea—the goal is to encourage you to select the word that best represents the idea you wish to communicate.

Specificity

In ordinary conversation, under the pressure of having to talk with little or no previous planning, we tend to speak in general terms. But general and vague language inhibits clear communication. For purposes of improvement, the time to test whether or not your language is specific is during your practice periods after the speech has been planned, but before the actual delivery. Listen critically to yourself to see which list of words below illustrates your word selection.

things	characteristics or objects or sayings
large stick	baseball bat
car	red sedan
five trees	three elms and two maples
writing instrument	pen or pencil
a container	a square, cardboard box
selected fruit	apples and oranges

If the words in the left-hand column represent your style, then your language may be vague, general, and unclear. If the words in the right-hand column represent your word selection, then your style is specific. A good method of practice is to recall objects, places, and events and try to describe them. If you have a tape recorder, record your statements. If not, perhaps a friend or relative could help you with your analysis. After each sentence, reexamine every word to see whether your language was specific enough to communicate clearly. If not, try for a more specific statement of the general words and phrases.

Concreteness

Just as we tend to speak in general rather than specific terms, we also tend to speak in abstract rather than concrete terms. Although use of some abstract language is unavoidable (in fact, high-level abstraction may be a sign of high intelligence), abstraction often substitutes for lack of concrete knowledge. You want to use words that communicate to the audience the same meaning you intended. With overuse of abstractions, clear communication becomes nearly impossible. For instance, in the 1972 Democratic primary campaign, George McGovern, George Wallace, and Hubert Humphrey all talked about justice. Probably 100 percent of their audiences concurred that justice is a desirable goal. But what did McGovern mean by "justice"?

What did Wallace mean? and Humphrey? Or equally important, what did their audiences think they meant? What does "justice" mean? Could you write a one-sentence definition? Ask your roommate what he thinks "justice" means. Ask three or four other persons for their definitions. Experiments of this kind reveal how the use of abstract terms can block communication. Whenever you hear yourself using an abstract word, ask whether your meaning would be clearer if you used a concrete expression. Increased use of the expressions in the right-hand column would make your speech more clear:

Honesty	Returning a five dollar bill to someone who dropped it in the street.
Equality	Being able to buy a home in the suburbs if you can afford to.
Loyalty	Defending a friend's character when it is being attacked in his absence.
Justice	Equal application of the law regardless of your color, whether you have long hair, or whether you are poor.

Economy of Words

Not only must language be specific and concrete, it should also be free from the senseless repetition, extraneous words, and excessive qualification and detail that creep into our speech. In several parts of this text we will have occasion to recommend repetition of key ideas for emphasis. Unfortunately, we often repeat words, phrases, and occasionally entire sentences for no apparent reason. The speaker who says, "Yesterday, ah, yesterday we went to the store," probably hadn't decided what he was going to say. In order to give himself some time to think, he repeated "yesterday." You may repeat words and phrases for this reason occasionally. Minimal repetition of this kind will not hinder communication. In fact, without memorizing speech, it is nearly impossible to avoid some repetitions. If, however, you find yourself repeating words and phrases constantly, for no apparent reason, you should take steps to check the bad habit.

In addition to senseless repetition, some people clutter their speech with extraneous words. On the printed page, breaks in thought are noted by commas, periods, semicolons, dashes, and other punctuation. While speaking, you can punctuate effectively with pauses of varying lengths. An unacceptable way is with extraneous, meaningless words and sounds used to fill the pauses. Most individuals have their own pet fillers. Are you one who says, "uh," "er," "well uh," "like," "you know uh"? Although we accept these irritating expressions from our friends, we do not accept them from public speakers. The speaker who turns the extraneous words and sounds on, turns the audience off. If your professor calls such uses to your attention, you must learn to listen to your speech. Once you hear what you are doing, correction of the habit is rather easy. Of course, you shouldn't be too hard on yourself for a few lapses. Not many speakers can talk for five to ten minutes without using an occasional extraneous filler—the test is whether you can keep these to an absolute minimum.

Economy of words also refers to the number of words it takes you to get a point across. The sentence "Yesterday about 3:00 P.M. I was almost run over by a very large, red Cadillac sedan, license AB34456, turning right at the corner of Center and Main, while I was approximately two fifths of the way across the street" is ludicrous, because it is so cluttered with excessive detail. Such excessive detail, use of endless qualifiers, and reliance on that overused admission of lack of clarity, "in other words," all hinder effective communication. Examine your communication to make sure that you say all that is necessary —but only what is necessary. Once you learn selectivity, the ability to tell what is important enough to say and what should be left out, you will increase your clarity.

In the following example, note how John Cunningham, author and historian, uses accurate word selection and specific, concrete language to sharpen the clarity of his point that the good old days weren't really so good:

> I could take you through a full century, chick by chick, onion by onion, Irish potato by Irish potato. I could read some poetry from William Cullen Bryant and a stanza or two from Longfellow to prove in lyrics that for farmers those long-ago times were the good old days.

> I will spare you that, for in truth those were NOT the good old days, regardless of poetry and Currier and Ives Lithographs. Those were days of backbreaking toil, of horrible farm failures brought on by unknown natural killers of plants and animals. Those were days when farmers stayed down on the farm chiefly because they were born down on the farm and knew no way out. It was much easier for William Cullen Bryant to catch the charm of farming on a weekend visit down from Boston than it was for the farmer's wife who toiled in the farm house 365 days a year. And Currier and Ives never seemed to be around when disease felled a half-dozen cattle.

> But it can be useful to look at agriculture in New Jersey a century ago. Farming was then the chief way of American life, for better or for worse. Only about 900,000 people lived in New Jersey in 1870—about one-eighth of today's population. Only Newark and Jersey City were genuine cities. Most county seats had populations

of 2,000 people or less. All else was either farmland, woodlots, or wasteland—and sometimes it was difficult to tell the difference.[1]

Vividness

Clarity of language allows you to secure understanding; vividness of language allows you to arouse and sustain interest in what you are saying. Literally, vividness means creating pictures or evoking lifelike mental images. A visual aid allows the audience to see details; vividness allows an audience to picture the details *in their imaginations*. This vivid imagery makes it possible for an audience to gain immediate understanding. Perhaps more important, this vivid imagery makes it possible for an audience to recall the experience itself. Since the imagery you are attempting to create is based upon sensory impression, you should try to heighten the image of the sensory impression. For instance, when you think vividly about pizza, you can see the round, flat pie, about 15 inches in diameter, with the crust cooked to a golden brown; you can hear the crackling of the crust and the popping of the sauce as it cooks; you can smell the savory tomato sauce, the pungent aroma of the pepperoni; you can taste the plump, juicy mushrooms, the spicy anchovies, the subtle flavor of oregano, the tang of the tomato sauce; you can feel the firm crust as you bite into it. And just as you can imagine these impressions, you can create them for an audience in your speech. As with clarity, some economy of words (especially adjectives) is appropriate. Too many will wear your audience out or give an artificiality to your speech. Judicious use of vivid words is the key.

Vividness of speech must begin with vividness of thought. You must have a mental picture before you can communicate one to your audience. If you can't feel the bite of the wind and the sting of the nearly freezing rain, if you can't hear the thick, juicy T-bone steaks sizzling on the grill, if you can't feel that empty yet exhilarating feeling as the jet climbs from takeoff, you won't be able to describe these sensations to your audience.

Here, Philip Lesley, President, Philip Lesley Company, uses vivid imagery to show that America, a nation built on selling, has greatly oversold what it can deliver:

---

[1] John Cunningham, "How Are You Going to Keep Them Down on the Farm?" *Vital Speeches*, March 15, 1971, p. 346.

And in a period when the overheating of expectations threatens to consume our civilization in flames, the effect of many of our political and opinion leaders, who build up still greater expectations, is to pour gasoline on it.

In this climate of expecting everything and accepting nothing, the acceptance of the law itself is in doubt. We cannot assume that people understand the basis of the law and its merits.[2]

Vividness is not solely the product of speaker imagery. It can also be achieved by appropriate stories, definitions, humor, comparison and contrast, and parallel structure.

William Arrowsmith, Visiting Professor of Humanities, Massachusetts Institute of Technology, uses careful word selection and illustration to achieve vividness for his point that the academic world is acting in bad faith:

Again. But the faculty defers to, concurs in, the mindlessness, this isolation and arrogance of youth—and minority-culture. Options are abandoned before ever being looked at; permission is granted for any project even though there may be serious doubt of any real educational result. A freshman, for instance, recently decided that the curriculum was not for him. He was an artist. He appeared before the faculty independent-studies committee and demanded that he be given credit and equipment for making a film of the deplorable conditions in the local hospital. By questioning him, a member of the committee ascertained that the student had never used a camera, that he knew nothing of composition or even the most ordinary technical skills, and that he had never, except to have his tonsils removed, been in a hospital. Yet the committee promptly and mindlessly voted the student $7000 worth of equipment and credit for an entire year for making this film. He would learn more by failing, or succeeding, it was said, than he could conceivably learn as a student. The principles at work behind this little true story explain perhaps why John Holt's argument that the faculty should be used as a resource rather than a body of teachers has found so many adherents among students and faculty.[3]

In his speech on "Economy and Environment," Lowry Wyatt, Senior Vice President of Weyerhaeuser, makes his point more vivid by blending humor, definition, and contrast:

This will not be an easy task. In industry, we often criticize the "nuts" of the environmental movement. We tend to regard some

---

[2] Philip Lesley, "Respect for the Law and Lawyers," *Vital Speeches*, March 1, 1971, p. 301.

[3] William Arrowsmith, "The Great Academic Refusal," *Vital Speeches*, July 15, 1971, p. 594.

of the more moss-backed in our ranks, however, as being merely "overly zealous." We have to recognize that the only essential difference between a "nut" and a "zealot" is one of perspective. One who overstates an issue in opposition to ours is a "nut." One who overstates our own issue is a "zealot." Both are equally dangerous to environmental solutions.[4]

A quite artful way of making ideas vivid is through the use of parallel structure. Here, U. S. Secretary of Commerce Maurice H. Stans combines repetition of his speech title, "Wait a Minute," with parallel structure to bring about an extremely vivid effect. This example not only illustrates vividness, but serves as a nice transition into the third major element or oral style—emphasis.

If we settle for quick, immediate solutions to one set of problems, we can catapult ourselves into others that are much more serious, and we are beginning to find that out.

So we have to begin to look a little farther down the road.

I think it is high time for the entire nation to weigh the needs against the demands and say: "Wait a Minute, what are our priorities?"

We need to weigh the requirements against our resources and say: "Wait a Minute, which can we afford? Which can we achieve?"

We need to weigh technological capabilities against the timetables and the options and say: "Wait a Minute, how can we get there from here?"

We need to weigh environmental goals against economic reality and say: "Wait a Minute, how do the benefits compare with the costs?"

In other words, the problem is: how do we develop public and private policies in which economies and technology are factored into every environmental assessment?[5]

Emphasis

In a 500-word speech, all 500 words are not of equal importance. We neither expect nor necessarily want an audience to

---

[4] Lowry Wyatt, "Economy and Environment," *Vital Speeches*, June 1, 1971, p. 510.

[5] Maurice H. Stans, "Wait a Minute," *Vital Speeches*, September 1, 1971, p. 690.

retain the memory of every word uttered. Thus, throughout your speech preparation you are concerned with ways of emphasizing those words and ideas that are more important than others and should therefore be remembered. Emphasis may be made through organization by idea subordination, through delivery by voice and bodily action, and through language itself. Let's consider three elements of language that will enable you to make ideas stand out: proportion, transition, and repetition.

Proportion

One way of emphasizing points is through proportion, the amount of time spent on each of the ideas in the speech. The psychological importance of proportion can be illustrated by a hypothetical example. Assuming for a moment that proportion can be considered independently, if in a ten-minute speech on the causes of juvenile delinquency, the three main points (poverty, broken homes, and permissiveness) were discussed for about three minutes each, the audience might perceive the ideas as having equal weight. If, however, the speaker spent five minutes on poverty and only two minutes on each of the other two causes, the audience would perceive poverty, the five-minute point, as the most important one in the speech. Now, if poverty was indeed the most important cause, proportion would emphasize the point; if, however, broken homes was really a more important cause of juvenile delinquency, audience perception would differ from speaker intent.

You will probably find that your ideas have the greatest effect if proportion is correlated with position. Thus, in a ten-minute speech, if you put the most important point first, it should be the one you spend four or five minutes on. If you put the second most important point last, spend three or four minutes on it. The remainder of the time should be divided among the points you put in the middle. Since audiences are likely to remember best those points that were discussed in greater detail, the artful speaker takes care that the most important points receive the greatest amount of discussion.

Proportion is brought about by amplification. If a point is important but is not receiving proper development, you should add a few examples or illustrations to build its strength. Remember, don't add words for the sake of words. If a point really is important, you should have valuable information to include. If you find that you have to invent "padding," you might want to reevaluate the importance of that particular point.

Transition

A second means of emphasis is by means of carefully phrased transitions. Transitions are the words, phrases, and sentences that show idea relationships. Transitions summarize, clarify, forecast, and in almost every case, emphasize. Of the three methods of emphasis discussed here, phrasing good transitions is perhaps the most effective, yet is the least used. If you understand both internal and external transitions you can increase idea impact.

Internal Transition   Internal transitions grow from the relationships between the ideas themselves. Our flexible language provides us with numerous words that show relationships. Although the following list is not complete, it indicates many of the common transition words and phrases that are appropriate for speech.[6]

Transitions	Uses
also and likewise again in addition moreover	You will use these words to add material.
therefore and so so finally all in all on the whole in short	You will use these expressions to add up consequences, to summarize, or to show results.
but however yet on the other hand still although while no doubt	You will use these expressions to indicate changes in direction, concessions, or a return to a previous position.
because for	You will use these words to indicate reasons for a statement.
then since as	You will use these words to show causal or time relationships.

---

[6] After Sheridan Baker, *The Complete Stylist* (New York: Thomas Y. Crowell Co., 1966), pp. 73–74.

Transitions	Uses
in other words in fact for example that is to say more specifically	You will use these expressions to explain, exemplify, or limit.

Because these particular words and phrases give the oral clues needed to perceive idea relationships, you should accustom yourself to their use.

External Transition   External transitions call special attention to words and ideas. Since internal transitions can be missed if the audience isn't paying close attention, both for the sake of variety and for additional emphasis you can utilize direct statements to call attention to shifts in meaning, degree of emphasis, and movement from one idea to another. These statements tell the audience exactly how they should respond. Consider the following list:

Now I come to the most important idea in the speech.

If you haven't remembered anything so far, make sure you remember this.

Pay particular attention to this idea.

Remember, this is the second step of the process.

Are you sure you have this point? It is one of the most important.

But maybe I should say this again, because it is so significant.

These examples represent only a few of the possible expressions that leave the flow of ideas and interject subjective keys, clues, and directions to stimulate audience memory or understanding. Although these are not very subtle, experimental studies have indicated that they are effective in helping emphasize points.[7]

Repetition

The third, and perhaps most common means of emphasis is by repetition. Repetition may be an exact duplication of idea

---

[7] Ronald Stingley, "An Experimental Study of Transition as a Means of Emphasis in Organized Speeches," unpublished Master's thesis, The University of Cincinnati, 1968, p. 36.

or it may be a restatement. If you want the audience to remember the exact words, you should use repetition. If you want the audience to remember the idea, restatement is probably preferable. For instance, the explanation "Even a three hundred hitter only gets three hits in every ten times at bat—That means for every three hits he gets, there are seven times he is put out" reiterates the idea and not the words.

The speech by Maurice H. Stans cited previously as an example of vividness achieved through parallel structure was also an excellent example of emphasis achieved through repetition. If you return to page 62, you will notice that his speech title and key idea, "Wait a Minute," is repeated throughout the excerpt.

Appropriateness

Almost everyone at one time or another in his childhood replied to a particularly scathing remark, "Sticks and stones may break my bones, but words will never hurt me." I think this little rhyme is so popular among children because they know it is a lie, but they don't know how else to react. Whether we are willing to admit it or not words do hurt—sometimes permanently. Think of the great personal damage done to the individual throughout our history as a result of his being called a "hillbilly," "nigger," "wap," "yid." Think of the fights started by one person calling another's mother, sister, or a girlfriend a "whore" or a "slut." We all know, however, that it is not the words alone that are so powerful, it is the context of the words, the situation, the feelings about the participants, the time, the place, or the tone of voice. Recall how under one set of circumstances someone called you a name or used any four-letter word to describe you and you didn't even flinch; yet under another set of circumstances someone else calls you something far less antagonistic and you become enraged.

The key to the understanding of this phenomenon and to language usage in general is appropriateness. Words are symbolic. Of and by themselves they have no meaning. A symbol doesn't take on meaning until the sender and the receiver agree to accept that symbol for some concrete object, specific idea, mood, or feeling. And then, of course, regardless of the "standard" meaning of the word, how we take it is affected by all the factors of context mentioned above. Thus words like "mother," "traveling man," "zoo," "horse" and other very ordinary words take on meanings that evoke a variety of reactions, depending upon the experience of the sender and the receiver.

As a result, we must always be aware that our language may have accidental repercussions. When the sender doesn't understand the frame of reference of his audience, he may send messages in language that distorts the intended communication. And it doesn't take a whole speech to ruin a speaker's effect—a single inappropriate sentence may be enough to wreak havoc with his total message. For instance, the speaker who says, "And we all know the problem originates downtown," may be referring to the city government. But if the audience is composed of people who see downtown not as the seat of government but as the home of an ethnic or a social group, the sentence takes on an entirely different meaning. Being specific can help to avoid problems of appropriateness; recognizing that some words communicate far more than their dictionary meanings will help even more.

In addition to accidental repercussions of our language, we should caution against using words for their shock value. The entire fabric of protest rhetoric is imbued with shock language; yet shock language often backfires on the user. The goal of arousing anger and hostility toward an issue often results in anger and hostility toward the speaker. Eldridge Cleaver, Jerry Rubin, Abbie Hoffman, and Stokely Carmichael might be telling it like it is, but the effectiveness of their shock language will probably be limited solely to partisans and may alienate others in the audience.

Appropriate language has the positive value of cementing the bond of trust between the speaker and his audience. During the last two decades or so of experimentation with the principles of speaking, we have learned a great deal about what makes people behave as they do. One concept proven to be at the base of effective communication is the effect of speaker personality on an audience. If an audience likes a speaker, they often believe him. Through appropriate language we can help ourselves to achieve this goal. The more hostile the audience is likely to be to our person or to our ideas, the more care we need to take to use language that will be accepted by that audience. Under strain we can and we often do lose our temper. When we lose our temper, we often say things we don't really mean or we express our feelings in language that is unlikely to be accepted by strangers. If we do that, we may lose all we have gained.

Exercise 8

Take any point of the outline you developed for the last exercise and tape record a minute or two of development of the point. Transcribe your oral statement. Test it for clarity, vividness, emphasis, and appropriateness of language. Take various sentences of the transcription and work for greater clarity, vividness, emphasis, and appropriateness. As you become more conscious of the use of good oral style, you will find that your first drafts will become better and better.

Practicing
Speech Delivery

6

Principle 4   Effective speaking requires good delivery.

The final step of speech preparation is to practice the delivery of the speech. If we were to ask famous speakers what they regarded as the single most important element of their success, many would respond as the famous classical orator Demosthenes did—delivery. Delivery is what we see and hear; it is the physical medium through which the ideas are perceived. The best of ideas will have little chance with an audience if they are not well delivered.

Now because most of us have been getting our ideas across to people reasonably well for many years, we are seldom willing to admit that any success we have had in communicating may be in spite of and not because of our oral ability. Even Demosthenes had weaknesses of delivery that he had to work for years to overcome in order to develop his powers fully. Whether or not he really did speak with pebbles in his mouth or run up and down the hills of Greece declaiming at the greatest volume he could achieve, it is well documented that he spent hours every week on improving delivery. In this chapter we want to focus on the elements of speech delivery that can be perfected or improved upon with practice. Then we want to consider how we can go about practicing the speech itself.

What to Practice: Standards of Delivery

Delivery is the use of voice and body to help convey the message of the speech. Although the best delivery will not save the poorly prepared speech, particularly poor delivery may well harm your speech so much that even exceptional content and organization are negated. Speech delivery may be the deciding factor in the audience's estimation of your effectiveness. What then are the minimum common elements of delivery that you should master? Effective speakers convey a desire to communicate, a sense of audience contact, and a spontaneity, all contributing to a conversational quality. If you master these three characteristics and meet minimum standards of voice, articulation, and bodily action, your speech delivery will contribute to your effectiveness.

Desire to Communicate

Have you ever listened to a speaker whose convictions were so strong that you found yourself saying, "He's got to be right—no one could speak with such strength of conviction unless he were." Likewise, have you ever heard a speaker who so bubbled with enthusiasm that you were caught up in his every word? One such spellbinder today is Billy Graham. Regardless of your religious persuasion, you can hardly escape the force of Graham's delivery. Speakers like Graham today and Henry Clay, William Jennings Bryan, and Franklin Delano Roosevelt in the past all have had a deep and overpowering desire to communicate. They have wanted to speak; they have wanted people to listen.

If you really want to communicate, your voice will have a quality in it that audiences will recognize and respond to. If you really care about your topic and your audience, your voice will usually reflect that attitude. And if you really want to communicate, your audience will usually listen.

Of course, you might be saying, "It's easy enough to talk about wanting to communicate, but I'm scared stiff." This nervousness about speaking in public is often called stage fright. All right, let's face it, stage fright is a very real thing that we've got to face. But everyone, beginner and experienced speaker alike exhibit degrees of nervousness about speaking. If before your speech, your palms perspire, your stomach feels queasy, and your mouth gets dry, remember that, like it or not, such reactions are normal. In fact, it would be quite abnormal if you did not show some nervousness. You're being observed, your ideas are being weighed and considered, your every movement and word is a matter of public record—of course, you're going to be nervous.

The question, then, is not whether you will be nervous, but what you can do about it. Speakers past and present have learned to cope with and have often lessened their nervousness by recognizing the following three realities. First, if you are really well prepared, you will be less nervous than if you are only partially prepared. Nervousness is based in part on expected audience reaction. If you know you have nothing of value to say or that you haven't prepared fully enough, you will and should be nervous. If you have prepared and practiced five to ten hours for a five-minute speech, there's no need to be nervous. Second, if you will try to think about communicating the subject and not about yourself, you will be less nervous. Speakers who become an active part of the communication process don't have the time to worry about themselves. Third, and perhaps most important, once you realize that you can succeed (and you can), you will be less likely to be concerned about your nervousness. Success breeds confidence. You will begin with easy speaking tasks—as you succeed with them you will build confidence for the next task. Eventually you will have enough confidence to attempt and accomplish very complex speaking assignments. So even if you are rather nervous about your first speech, as long as you are well prepared and as long as you think about the speech and not yourself, you will be amazed to find that each time you speak you will be better able to control your nervousness.

Nervousness is related to self-concept. Some of us have a high opinion of ourselves. If we fail, and everyone fails at something at some time, we know that our failure is only temporary. We think of ourselves as winners and, of course, winners succeed. Likewise some of us have a low opinion of ourselves and our abilities. We expect to fail and we usually do. In fact, it is only when we succeed that we are surprised. One of the goals of an effective speaking course is to strengthen the self-concept. Low self-esteem is often a matter of how we think about ourselves and may have no relationship to our actual abilities. Research shows that in most classes a high percentage of individuals reinforce a good self-concept or strengthen a weak one. All we can ask you to do is to try. In trying, you will probably be surprised with the results. Still, don't expect miracles overnight. You may see only a little improvement in the first two or three speeches— by the end of the term, however, chances are the improvement will be considerable.

Aside from being inhibited by nervousness or by low self-esteem, some of us may be inhibited by our natural tendency to be less demonstrative than is needed for effective delivery. As individuals, each of us exhibits personality traits that make him distinct. These traits combine to make some of us more outgoing than our neighbors and some of us more reserved. The relationship to speechmaking is that if you are outgoing, you may find it easier to project your attitude about your topic. If, however, you are rather reserved, the audience may not be able to pick up the cues showing your attitude so readily. If you seldom show much overt responsiveness to your feelings, you must do a little more than "what comes naturally." Whereas the extrovert shows emotional responsiveness even when his feeling is not very strong, the introvert registers the same level of expressiveness only when he has reached a high degree of emotion. If you tend to be more reserved, you must intensify your feelings about what you are doing in order for the emotions to be communicated. Make sure your topic pleases you; get involved with the developmental material; and constantly remind yourself that what you are planning to say will benefit the audience. Audiences do not listen without some motivation; they will expect some effort on your part.

Audience Contact

Although perception of speech communication seems to be primarily auditory, we concentrate better on the message when a visual bond is established between speaker and audience. In fact, in face-to-face communication we expect the speaker to look at us while he is talking. If the source of the sound, the speaker, does not look at us, we will lose our need to look at him, and, thus, our desire to pay attention to him. The result is a break in the communication bond and a proportional loss of attention. As a speaker then, you have a certain amount of control over your audience's attention simply by looking at them.

Not only does good eye contact help attention, it also increases audience confidence in the speaker. What do you think of an individual who will *not* look you in the eye when he speaks with you? Your attitude toward him is probably negative. On the other hand, when a speaker does look you in the eye, you are probably more willing to trust him. Eye contact is not material evidence of a speaker's sincerity. We do, however, regard it as psychological evidence.

But as you gain skill in speaking you will become aware of the most beneficial aspect of good eye contact; that is, your ability to study audience reaction to what you are saying. Communication is two-way. You are speaking with an audience, and they in turn are responding to what you are saying. In daily conversation, their response would be verbal; in public speaking, their response is shown by various cues they give. An audience of people who are virtually on the edges of their seats with their eyes upon you is paying attention. An audience of people who are yawning, looking out the window, and slouching is not paying attention. You can determine what adjustments, what additions, changes, and deletions you need to make in your plans by being aware of audience reaction. As you gain greater skill, you will be able to make more and better use of the information learned through eye contact.

How do you maintain audience eye contact? It is, of course, physically impossible to look at your whole audience all at once. What you can do is to talk with individuals and small groups in all parts of the audience throughout your speech. Don't spend all of your time looking front and center. The people at the ends of aisles and those in the back of the room are every bit as important as those right in front of you.

Spontaneity

The third interrelated quality or characteristic that is fundamental to effective speech delivery is a spontaneity, the impression that the idea is being formed at the time it is spoken. At some time in your academic career, you may have had the opportunity, or the misfortune, to memorize some bit of prose or poetry. Remember when you were working on the assignment, you were not nearly as concerned with the meaning of the words as you were with the process of memorizing the flow of words. If you or other classmates had to recite, you will remember that the class was seldom inspired by the presentations. Why? Since the words sounded memorized, any semblance of meaning was lost. Spontaneity, the particular characteristic of voice that makes an idea sound new, fresh, and vital even if it has been practiced for days, was missing. Although our best actors and actresses can make lines they have spoken literally thousands of times sound original, most of us do not have the ability or the know-how. Have you ever wondered why a public official often sounds so much better in off-the-cuff interviews than he does when reading a speech? Once the word is memorized or written down, it is no longer spontaneous communication and the speaker is then required to become somewhat of an actor to make the idea sound spontaneous.

How can you make a planned speech seem spontaneous? The answer lies in the utilization of characteristics of your own conversational method. Since there is a tremendous difference between knowing ideas and memorizing them, you need to have a mastery of content, not words. If I asked you to tell me how to get downtown, you would be able to tell me spontaneously because you have made the trip so many times the knowledge is literally a part of you. If I asked you to tell me about the handball game or the field hockey game you just finished, you could do it spontaneously because key parts of the game would be vivid in your memory. If, on the other hand, I asked you to tell me a little about the material you studied for a history class, your ability to do it spontaneously would depend upon the quality of the effort you had made to master the material. If you had weighed and considered the material, if you had tried to understand the concepts rather than just memorize the details, you would have enough understanding to discuss the content spontaneously. Spontaneous presentation of prepared materials requires experience with the facts, vivid images of the facts, and true understanding of the facts.

Students will often say that they can speak so much better on the spur of the moment than when they try to give a prepared speech. What they mean, of course, is that given a topic about which they have had experiences, vivid images, and understanding they can communicate reasonably well on the spur of the moment. Since you have the opportunity to weigh and consider your subject matter, there is no reason why you should not be equally spontaneous with the prepared speech. How to show spontaneity will be considered further when we examine speech practice later in this chapter.

These three concepts—desire to communicate, eye contact, and spontaneity—when taken together, give a speaker what has come to be called a conversational quality. Speechmaking and conversation are not really quite the same. However, by utilizing the best characteristics of conversation in the formal speech situation the speaker will give the audience the feeling that he is conversing with them. These three characteristics of conversational quality are so important that their presence will guarantee good delivery for the speaker whose voice is acceptable, who articulates clearly, and who is physically responsive to his own ideas.

Voice

Speech is a product of breathing, phonation, resonation, and articulation. During inhalation, air is taken in through the mouth or nose, down through the pharynx (throat), larynx, trachea, bronchial tubes, and into the lungs. We get the power for speech from exhaling the air we breathed. As air is forced from the lungs back up through the trachea and larynx by controlled relaxation of the diaphragm and contraction of abdominal and chest muscles, the vocal folds that help protect the opening into the trachea are brought closely enough together to vibrate the air as it passes through them. This vibration is called phonation, the production of sound. The weak sound that is emitted (like the sound made by vibrating string) travels through the pharynx, mouth, and in some cases the nasal cavity. Each of these three cavities helps to resonate the sound. This resonated sound is then shaped by the articulators (tongue, lips, palate, and so forth) to form the separate sounds of our language system. These individual sounds are then put together into words, or distinguishable oral symbols. We call the sound that we produce voice. Now let's examine the major characteristics of voice that work together to give us the variety, expressiveness, and intelligibility that assist communication.

Pitch   Pitch refers to the highness or lowness of the voice. As mentioned above, voice is produced in the larynx by vibration of the vocal folds. In order to feel this vibration, put your hand on your throat at the top of the Adam's apple and say "ah." Just as the change in pitch of a violin string is brought about by making it tighter or looser, so the pitch of your voice is changed by the tightening and loosening of the vocal folds. Although you have no conscious control over the muscles that change the tension in the vocal folds, you can feel the change of position of the entire larynx by placing your hand on the Adam's apple again and saying "ah" first at a very high pitch and then at a low pitch. The pitch that a speaker uses most frequently is called the "key" of his voice. Fortunately, most people talk in a pitch that is about right for them. Occasionally a person talks in a pitch that seems abnormally high or low. If you have questions about your pitch, ask your professor. If you are one of the very few persons with a pitch problem, he will refer you to a speech therapist for corrective work. Since for most of us our normal pitch is satisfactory, the question is whether we are making the best use of the pitch range that we have at our disposal.

Volume   Volume is the loudness of the tone we make. When we exhale normally, the diaphragm relaxes, and air is expelled through the trachea. When we wish to speak, we need to supplement the force of the expelled air on the vibrating vocal folds by contracting our abdominal muscles. This greater force behind the air we expel increases the volume of our tone. To feel how these muscles work, place your hands on your sides with your fingers extended over the stomach. Say "ah" in a normal voice. Now say "ah" louder. Now say "ah" as loud as you can. If you are making proper use of your muscles, you should have felt the stomach contraction increase as you increased volume. If you felt little or no muscle contraction you are probably trying to gain volume from the wrong source, resulting in tiredness, stridency, and lack of sufficient volume to fill a large room. Under ideal circumstances, you should be able to increase volume without raising pitch. Each of us, regardless of size, is capable of a great deal of vocal volume. The problem is that most of us don't use our potential. If you have trouble getting sufficient volume, work on exerting greater pressure from the abdominal area.

Rate   Rate is the speed at which we talk. As mentioned earlier, a normal rate is somewhere between 140 and 180 words per minute. Rate, like pitch, is an individual matter. There is no one rate that is best for everyone. Since some people talk more rapidly and some more slowly than others, the test is whether an audience can understand what a speaker is saying.

If your professor believes you talk too rapidly or too slowly, he will tell you; and before improvement in normal conversation is possible, you must adjust your ear to a more appropriate rate. The most effective method is to read passages aloud, timing yourself to determine the exact number of words per minute you speak. Then you must make a conscious effort to decrease or increase the number of words per minute accordingly. At first, a different speech rate will sound very strange to your own ear. But if you practice daily, within a few weeks you should be able to hear an improvement and you should be able to accustom your ear to the change.

Quality   Quality is the tone, timbre, or sound of your voice. Voices are characterized as being clear, nasal, breathy, harsh, hoarse, strident, and by other such adjectives. If your voice has too great a degree of some undesirable quality, consult your professor. Although you can make some improvement on your own, improvement requires a great deal of work and a rather extensive knowledge of vocal anatomy and physiology. Severe problems of quality should be referred to a speech therapist.

Vocal Variety and Expressiveness   In determining effectiveness of delivery, these variables are not nearly so important individually as they are in combination. It is through the variety of pitch, volume, rate, and occasionally quality that you are able to give the most precise meaning to your words. An expressive voice is not flawed by the two most common faults of speech melody: monotone and constant pattern.

A monotonous voice is one in which the pitch, volume, and rate remain constant, with no word, idea, or sentence differing from any other. Although very few people speak in a true monotone, many limit themselves severely by using only two or three tones and relatively unchanging volume and rate. The effect of an actual or near monotone is that the audience is lulled to sleep. Without vocal clues to help them assess the comparative value of words, an audience will usually lose interest. To illustrate what proper vocal emphasis can do for meaning, say the sentence, "I want to buy ice cream," in such a way that the pitch, rate, and volume are held constant. Such a delivery would require the auditor to decide what the sentence meant. Now say "buy" in a higher pitch, louder, or perhaps more slowly than the other words in the sentence. Through this vocal stress alone, you are communicating the idea that you want to buy ice cream rather than making it or procuring it in some other way. With this sentence, meaning can be changed significantly by changing only vocal emphasis of "I," "want," "buy," or "ice cream." During an actual speech, you should give such vocal clues in almost every sentence to insure audience interest and understanding.

The other prevalent fault detracting from expressiveness is the constant vocal pattern in which vocal variation is the same for every sentence regardless of meaning. The resulting vocal pattern is nearly as monotonous as a true monotone. For instance, a person may end every sentence with an upward pitch, or he may go up in the middle and down at the end of every phrase. Vocal variety is of little value unless it is appropriate to the intended meaning. The best cure for a constant pattern is to correlate changes in voice with meaning. If you suffer from a relatively severe case of monotone or constant pattern you should set up a work program that you can pursue every day. One method is to read short passages aloud to a friend. Ask your friend to tell you which words were higher in pitch, or louder, or faster. When you find that you can read or speak in such a way that your friend will recognize which words you were trying to emphasize, you will be showing improvement in using vocal variety to clarify meaning.

Articulation

Articulation is the shaping of speech sounds into recognizable oral symbols that go together to make up a word. Articulation is often confused with pronunciation, the form and accent of various syllables of a word. Thus in the word "statistics," articulation refers to the shaping of the ten sounds (s, t, a, t, i, s, t, i, k, s); pronunciation refers to the grouping and accenting of the sounds (sta-'tis-

tiks). If you are unsure of a pronunciation, look it up in a dictionary. Constant mispronunciation labels a person as ignorant or careless or both.

Although true articulatory problems (distortion, omission, substitution, or addition of sounds) need to be corrected by a speech therapist, the kinds of articulatory problems exhibited by most students can be improved individually during a single term. The two most common faults among college students are slurring sounds (running sounds and words together) and leaving off word endings. "Wutcha doin" for "What are you doing" illustrates both of these errors. If you have a mild case of "sluritis," caused by not taking the time to form sounds clearly, you can make considerable headway by taking ten to fifteen minutes a day to read passages aloud, trying to overaccentuate each of the sounds. Some teachers advocate "chewing" your words; that is, making sure that you move your lips, jaw, and tongue very carefully for each sound you make. As with most other problems of delivery, you must work conscientiously every day for weeks or months to bring about significant improvement.

Bodily Action

Recently books on nonverbal communication have made us aware that ideas are not communicated by voice and articulation alone. A speaker may supplement what he says by appropriate movement of face, arms, hands, and body.

Facial Expression   The eyes and mouth communicate far more than some people realize. You need only recall the icy stare, the warm smile, or the hostile scowl that you received from someone to validate the statement that the eyes (and mouth as well) are the mirror of the mind. Facial expression should be appropriate to what we are saying. We are impressed by neither deadpan expressions nor perpetual grins or scowls; we are impressed by honest and sincere expression reflecting the thought and feeling being communicated. Think actively about what you are saying and your face will probably respond accordingly.

Gesture   By gesture we mean the movement of hands, arms, and fingers. Gestures are usually descriptive or emphatic. When the speaker says "about this high" or "nearly this round," we expect to see a gesture accompany the verbal description. Likewise, when the speaker says "We want you" or "Now is the time to act," we look for him to point a finger, pound his fist, or use some other gesture that reinforces his point. If you gesture in conversation, you will usually gesture in a speech; if you do not gesture in conversation, it is probably best not to force yourself to gesture in a speech. As aids in helping you "do what comes naturally," I would suggest that you try to leave your hands free at all times. If you clasp them behind you, grip the sides of the speaker's stand, or put your hands in your pockets, you won't be able to gesture even if you want to. If you wonder what to do with your hands at the start of the speech so that they won't seem conspicuous, you may either rest them on the speaker's stand partially clenched or hold them relaxed at your sides, or perhaps with one arm slightly bent at the elbow. Once you begin the speech, forget about your hands—they'll be free for appropriate gestures. If, however, you discover that you have folded your arms in front of you or clasped them behind you, put them back in one of the two original positions. After you have spoken a few times, your professor will suggest whether you need to be encouraged to be more responsive or whether you need to be somewhat restrained.

Movement   Some speakers stand perfectly still throughout an entire speech. Others are constantly on the move. In general, it is probably better to remain in one place unless you have some reason for moving. Nevertheless, because a little movement adds action to the speech, it may help you maintain attention. Ideally, movement should occur to help focus on transition, to emphasize an idea, or to call attention to a particular aspect of the speech. Avoid such unmotivated movement as bobbing and weaving, shifting from foot to foot, or pacing from one side of the room to the other. At the beginning of your speech, stand up straight and on both feet. If during the course of the speech, you find yourself in some peculiar posture, return to the upright position standing on both feet.

With all kinds of bodily action, be careful to avoid those little mannerisms that often are so distracting to the audience, like taking off or putting on glasses, smacking the tongue, licking the lips, or scratching the nose, hand, or arm. As a general rule, anything that calls attention to itself is bad, and anything that helps reinforce the idea is good.

A Program of Speech Practice

The first thing we need to consider in terms of speech practice is the mode of delivery we will be using. Speeches may be delivered impromptu, by manuscript, by memorization, or extemporaneously. Impromptu speaking is done on the spur of the moment without previous specific preparation. Although nearly all of our conversation is impromptu, most people prefer to prepare their thoughts well ahead of time before they face an audience. Regardless of how good you are at daily communication, you would be foolhardy to leave your preparation and analysis for formal speeches to chance. Audiences expect to hear a speech that was well thought out beforehand.

A common and often misused mode is the manuscript speech. Because the speech is written out in full (and then read aloud), the wording can be planned very carefully. Although Presidents and other heads of state have good reason to resort to the manuscript (even the slightest mistake in sentence construction could cause national upheaval), most speakers have little need to prepare a manuscript. Often their only excuse is the false sense of security that the written speech provides. As you can attest from your listening experience, however, few manuscript speeches are very interesting. Because manuscript speeches are not likely to be very spontaneous, very stimulating, or very interesting and because of the natural tendency to write a speech in written style devoid of audience adaptation, you should avoid manuscript speaking except as a special assignment.

A memorized speech is merely a manuscript committed to memory. In addition to the opportunity to polish the wording, memorization allows the speaker to look at his audience while he speaks. Unfortunately for beginning speakers, memorization has the same disadvantages as the manuscript. Few individuals are able to memorize so well that their speech sounds spontaneous. Since a speech that sounds memorized affects an audience adversely, you should also avoid memorization for your first speech assignment.

The ideal mode is one that has the spontaneity of impromptu, yet allows for careful preparation and practice. The extemporaneous speech (the goal of most professional speakers) is prepared and practiced, but the exact wording is determined at the time of utterance. Most of the material in this text relates most directly to the extemporaneous method. Now let's consider how a speech can be carefully prepared without being memorized.

All that we have discussed so far is concerned with the standards of delivery, or what you should practice. Now we can apply the theory showing *when* and *how* you should practice your delivery. Novice speakers often believe that preparation is complete once the outline has been finished. Nothing could be further from the truth. If you are scheduled to speak at 9:00 A.M. Monday and you have not finished the outline for the speech until 8:45 A.M. Monday, the speech is not likely to be nearly as good as it could have been had you allowed yourself sufficient practice time. Try to complete your outline a day in advance of a two- to five-minute speech and two or even three days in advance of longer speeches. The only way to test the speech itself is to make proper use of the practice period. Practice gives you a chance to revise, evaluate, mull over, and consider all aspects of the speech.

Like any other part of speech preparation, speech practice must be undertaken systematically. In order to make the practice period as similar to the speech situation as possible, you should stand up and practice aloud. The specific procedure may be outlined as follows:

1. Read through your outline once or twice before you begin.

2. Put the outline out of sight.

3. Look at your watch to see what time you begin.

4. Begin the speech. Keep going until you have finished the ideas. If you forget something, don't worry about it—complete what you can.

5. Note the time you finish.

6. Look at your outline again.

Now the analysis begins. Did you leave out any key ideas? Did you talk too long on any one point and not long enough on another? Did you really clarify each of your points? Did you try to adapt to your anticipated audience? Unless you are prepared to criticize yourself carefully, your practice will be of little value. As soon as you have completed the analysis of your first attempt, go through the six steps again. After you have completed two sessions of practice and criticism, put the speech away for a while. Although you may need to practice three, four, or even ten times, there is no value in going through all the sessions consecutively. You may well find that a practice session right before you go to bed will be extremely beneficial. While you are sleeping, your subconscious will continue to work on the speech. As a result, you will often note a tremendous improvement at the first practice the next day.

Should you use notes in practice or during the speech itself? The answer depends upon what you mean by notes and how you plan to use them. My advice would be to avoid using notes at all for the first short speech assignments. Then, when assignments get longer, you will be more likely to use notes properly and not as a crutch. Of course, there is no harm in experimenting with notes to see what effect they have on your delivery.

Appropriate notes are composed of key words or phrases that will help trigger your memory. Notes will be most useful to you when they consist of the fewest words possible written in lettering large enough to be seen instantly at a distance. Many speakers condense their written preparatory outline into a brief word or phrase outline. A typical set of notes made from the preparatory outline illustrated on pages 51–53 would look like this:

> What compels selection of clothes?
>   Physical comfort
>   Temperature
>   Weather
>   Modesty
>   Religion
>   Culture
>   Appeal to opposite sex
>   Women
>   Attraction
>   Approval
>   Men
>   Distinction
>   Status

For a speech in the five- to ten-minute category a single 3 x 5 note card should be enough. When your speech contains a particularly good quotation or a complicated set of statistics, you may want to write them out in detail on separate 3 x 5 cards.

During practice sessions you should use notes the way that you plan to use them in the speech. Either set them on the speaker's stand, or hold them in one hand and refer to them only when you have to. Speakers often find that the act of making a note card is so effective in helping cement ideas in the mind that during practice or later during the speech itself they don't need to use the notes at all.

How many times should you practice? This depends upon many variables including your experience, familiarity with subject, the length of the speech, and so on. What you don't want to do is to practice the speech the same way each time until you have it memorized. An effective speaker needs to learn the difference between learning a speech and memorizing it. One has to do with gaining an understanding of ideas; the other has to do with learning a series of words.

When a person memorizes, he repeats the speech until he has mastered the wording. Since emphasis is then on word order, any mistake requires backtracking or some other means of getting back to the proper word order. Unfortunately, this kind of practice does not make for mastery of content, it does not give additional insight into the topic, and it does not allow for audience adaptation at the time of presentation. Another way that speakers memorize is to say the speech once extemporaneously and then repeat the same wording over and over again. The result is about the same in both instances.

When a person stresses the learning of ideas, he practices his speech differently each time. Utilizing the principles of proper speech practice, a description of the shaft of a pencil would take the following forms:

1. The shaft is a cylindrical piece of wood about 6 inches in length. Its color is yellow. It houses a piece of graphite of about $\frac{1}{16}$ of an inch in diameter.

2. It's the shaft that houses the graphite. The yellow shaft is about 6 inches long and is cylindrical in shape. The piece of graphite that does the actual writing is about $\frac{1}{16}$ of an inch in diameter.

3. The main part of the pencil is made out of a soft piece of wood. Its shape is cylindrical. Its color is yellow. Its length is about 6 inches long. It houses a $\frac{1}{16}$-inch piece of graphite that runs the entire length of the shaft—and of course, it's the graphite that leaves the imprint on paper.

4. The main part of the pencil is a cylindrical shaft that houses the graphite writing compound. The shaft, painted a bright yellow, is about 6 inches long. The graphite runs the length of the shaft and is about $\frac{1}{16}$ of an inch in diameter.

Notice that in all four versions the same essential facts were included: the shaft is a cylindrical piece of wood; it is about 6 inches long; it is painted yellow; it houses a $\frac{1}{16}$-inch piece of graphite. These are the facts that would appear on the outline and that the speaker would attempt to include in every practice and in the speech itself. An interesting phenomenon is that each practice usually gets a little better. As a result, more often than not the actual speech will be similar to the best practice period rather than to the worst. Because the speaker would not be tied to a particular phrasing, he could adapt to audience reaction at the time of delivery.

Exercise 9

Make a diary of your program of practice for your first formal speech. How many times did you practice? At what point did you feel you had a mastery of substance? How long was each of your practice periods?

Assignment

Prepare a two- to five-minute speech. Outline is required. Criteria for evaluation will include (1) *content*—whether topic was well selected, whether the purpose was clear, and whether good material was used to develop or to prove the points; (2) *organization*—whether speech had a good opening, clear main points, and a good conclusion; (3) *style*—whether language was clear, vivid, emphatic, and appropriate and (4) *delivery*—whether voice and body were used effectively to show a positive attitude, spontaneity, and to achieve directness.

Outline: First Speech

Since this outline is for the first speech given, notice the way it is written. Test each part against the recommendations for outlining on pages 50–53. Also note that this outline contains only 211 words, a good length for the assigned speech.

Specific Purpose: To explain three aspects of dining with a Spanish family.

Introduction

I. Have you ever been ravenously hungry, but no dinner until 10.00 P.M.— or faced enough food for two people at one meal—or tasted nothing but olive oil while eating?

II. Then you've been to Spain!

Body

I. The dining hours of Spanish families are completely different from an American household.
   A. Breakfast is served at 10:00 A.M.
   B. Lunch is eaten at 2:00 or 3:00 P.M.
      1. People take a siesta during the hottest part of the day.
   C. Dinner is served late at night, around 10:00 or 11:00 P.M.

II. The amount of food served at the various meals is not at all in balance with the way I am accustomed to eating.
   A. Breakfast consists of a roll and coffee or tea.
   B. Lunch is normally the big meal of the day.
   C. Dinner is also a large meal.

III. The taste of food in Spain is entirely different from what I expected.
   A. There is an erroneous belief that Spanish food is spicy.
   B. The Spanish women use a lot of tomato sauce in their cooking.
   C. Due to the heavy use of olive oil, the food tastes quite different.

Conclusion

I. People expecting to live and dine in Spain should be prepared to face different dining hours, larger amounts of food, and no spices.

II. If you can adjust to this situation—*Bien Viaje.*

Read the speech in the inside column through aloud in its entirety.[1] After you have judged its quality read the speech again noting the criticism included in the outside column.

Dining in Spain

Speech

Analysis

Have you ever been ravenously hungry at 10:00 p.m. with no dinner in sight until 11 or so? Have you ever eaten enough food for two at one meal daily? Or have you ever sat down and eaten food that tasted as bland as Cream of Wheat every meal? If you have, then you have eaten in Spain.

One way to begin a short speech is with a series of questions. These three questions are particularly good because they relate to student experiences and they forecast the main points of the speech. The final sentence is a short but effective lead into the body.

The visitor soon finds that in Spain the dining hours are quite different from an American household. In Spain breakfast is served at approximately ten in the morning—I guess mostly because the people don't go to bed until two, three, and sometimes four o'clock. Of course, there's no need to get up at six o'clock and rush around to make it to work on time or to school by eight. Lunch isn't served until two o'clock. It's eaten during the hottest part of the day, and the hottest part of the day in Spain is from about two until four. So, they have a long lunch hour. Dinner, as I mentioned, is served at about ten or eleven in the evening. If you are lucky, your family will give it to you by twelve. At dinner time, they just sort of take the time to relax and talk over what happened during the day, and afterwards they just let the dishes go until morning.

This one-sentence transition and main point move satisfactorily into the first area to be considered. The first point is developed with the particulars of when the meals are served. The speaker has tried to draw comparisons and contrasts to emphasize the explanations.

Just as the dining hours are quite different from an American household, the amount of food is just

Here is another effective use of transition. By summarizing the first point and forecasting

---

[1] Speech given in Fundamentals of Speech class, University of Cincinnati. Printed by permission of Susan Woistmann.

the second, the speaker has let us know that we are leaving a main point, she has reminded us of the substance of the point we are leaving, and she gives us a clue about what we should be listening for. This kind of transition will help even a poor listener to follow the flow of ideas.

Again the speaker supports her generalization with specific examples. As a result of economy of words, she gets quite a lot of information into only slightly more than a minute's worth of speech.

This particular transition serves two important purposes. First it takes us smoothly from the second to the third main point of the speech. In addition, it conveys the idea that this is the most important contrast of the three. The latter part of this development doesn't support the main point as well as it could. Notice, she is trying to show that the Spanish food is bland. Although her experience with the absence of pepper shakers develops the idea when she speaks of the excessive salt on salads, the use of tomato sauce, and the olive oil, we wonder whether bland was really the most descriptive term. This part of the speech needs some re-evaluation.

The speaker elects to end her speech with the simple summary. When the assignment is a short, informative speech, this is perhaps the best choice available. The final sentence of the speech makes the summary conclusion a little more vivid.

absolutely out of balance with what you are accustomed to here. For breakfast, you may eat scrambled eggs, bacon, or whatnot. There you get a roll, coffee, or milk and that's all. Then for lunch you get a four-course meal. A big, huge, heaping plate of potatoes or rice is your first course. Your second course usually consists of a large dinner-sized plate full of potatoes, vegetable, and meat, fish, or chicken. Dinner is also a large meal, but the food isn't as heavy. Rather than having a first plate of potatoes and rice, you'd be served a bowl of soup. And for desert, you usually get a fruit.

Perhaps more than even the contrast in dining hours or the amount of food, the taste of Spanish food is quite different from what you expect. There's an erroneous belief that Spanish food is very, very spicy. Well, it's just not true. During the entire three months while I was in Spain, I didn't find one pepper shaker, either in my house, a hotel, or a restaurant. No pepper shakers! And the only thing that I really found to be spicy was the lettuce salad, and it was so salty you had to choke it down—you couldn't even taste the lettuce. And the Spanish people use a lot of tomato sauce, mostly for its coloring, but you can taste it. That's about the only really special thing that you can have. And due to the heavy use of olive oil, your digestive system has quite a lot to get used to. They cook everything in olive oil. All the way from boiling the rice, which I didn't believe at first, down to frying the chicken or meat—they even boil their potatoes in olive oil.

People who expect to live and dine in Spain should learn how to become accustomed to the dining hours, to the amount of food, and also to the taste. So, if you can become adjusted to this situation, *Bien Viaje!*

**Putting
Fundamentals
into Practice**

Three

Adapting
to Audiences

7

In our discussion of fundamental principles of speech preparation, we have already talked about audience needs and expectations. Our concern for our audience is of course well founded—our very reason for speaking is to affect our listeners' understanding and attitudes. Because this concern is so important to the successful accomplishment of any speech purpose, in this chapter we want to explore the specific process of audience adaptation in detail. It is my hope, by placing this chapter and the chapter on visual aids in a special unit, to give special emphasis to their importance and applicability to any speech regardless of subject, purpose, or means of development.

Audience Analysis

Audience adaptation begins with analysis, the process of determining audience similarities and differences. When we understand our audience, we can best adapt to it. In conversation, our audience is composed of one individual or a small, often homogeneous, group. For a speech, however, an audience is composed of many individuals, who provide us with a far more complex problem of analysis. When you and a friend walk from one class to another, you have no difficulty discussing a topic because you know each other's knowledge, interests, and attitudes and you are able to relate to each other. But as a group gets larger, it becomes more difficult to anticipate and respond to the larger numbers. The next time you are at a large party, note how many times the groupings of individuals change depending upon the topics of conversation. People "drop out" of the conversation if the subject no longer relates to them. Everyone lives in many worlds at the same time. Each world reflects different interests, degrees of knowledge, and attitudes. Your analysis of your speech audience will enable you to understand its frame of reference and enable you to adapt to it. Specifically, you will need to find answers to the following questions:

1. What is the nature and extent of my audience's knowledge of this topic?

   Is my audience's knowledge of the subject area sufficient to allow them to understand my topic?

   Would the material on my topic provide new information to most of the audience?

   What kinds of development will be most suitable in meeting their level of knowledge?

2. What is the nature and the extent of my audience's interest in this topic?

   Does my audience already have an immediate interest?

   If not, can I relate my topic to their interest?

   What kinds of material are most likely to arouse or to maintain their interest?

3. What is the nature and the intensity of my audience's attitude toward this topic?

   Will my audience be sympathetic? apathetic? or hostile?

   Can I expect my audience to have any preconceived biases that will affect their listening, understanding, or emotional reactions?

   If sympathetic, how can I present my material so that it will take advantage of their favorable attitude?

   If apathetic, how can I present my material so that I can create a favorable attitude?

   If hostile, how can I present my material in a way that will lessen or at least not arouse their hostility?

If you could give your audience a comprehensive exam and an aptitude test and then if you could take an opinion poll, you could answer these questions with no difficulty. Since such methods are impracticable, you have to approach the problem in a more indirect manner. The procedure requires that you gather as much data about the audience as you possibly can, and then use that data in making judgments about knowledge, interests, and attitudes.

Gathering Data

Data about your audience is gathered in a variety of ways. If you know the audience, if you've spoken to them before, you can gather data by direct observation and experience. Any familiar group such as your family or the group you live with, your political group, your service organization, or your speech class can be analyzed in this way.

The problem of gathering data becomes more difficult when you are not familiar with the group that will make up your audience. If you are being called upon to speak to such a group, you will have to ask the chairman or your group contact to provide information about that audience. Usually, before you speak you will have a chance to observe the audience and often you will have an opportunity to talk with a few of the members. For instance, if you are scheduled to speak after a dinner, you can observe the physical characteristics of your audience directly; your informal conversation with those around you will often reveal information that substantiates and supplements your observations.

The most difficult situation presents itself when you are scheduled to speak before a heterogeneous group, of which you have no prior knowledge. Although you cannot determine the exact makeup of the prospective audience, you can make qualified guesses based upon such things as the kind of group most likely to attend a speech on this subject, the location of the meeting place, and the sponsor of the speech. Again, you may be able to verify your analysis through observation before you begin your speech. Although it is better to get audience information before you finish your preparation, you can learn to make adjustments in your plans based upon last-minute information. As you gain experience, you will find that you can make such adjustments more easily.

Judgments about audience knowledge, interests, and attitudes can be made by gathering the following data:

Age: What is the average age? What is the age range?

Sex: Is the audience all or predominantly male? female? Or is the sex of the group reasonably evenly balanced?

Occupation: Is everyone of one occupation such as nurses? bankers? drill press operators? Is everyone of a related occupation such as professional men? educators? skilled laborers?

Income: Is average income high? low? average? Is range of income narrow? large?

Race, religion, nationality: Is the audience primarily of one race, religion, or nationality? Or is the audience mixed?

Geographic uniqueness: Are all the people from one state? city? region?

Group affiliation: Is the audience a member of one group such as a fraternity or sorority? professional organization? political group?

Remember, your goal is to determine how the members of the audience are alike and in what ways they differ. The more homogeneous the group, the easier it will be to answer questions about knowledge, interests, and attitudes. Suppose, for instance, that you are scheduled to talk to a group of Boy Scouts about the uses of plastics; and that the members have certain things in common: (1) they are all boys, (2) they are of roughly the same age range, and (3) they are all scouts. Their total knowledge will be far more limited than an adult audience—especially about plastics in general; their interests will relate to scouting and other boys' activities; their attitude about plastics will be unlikely to close their minds to the subject. In your speech, then, by alluding to uses of plastics in scouting equipment and in boys' activities and by alluding to boyhood experiences, you will be able to adapt directly to them.

Yet, even when the audience is heterogeneous, you can uncover similarities that will provide a base for adaptation. Suppose the speech on the uses of plastics is to be given to a local adult community organization. If that was the only information you have available, you could still make some good guesses about similarities: (1) because the organization is an adult organization you can assume that the audience will be mostly adult—most will be married, many will have homes and families; (2) because the organization is a local community organization, they have a geographic bond. As adults their knowledge about plastics in general can be assumed; their interests will relate in part to home, family, and neighborhood; their experience with plastics will be varied—some may regard plastics as a cheap substitute for wood, steel, or aluminum. In your speech then, by alluding to uses of plastics within the range of adult experiences, by talking about home, garden, neighborhood, and community, and by stating ideas that will show comparative strength and durability of plastics, you will be able to adapt to that audience.

Characteristics of Direct Adaptation

On the basis of your audience analysis, you will know the kinds of adjustments you will have to make in your material to meet audience knowledge, interests, and attitudes. The question now is what are the characteristics of direct adaptation that you can employ. What can you do to get each member of the audience to feel that the speech is meant for him? Although no device will give the impression of adaptation if you do not have a sincere interest in your audience, the following suggestions will help you to show your audience concern more directly.

Use Personal Pronouns

Personal pronouns by themselves are a form of direct audience adaptation. Saying "you," "us," "we," "our," whenever possible will give the audience a verbal clue to your interest in them. Too often, speakers ignore this simplest of devices by stating ideas impersonally. Suppose you wanted the audience to consider buying a house. You could say: "When an individual eventually gets enough money for a down payment on a house, he needs to ask himself some very serious questions." Notice the psychological difference if you were to phrase the same idea this way: "When you eventually get enough money for a down payment on a house, you need to ask yourself some very serious questions." In one sentence you would be able to show *three* times that you are thinking about your audience. Although this may seem a very small matter, it may make the difference between audience attention and audience indifference. You will notice that each of the four speeches in the Appendix illustrates this form of adaptation.

Use Audience Questions

One of the secrets of audience adaptation is inducing audience involvement. Public speaking is not direct conversation; your audience is not going to respond vocally to each of your ideas. How then can you create the impression of direct conversation? How can you generate some sense of personal involvement? One way is by asking audience questions.

In her classroom speech explaining man's reasons for wearing clothing, a girl said: "There are certain decisions you must make and there are factors affecting these decisions. One reason we wear clothing is to protect our body from any visible harm." Although she included personal pronouns, she might have augmented the directness of the statement and improved the adaptation by saying:

> There are certain decisions you must make and there are factors affecting these decisions. Why do we wear clothes at all? What is a motivation for anyone to wear clothes? One reason we wear clothing is to protect our body from any visible harm.

Audience questions generate audience participation; and, of course, once an audience is participating, the content will be even more meaningful to them. Because direct audience questions seeking verbal audience responses may disrupt your flow of thought (and sometimes yield unexpected answers), the rhetorical question, a question seeking a mental rather than a verbal response, is usually safer. Rhetorical questions encourage the same degree of involvement and they are easier to handle. Moreover, questions are appropriate at any place in the speech where special emphasis is needed.

Notice how Eric A. Walker, retired President of the Pennsylvania State University, uses three audience questions to encourage the audience to think with him as he explores the issue of student rate of learning—specifically whether we should force all students into a pattern designed for the mythical average student:

> We take four nine-month years to get a bachelor's degree. Is there anything sacrosanct in this schedule? How can we really justify it? In England they use three years, and shorter years at that. Other countries use five years. But students learn at different rates and they come to college in different stages of advancement. Isn't it time we ask ourselves very seriously whether we are right in trying to tie everybody to a standard four-year curriculum?[1]

Despite their value, one caution about the use of questions is in order: Unless the speaker is really interested in asking a question, his delivery will sound artificial. Get used to asking questions naturally and sincerely.

---

[1] Eric A. Walker, "High Education Faces Real Disaster," *Vital Speeches*, February 15, 1971, p. 272.

Alluding to Common Experience

Alluding to common experience also brings about audience involvement. Earlier we were talking about giving a speech to a group of Boy Scouts. If you were a scout, your job of adapting to the audience would be much easier because you could refer to common experiences. You can often adapt directly by relating an anecdote, narrative, or illustration that will be common to the speaker and the audience alike. For instance, if you were expressing the idea that a store in a shopping center often doesn't have a person's size or color, you might say:

> I'm sure we've all had the experience of going to a shopping center for some item that we had particularly in mind only to find when we got there that either the store didn't have the color we wanted or they didn't have our size.

You want the audience to identify with the common experience. Identification stimulates thought. If an audience is thinking with you, they will be listening to you.

In his speech, "The Critical Consumer Need," Edward Reavey, Vice President and General Manager, Consumer Products Division, Motorola Inc., shows how this method can be built into the speech unobtrusively and effectively. Reavey himself is a businessman, so he can discuss the problem as common to speaker and audience:

> The deterioration of costly service is partly our fault, Gentlemen. We experience the consumer's service problems every day. As businessmen, we know that the same kind of treatment is being given to our customers. Still, we don't do much about it. We tolerate the terrible, when it comes to service.[2]

Build Hypothetical Situations

Since audience involvement is so important to audience attention, you can often simulate involvement by placing the audience into a hypothetical situation. The hypothetical situation can incorporate the entire framework for the speech, or it can be utilized to reinforce a single item of information. Suppose you wanted to show

---

[2] Edward Reavey, Jr., "The Critical Consumer Need," *Vital Speeches*, October 15, 1971, pp. 25–26.

the audience how they could turn a cast-off table or chair into a fine piece of refinished furniture. You could start the speech by placing the audience into the following hypothetical situation:

Many times we relegate our cast-off end tables, a desk, a record cabinet to the land of the lost—the storage room of our basement. We know the piece of furniture is worth saving—but we don't know why. That cast-off is probably a lot heavier and a lot more solid than most furniture being made today. So, what are we going to do with it? Why not refinish it? Let's assume for this evening that you have just such a piece of furniture in your basement. Let's take it out of that storage room and go to work on it. Where do we start? Well, first of all, we have to gather the right material to do the job.

Whether members of the audience actually have such pieces of furniture is somewhat irrelevant. Because of the hypothetical situation, they can involve themselves in the procedure.

The hypothetical situation can also be used to illustrate a single portion of the speech. In your speech on the same topic, refinishing furniture, you might explain the final step, putting on the varnish, by saying:

The final step in the process is to varnish the piece of furniture. Now, varnishing appears to be a very simple task—and it is if you do it the right way. Let's assume that you've got a good-quality 2-inch brush in your hand, with a good quality of transparent varnish open and ready to go. Now, how are you going to apply that varnish? Many of you may be used to the paintbrush method, you know, back and forth until the piece is covered. But in varnishing, this may well lead to a very poor finish. Instead, start about 4 inches from the edge with the grain, and move your brush to the edge. Now, don't go back the other way. Pick the brush up and make another stroke adjacent to the first—always keep the stroke in the same direction. After you've covered the width go back another 4 inches (now 8 inches from the edge). Move the brush in one direction and continue right over the part you did first. If you will continue doing it in this way you will leave no brush marks in your work and you will have a smooth, even finish.

Whether you used a visual aid or not to visualize the procedure, the hypothetical example would involve each member of the audience in the actual varnishing. The hypothetical situation is just another way of inducing audience involvement.

Show the Relationship of the Topic to the Audience

As human beings, we are interested in *our* appearance and *our* welfare. Although self-interest can be carried to an extreme, a degree of vanity is innate with all of us. Suppose that at the start of the next class period, your professor took a class picture with his Polaroid camera. After waiting the required fifteen seconds to develop it, suppose that he passed the picture around the class. When it came to you, whom would you look for first? In all probability, you would look for yourself. Later, perhaps you would look for that boy or girl who had caught your eye; but first, you would look for yourself.

Because of this degree of self-interest, each member of a listening audience expects a speaker to say something that will relate to him. If he sees some relationship between the subject and himself, he will listen; if he sees no relationship, he may not listen. Since a successful speaker does not leave the decision to listen or not to chance, at every opportunity you should attempt to demonstrate the need for the audience to listen. Sometimes this is very easy. In talking to a classroom of young ladies on the topic "how to protect yourself if you are attacked," your topic itself would probably hold the attention of most girls. Even those who already know some of the suggestions for self-defense would probably listen for new pointers. Suppose, however, that you are talking about "air pollution," "the stock market," or "emerging nations of Africa." Before you give the speech, you must think of some way that you can make the topic relate to individual members of the audience.

The following excerpt, from a speech by F. Ritter Shumway, President, Chamber of Commerce of the United States, is a particularly good example of at least three important elements of audience adaptation. Not only does it develop the relationship between the topic and the audience, it also incorporates hypothetical situations and, through narrative development, really brings the point to focus.

A society's standard of living and indeed its very security of existence bears a direct relationship to its use and consumption of energy. With less than $\frac{1}{17}$ of the world's population, the United States consumes more than $\frac{1}{3}$ of the world's energy. Or to put it in slightly different terms, the average consumption of energy per person in the United States is six times the world average. Our standard of living is five times the world's average. Energy and the materials which provide energy are basic to all national economies. No government anywhere can fail to be aware of the place of energy supplies in its political-economic life, nor can—nor should—any individual be unconcerned.

To bring this home more forcibly, consider for a moment what would happen if on returning home after a hard day of work at the office your wife were to tell you that there was no gas or electricity with which to cook, that when darkness fell there was no electricity for lights or to operate the furnace to heat your home. Perhaps the matter of heat would not be a great problem for Floridians who, I understand, would rather shiver than admit that it could be cold in this fair state. Add to this domestic scene a picture of all manufacturing operations and many businesses shut down completely and you get an idea of the disastrous chaos that would reign in our society.

Along with millions of other citizens of the northeast, I had a dramatic experience of just this sort of thing in November 1965. I was on the 55th floor of the Chase Manhattan Bank building when the lights flickered and then went out all over the northeast. For quite a while it was impossible to obtain any information as to just what had happened. Most radio stations had gone off the air and even though some managed to operate on emergency power it was not possible to hear them unless one happened to have a battery operated receiver. It was an impossibly long walk down 55 flights of stairs to the street level. Even if one managed to get to the street later in the evening by way of the one elevator that was finally put in service through the use of emergency auxiliary power, what then? The subways, loaded with rush hour people caught in stygian darkness, were not running. With thousands of people looking for taxis, the chance of getting one was very slim. A walk to my midtown hotel in total darkness was not appealing in "fun city." Even if I had made it to the hotel, I would have faced another impossible climb up 21 flights of stairs to get to my room.

It was a terrifying experience, believe me. It was also cause for reflection. I began to understand how basic our energy supply is to virtually everything we do.[3]

If at the conclusion of the speech members of the audience still felt that the entire speech was relevant to them, attention and retention would be excellent. Remember what happens to a student's attention when the professor mentions casually, "You'd better make note of this point, it will be on the test." The students see the relevancy, and they listen. Now, of course you can't threaten your audience with a test. But you can stress relevancy enough to keep motivation high.

Associate the Most Important Points of the Speech with a Story

In various places in this textbook, we have spoken of the importance of anecdotes, narratives, illustrations, and other forms

---

[3] F. Ritter Shumway, "The Energy Crisis," *Vital Speeches*, January 15, 1971, p. 209.

of idea development that are storylike. A story may be a good form of audience adaptation even if it doesn't relate to the individual. We all like to tell and listen to stories. When a story is relevant to the topic or audience, it is even better.

You'll notice that in the following instance the story does relate to the point being made. Even though the story does not represent any direct audience adaptation, it has much the same result:

> A warm friend of mine moved to North Carolina about 15 years ago and bought a piece of property in the Smoky Mountains. The real estate man who showed him the property said: "By the way, this farm carries a subsidy for not growing a quarter acre of tobacco."
>
> My friend, who had never ever seen tobacco growing, said, "I am not planning to grow any tobacco."
>
> "Fine," answered the real estate man. "It won't cause you any extra work. You couldn't grow it in these rocks anyway."
>
> So he has not been growing any tobacco that he had not intended to grow on a hillside where it wouldn't grow. He has learned to enjoy the whole thing. His neighbors don't grow any tobacco either, a noble thing in a time when smoking is regarded as a health hazard. This matter of not growing anything and getting paid for it is a new agricultural science, considerably more lucrative than walking behind a plow. I assume that it is taught as a major subject in southern and western agricultural colleges. They are so good at it.
>
> Don't laugh. You're paying for it.[4]

We have discussed some of the direct and indirect methods of audience adaptation that will emphasize your concern for the audience. Whether you use them individually or in combination, your speech will profit by their use.

Remember, however, that the time to begin work on developing these means of adaptation is after you have completed your speech outline. Direct audience adaptation does not necessarily affect the speech structurally: you could discuss three rules for investing in the stock market before your class, the women's gardening club, the Young Democrats, and the local Kiwanis; and the outlines for speeches to all four of these audiences might be nearly the same. After you are satisfied with the speech structure, you can determine how you will use these methods of direct audience adaptation.

As a summary to our discussion, let's look at a full speech to see these methods of adaptation in practice. Our concern in this analysis

---

[4] John Cunningham, "How Are You Going to Keep Them Down on the Farm," *Vital Speeches*, March 15, 1971, p. 348.

is to identify and to comment specifically on the means of direct adaptation.

Assignment

Prepare a three- to five-minute speech. Criteria for evaluation will include how well the speech was adapted to the audience.

Papermaking Process[5]

Analysis

Speech

Mr. McMillian begins his audience adaptation with a personal reference introduction.

Notice that throughout the speech he talks in terms of "you," "us," "we," and "our."

This audience question leads directly into the specific procedure he will explain in the speech.

With this topic, Mr. McMillian decides that he can adapt most directly by building hypothetical situations. His use of the method throughout this speech is excellent.

Mr. McMillian continues his hypothetical situation throughout the steps of the process.

In front of each one of you this morning are several products made of wood. I would like to spend a few moments and talk with you about the lightest wood product made—a piece of paper. As we all know, a piece of paper has many and varied uses, ranging from the test that we record our results on, for instance, in our speech class to our grade results recorded in the office of the summer school. But did you ever wonder how that piece of paper was made? There are two ways that we will explore this fascinating process this morning.

The first way is to actually make a piece of paper in our own kitchen. Now paper is made of many millions of wooden fibers to make up a single sheet of paper. If we take a sheet of paper and tear it across, we can notice that many individual wood fibers are sticking up where we tore the paper. In our speech book are several pages, just one of those pages contains anywhere from 3 to 5 million individual wood fibers. No wonder it costs so much. Basic papermaking is a process involving essentially four main ingredients: wood, chemicals, machines, and humans. To see how these four main ingredients work together, let's go into our kitchen and make that piece of paper. The first thing we need are wood chips. About this size would do fine. So let's go into our backyard, cut a limb from our tree and get about two cups of wood chips. Next let's

[5] Speech given in Fundamentals of Speech class, University of Cincinnati. Printed by permission of Terry McMillian.

place them in our pressure cooker with a cup of caustic soda or lye. This will separate the individual wood fibers. After about four hours, we'll take the, by then, wood pulp, from the pressure cooker, wash it, and if it isn't white enough for everyone, we'll bleach it. After that, we'll take about a cupful, put it into our blender, fill three fourths of the way with water and turn it on for about a minute. While this is in process, go over to your windows and remove two screens from them. Place them on top of each other, then take that mixture—we're outside, of course, we won't mess up anything in the house—and pour it over the screens in about a 10″ square area. Let dry, remove it. Presto—you have a sheet of paper. Now if it isn't smooth enough for you, just take your iron to it and iron it a little smoother.

By talking in terms of common materials and common experiences, he helps us "see" the process work. Because his explanation is personal as well as clear and vivid, we are likely to remember the steps.

Now for the second way to explore paper making. Let's take our kitchen process and enlarge it to a big commercial operation—the paper mill. Of course, this larger operation naturally requires larger machines. They have large pressure cookers and large paper mills. This is a papermaking machine that they have in one of our large paper manufacturers. Like the ingredients that you use at home, they're the same only in a larger scale. At the beginning of this operation, the mixture that you poured onto your home screens begins here as 99 percent water, and it goes through their screen, which is about twice the size of our classroom. The series of drums that you see there are nothing but drying drums, continually drying the paper, adding different ingredients to it, and smoothing it down so it is completely smooth all the way across. The other rollers that you see there and drums are different coating machines to make the paper glossy and the other drums to dry the paper. As you can see, they made this visual as long as the length of my arms, and if we turn it over we can see a photograph of the actual paper mill.

Now Mr. McMillian switches from the familiar to the unfamiliar. Because we saw the process in terms of home materials and experiences, we will be able to apply our knowledge to the commercial process.

Here Mr. McMillian used a large sketch as a visual aid.

Thus, with wood, a few chemicals, machines, and labor the paper mills produce millions of paper sheets, using the same ingredients and much the same process as we used to make paper in our own kitchen.

Although this speech was prepared as an exercise in audience adaptation, it stands as a model of the kinds of adaptation that can be used in any speech.

When an audience sees the material relating to them, they are more likely to understand and to be influenced.

Using
Visual Aids

8

The visual aid is a unique form of speech amplification, for it gives the speech a new dimension. Speech, being primarily verbal, appeals to the ear; visual aids appeal to the eye. With the use of visual aids, the ideas of the speech gain a double sensory impact. Because of this unique feature, speakers have come to regard visual aids as one of the most impressive forms of speech amplification. Whether a picture is worth a thousand words or not, research has shown that people learn considerably more via the eye than the ear.[1] Although visual aids are used most in informative speeches and are usually a requirement of speeches explaining processes, visual aids can be used in any speech. Let's consider the various kinds of visual aids and how they can be used effectively.

Kinds of Visual Aids

By definition, anything that is used to appeal to the visual sense of the audience is a visual aid. Going from the simple to the complex, the most common types are the speaker; objects; models; chalkboards; pictures, drawings and sketches; charts; and slides, projections, and films.

The Speaker

Sometimes the best visual aid is the speaker himself. Through his use of gesture, movement, and attire the speaker can

---

[1] See *Speech Monographs*, Vol. 20 (November 1953), p. 7.

supplement his words. For instance, through descriptive gestures the speaker can show the size of a squash ball, the height of a volleyball net, and the shape of a lake; through his posture and movement, the speaker can show the correct stance for skiing, a butterfly swimming stroke, and methods of artificial respiration; and through his own attire, he can illustrate the native dress of a foreign country; the proper outfit for a mountain climber, a spielunker, or a scuba diver; and the uniform of a fireman, a policeman, or a soldier.

Objects

Objects are usually excellent visual aids in that they eliminate most of the possible distortions of size, shape, and color. If you talk about a vase, a basketball, a braided rug, or an épée, the object itself is most suitable for display. Unfortunately, most objects are too small to be seen or too large to be carried to class, maneuvered, or shown. As a result, even though the actual object might be the best visual aid, its use may be impracticable.

Models

A model is a representation used to show the construction or to serve as a copy. When the object itself is too large to bring to class, a model will usually prove a worthwhile substitute. If you were to talk about a turbine engine, a racing car, the Great Pyramid, or a dam, a model might well be the best visual aid. Especially if you are able to obtain or construct a working model, the speech will usually benefit from its use. Your most important test is whether the model is large enough to be seen by the entire audience. Some model cars, for instance, may be only 3 or 4 inches long—too small to be used for a speech; on the other hand, a model car made to the scale of 1 inch to 1 foot (perhaps 12 to 18 inches long) would be large enough. Although models distort size, their shape, color, and maneuverability make them excellent visual aids.

Chalkboard

Because every classroom has a chalkboard, our first reaction is to make use of it in our speeches. As a means of visually portraying simple information, the chalkboard is unbeatable. Unfortunately, the chalkboard is easy to misuse and to overuse. The principal misuse students and teachers make of it is to write a volume of material while they are talking. More often than not what we write while we talk is either illegible or at least partially obscured by our body while we are writing. Furthermore, the tendency is to spend too much time talking to the board instead of to the audience.

The chalkboard is overused because it is so readily available. Most people use it in an impromptu fashion, whereas good visual aids require considerable preplanning to achieve their greatest value. By and large anything that can be done with a chalkboard can be done better with a pre-prepared chart, which can be introduced when needed.

If you believe you must use the chalkboard, think about putting the material on the board before you begin, or use the board for only a few seconds at a time. If you plan to draw your visual aid on the board before you begin, get to class a little early so that you can complete your drawing before the period. It's not fair to your classmates to use several minutes of class time completing your visual aid. Moreover, it is usually a good idea to cover what you have done in some way. If you do plan to draw or to write while you are talking, practice doing that as carefully as you practice the rest of the speech. If you are righthanded, stand to the right of what you are drawing. Try to face at least part of the audience while you work. Although it seems awkward at first, your effort will allow your audience to see what you are doing while you are doing it.

Pictures, Drawings, and Sketches

Pictures, drawings, and sketches probably account for a majority of all visual aids used in speeches in or out of the classroom. Because they may be obtained or made so much more easily and inexpensively, their use is undoubtedly justified. Obviously, any picture, drawing, or sketch gives up some aspect of realism in size, shape, color, or detail. Nevertheless, the opportunities for emphasis of key features usually outweigh any disadvantages.

Pictures, of course, are readily obtainable from a variety of sources. In your selection, make sure that the picture is not so detailed that it obscures the central features you wish to emphasize. Colored pictures are usually better than black and white; and, above all, of course, the picture must be large enough to be seen. The all-too-common disclaimer, "I know you can't see this picture but . . ." is of little help to the audience.

Many times you will have to draw your own visual aid. Don't feel that you are at any disadvantage because you "can't draw." If you can use a compass, a straightedge, and a measure, you can draw or sketch well enough for speech purposes. If you were making the point that a water skier must hold his arms straight, his back straight, and have his knees bent slightly, a stick figure (see below) would illustrate the point every bit as well as an elaborate, lifelike drawing. In fact, elaborate detailed drawings are not worth the time and effort and may actually obscure the point you wish to make. Although actual representation is not a major problem, size, color, and neatness often are. For some reason, people tend to draw and letter far too small. Before

you complete your visual aid, move as far away from it as the farthest student in class will be. If you can read the lettering and see the details, it is large enough; if not, you should begin again. Color selection may also cause some problem. Black or red on white are always good contrasts. Chartreuse on pink and other such combinations just cannot be seen very well.

Charts

A chart is another graphic representation of material that enables a speaker to compress a great deal of material and to show it in a usable, easily interpreted form. A frequently used type is the word chart. For instance, in a speech on causes of juvenile delinquency the speaker may print:

<u>CAUSES</u>

1. Poverty
2. Permissiveness
3. Broken homes

To make the chart more eye-catching, the speaker may have a picture or a sketch to portray each word visually.

The chart is also used to show organization, chains of command, or steps of a process. The following chart illustrates the organization of a college department:

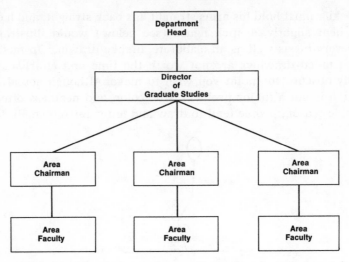

Charts of this kind lend themselves well to what is called a strip-tease method of showing. The speaker prints his words on a large piece of cardboard and covers each with pieces of cardboard or paper mounted with small pieces of cellophane tape. Then as he comes to each point, he removes the cover to expose that portion of the chart.

Maps are of great value to indicate key elements of a territory. For instance, through various maps you have the opportunity to focus on physical details such as mountains, rivers, valleys; or on the location of cities, states, nations, parks, and monuments; or on automobile, train, boat, and airplane routes. A professionally prepared map may have artistic advantages, but a map you make yourself can be drawn to include only the details you wish to show. Whether you use a professionally prepared map or your own drawing, the features you wish to point out should be easy to see. The following weather map is a good example of a focusing on selected detail:

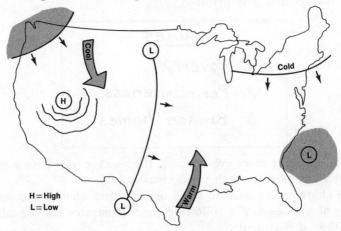

If your speech contains figures, you may want to find or to draw some kind of graph. The three most common types are the line graph, the bar graph, and the pie graph. If you were giving a speech on auto fatalities in the United States, you could use the following *line graph* to show the number of auto deaths in thousands for a thirty-five year period:

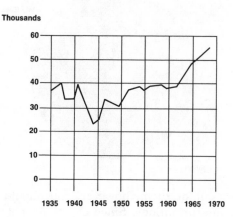

**Number of Motor Vehicle
Traffic Deaths Each Year in USA**

If you were giving a speech on gold, you could use the following *bar graph* to show comparative holdings of world governments:

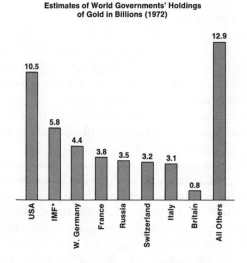

**Estimates of World Governments' Holdings
of Gold in Billions (1972)**

*International Monetary Fund

In any speech where you want to show distribution of percentages of a whole, a *pie graph* like the following can be used:

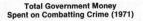

**Total Government Money
Spent on Combatting Crime (1971)**

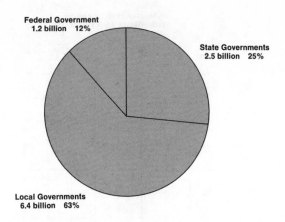

Federal Government
1.2 billion   12%

State Governments
2.5 billion   25%

Local Governments
6.4 billion   63%

To get the most out of them, however, you should be prepared to make extensive interpretations. Since charts do not speak for themselves, you should know how to read, test, and interpret them before you use them in speeches. The obvious tests of size and color are the same as for drawings.

Films, Slides, and Projections

Seldom will you have the opportunity to use films, slides, or projections. The scheduling of projectors, the need for darkened classrooms, and the tendency for these visual aids to dominate the speaker all combine to outweigh possible advantages of their use. Beginning speakers find it difficult enough to control the speaking situation without having to cope with the problems that films, slides, and projections involve.

Nevertheless, because they are used so much professionally and because they can make a classroom speech more exciting, we need to say at least a few words about three of the most easily used: slides, opaque projections, and overhead projections. Slides are mounted transparencies that can be projected individually. In a speech a few slides could be used much the same as pictures. For instance, for a speech on "Scenic Attractions in London," a speaker might have one or more slides on the Tower of London, the British Museum, Buckingham Palace, and the Houses of Parliament. He could show the slides and talk about each of them as long as he needed to. Opaque and overhead projections can be used much the same way. An opaque projector is a machine that enables you to project right from a book, a newspaper, or a typed page. It is especially useful for materials that would be too small to show otherwise. An overhead projector is a machine that requires special transparencies. The advantage of an overhead is that the room need not be darkened and you can write, trace, or draw on the transparency while you are talking. Overheads are especially useful for showing how formulas work, for illustrating various computations, or for analyzing outlines, prose, or poetry. Many of the kinds of things teachers use a chalkboard for could be done better with an overhead projector.

With each type of projection, you need to practice using the visual aid as often as you practice the speech itself. You will also notice that it takes longer to prepare mechanically projected visual aids than charts or sketches. It is often to your advantage to use a partner to run the machinery from the back of the room while you give your speech from a position next to the projection.

Using Visual Aids

Since visual aids are very powerful types of speech amplification, you should take care to use them to your advantage. The following are some of the guidelines that will enable you to get the most out of your visual aids:

1. Show visual aids only when you are talking about them. It takes a very strong-willed person to avoid looking at a visual aid while it is being shown. And while a person is looking at a visual aid, he will find it difficult to pay attention to the speaker's words if they are not related to that visual aid. So, when you show a visual aid, talk about it; when you have finished talking about it, put it out of sight.

2. Conversely, you should talk about the visual aid while you are showing it. Although a picture may be worth a thousand words, it still needs to be explained. You should tell your audience what to look for; you should explain the various parts; and you should interpret figures, symbols, and percentages.

3. Show visual aids so that everyone in the audience can see them. If you hold the visual aid, hold it away from your body and let everyone see it. Even when the visual aid is large enough, you may find

yourself obscuring someone's view inadvertently if you are not careful in your handling of your aid. If you place your visual aid on the chalk board or mount it on some other device, stand to one side and point with the arm nearest the visual aid. If it is necessary to roll or fold your visual aid, you will probably need to bring transparent tape to hold the aid firmly against the chalk board so that it doesn't roll or wrinkle.

4. Talk to your audience and not to your visual aid. Even though most of the members of the audience will be looking at your visual aid while you are speaking, you should maintain eye contact with them. The eye contact will improve your delivery, and you will be able to see how your audience is reacting to your visual material.

5. Don't overdo the use of visual aids; you can reach a point of diminishing returns with them. If one is good, two may be better; if two are good, three may be better. Somewhere along the line, there is a point at which one more visual aid is too many. Visual aids are a form of emphasis; but when everything is emphasized, nothing receives emphasis. If you have many places where visual aids would be appropriate, decide at which points the visual aids would be most valuable. Remember, a visual aid is not a substitute for good speechmaking.

6. Think of all the possible hazards before you decide to pass objects around the class. Since we are used to professors passing out materials, we sometimes became insensitive to the great hazards of such a practice. Audiences cannot resist looking at, reading, handling, and thinking about something they hold in their hands; and while they are so occupied, they are not listening to the speaker. More often than not, when you pass out materials you lose control of your audience— lessening your chances of achieving your purpose. Even when only two or three objects are passed around, the result may be disastrous. Most members of the class become absorbed in looking at the objects, looking for the objects, wondering why people are taking so long, and fearing that perhaps they will be forgotten. Anytime you pass something around, you are taking a gamble—a gamble that usually is not worth the risk.

Assignment

Because the kinds of visual aids have already been discussed, this chapter does not include a speech for illustration. Chapter 10 on "Exploring Processes," however, contains an assignment that requires the use of visual aids in that context, and that speech may well be used in conjunction with this chapter.

If a round of visual aids speeches seems appropriate to emphasize the points made in this chapter, the following assignment may prove valuable: Prepare a three- to five-minute speech in which visual aids are the major kind of speech amplification. Criteria for evaluation will include selection and use of visual aids.

Informative Speaking

Four

Principles of Informative Speaking

9

Up to now, we have considered the major principles and practices that underly the preparation and presentation of any and all speeches. In this chapter, we want to examine principles of informative speaking in particular. Although speech purposes overlap —in fact, as you read the speeches in the Appendix, you may have difficulty in deciding whether the speaker intended to inform or to persuade—studying informative speaking as a separate purpose gives us an opportunity to focus on the subjects of clarity and objectivity. Whether your intention is to explain how a zipper is made, to describe your new library, to discuss Thor Heyerdahl's findings on the Ra Expeditions, or to explain how scientists are working to predict earthquakes, your ultimate purpose is to create understanding based upon clear development and objective reporting. Each of the next four chapters considers different forms of presenting information. For now, let's examine some general principles of information exchange that will be useful to your development of any informative speech. Each of these principles will assist you in gaining your audience's reception, understanding, and retention of the information you present.

1. *Information is more readily received when it answers some stated question or meets some felt need.* If you ask your professor what the midterm test will be like, whether his reply is given in a few sentences or in a ten-minute statement, you are inclined to listen carefully because the information is intended to answer the stated question, which relates to a felt need of the entire class—because everyone will have to take the test, the more information he has about it, the better he will be able to prepare himself for it. Even if your speech is not an answer to a direct question, if it speaks to a felt need, your ideas will be received and probably retained by the audience.

2. *Information is more readily received when it is new to the audience.* Technically, any fact is information to someone. We think of the fact as information, however, only when it adds to our knowledge or gives new insights into the knowledge we already possess. For instance, the statement "the earth is a planet" is a fact. Since we already know that the earth is a planet, time spent by a speaker in explanation would be time wasted. Two key tests of "information," therefore, are whether it has added to our present knowledge or has given us a clarification in the form of deeper insight into knowledge we already possess.

3. *Information is more readily received when it is relevant.* Although new information alone is important to audience reception, the probability of careful listening is increased when that new information is regarded as personally important. The test of relevancy explains some reactions to various classroom lecturers. If one professor's lecture consists of a summary of the chapter he assigned last time, a chapter that the students had read before coming to class, they may reject his attempts with the comment, "He's just a book follower." On the other hand, if a professor gives a highly factual but theoretical fifty-minute lecture based upon entirely new material, his students might say, "That was too deep for me" or "He just bored us with a mountain of facts," meaning that the content did not relate to their prior knowledge or interests. However, if he relates the material to the class, regardless of whether he reviews a chapter or presents new material, he will be regarded as a stimulating lecturer. Thus, a lecture on Susan B. Anthony's efforts in behalf of woman's emancipation during the nineteenth century may spark some interest because the information would be new to them; however, the audience would be even more receptive if the professor showed the relevancy of Anthony's efforts to the goals of today's women's liberationists.

4. *Information is more likely to be understood and retained when it is repeated.* When you meet someone for the first time, you will be more likely to remember his name if you repeat it a few times immediately after being introduced; when you are trying to learn a new definition, a formula for a compound, or a few lines of poetry, you will master them only after you have repeated them often enough to remember. And as we all know, some of the most effective, as well as the most irritating, television commercials are based upon the simple device of repetition. As a student of public address, you should learn when and how to take advantage of this potent device. Unfortunately, for beginning speakers the words that are most often repeated are of the nature of "uh," "well," "now," and "you know." The artful speaker will determine the two, three, four, or five most important words,

ideas, or concepts in his speech, and he will think of ways that he can repeat them for emphasis.

Exact duplication is called repetition; duplication of idea but not of words is called restatement. If you want the audience to remember the exact word, repetition is the proper device to use; if you want the audience to remember the idea, restatement is probably better. Thus a speaker who wants you to remember a telephone number would say: "The number is 365–4217—that's 3, 6, 5, 4, 2, 1, 7." In contrast, a speaker who wants you to remember the approximate size of a city would say: "The population is 497,000—that's roughly half a million people." A speech with artful use of repetition and restatement will be remembered longer than a speech without them.

5. *Information is more likely to be understood and retained when it is well organized.* A clear, well-developed outline is the starting point of good speech organization. But in addition to your speech having a clear organization on paper, an audience must be consciously aware of the *presence* of that good organization. The old journalistic advice, "Tell them what you're going to tell them, tell them, and tell them what you've told them," recognizes the importance of emphasizing organization. The speaker who states, "In my speech I will cover three goals, the first is. . . the second is. . . and the third is. . ." will often have more success getting an audience to remember than one who doesn't. Likewise, such reminder statements as "Now we come to the second key point" or "Here's where we move from the third stage of development and go to the fourth" have proven effective in directing audience thinking. When listeners perceive the clarity of idea development, they are likely to remember the material.

6. *Information is more likely to be retained when it has emotional impact.* Think back over your life and recall what stands out most vividly about the past. What you recall is probably some happening, event, experience, or incident that had highly emotional impact. Was it your first date? The day you fell out of the apple tree? The spanking you got for rolling the new car into the telephone pole? The artful speaker can simulate this emotional impact through anecdotes, illustrations, and examples. A speaker trying to explain "permissive parent" to an audience might say:

> A permissive parent is one who tolerates or goes along with any request or demand of his children. A classic case of the permissive parent was Henry Fox, father of Charles James Fox, the famous eighteenth-century English Parliamentary speaker. Henry Fox's maxim was "Let nothing be done to break his spirit." Now we might say he carried the maxim to extremes. It seems that when Charles was about five he looked at his father winding his highly prized

watch and said: "I have a great mind to break the watch." At first his father said no, but when young Charles looked at him poutingly and cried "I must," Henry Fox in effect replied, "All right, if you must," whereupon he gave it to his son who instantly dashed it on the floor. Now that's pretty permissive!

The more vivid you can make your development, the more powerful the emotional impact will be. Repetition can become boring when used to excess, but audiences seldom tire of amplification that has sensory impact. And don't forget the value of visual aids to this end. They can be especially good for creating emotional impact because they appeal to two senses at the same time.

7. *Information is more likely to be understood and retained when it is associated.* Psychologically, association is defined as the tendency of a sensation, perception, or thought to recall others previously co-existing in consciousness with it or with states similar to it. That means when one word, idea, or event reminds you of another, you are associating. Effective speakers take advantage of this tendency by building association through vivid comparisons and contrasts. If I were trying to show you how a television picture tube worked, I would try to build some association between the unknown of the television tube and some knowledge you had. The metaphor "a television picture tube is a gun shooting beams of light" would be an excellent association to develop. The image of a gun shooting is a familiar one. A gun shooting beams of light is easy to visualize. If the association were made strikingly enough, every time you thought of a television picture tube, you would associate it with guns shooting beams of light. If you can establish one or more associations during your speech, you are helping to insure audience retention of key ideas.

Explaining Processes

10

Much of our daily information exchange involves explaining processes: telling how to do something, how to make something, or how something works. We give instructions to our partner on how to get more power on a forehand table-tennis shot; we share ideas with our neighbor on how to make gourmet meals with ground meat; and we talk with an employee of the water works on how the new water-purification system works. In this chapter we want to consider the means of clear, accurate explanation.

Selecting Topics

Chances are that the brainstorming lists you developed earlier contain several ideas that relate to explaining processes. Because topics of this kind are so abundant, you may be tempted to make your selection too hastily. For instance, "how to bowl" may sound like a good topic for a bowler. When we apply the tests outlined in Chapter 4, we see that it fails as a topic on at least two counts. First, because nearly all college students have bowled and because many bowl frequently, a topic this general is unlikely to provide much new information for most of the class. Second, the topic is so broad that it is unlikely that you would be able to get into much depth within the time limits. If bowling is your hobby, your brainstorming sheet should contain such ideas as "spare bowling," "scoring," "automatic pin setters," "selecting a grip," "altering the amount of curve," and "getting more pin action," any of which would be better than "how to bowl." For this speech, a principle for topic selection should be to reject such broad-based topics as "how to bake cookies," "how clocks work," and "how to play tennis," in favor of more informative and more specific topics such as "judging baked goods," "how a cuckoo clock works," or "developing power in your tennis strokes."

The Essentials of Explanation of Processes

Your explanation of a process is a success when an audience understands the process—or better yet, when an audience can apply what you've shown them. The more complicated the process, the more care you will need to take with your explanation. Although explanations of processes are often considered the easiest types of informative speeches to give—they deal with specific, concrete procedures—you will still need to consider the essentials carefully.

Knowledge and Experience

Good, clear explanation requires knowledge and experience of the process. Have you ever used a recipe? A recipe is an example of clear explanation of a process. If you can read a recipe, you can make the dish. Right? —Wrong. As many of us have found out, in the hands of a novice the best recipe in the world for beef stroganoff may still lead to disaster. Why? Because cooking requires both knowledge and experience. Just because Julia Child can turn the recipe into a gourmet's delight doesn't mean we can. But, after Julia Child explains how to make a dish, we can often come up with something that tastes quite good. A recipe indicates ingredients, quantities needed, and a way to proceed. The success of the dish depends upon the execution of that recipe. Only our knowledge and experience tell us whether two eggs are better than one, whether an additional few minutes in letting dough rise is beneficial or disastrous, or whether the end product will taste even better if one of the suggested ingredients is omitted or substituted. If you are experienced, you will have tried the many variations. During the speech, you can speak from that experience; and you will be able to guide your listeners by explaining whether alternate procedures will work equally well or whether such procedures might be ill-suited for this audience.

In addition to giving necessary know-how to barren instructions, knowledge and experience builds speaker credibility. In explaining a process, you are projecting yourself as an authority on that particular subject. How well an audience listens will depend upon your credibility as an authority. We listen to Julia Child tell us how to make chicken cacciatora, Ted Williams tell us how to hit a curve, and Neil Armstrong tell us how a moon rover works. And your audience will listen to you if you make them confident in your knowledge and experience of the process you are explaining.

Grouping Steps

All but the simplest processes will have many steps involved in the explanation. Earlier, in our discussion of outlining, we talked about limiting main points to no more than five, yet your process may have nine, eleven, or even fifteen steps. And of course, you can't leave any of them out. One of your problems will be to group the steps into units that can be comprehended and recalled. A principle of learning states that it is easier to remember and comprehend information in units than as a series of independent items. Although you should not sacrifice accuracy for listening ease, you should employ this principle whenever possible. The following example of a very simple process illustrates this principle:

A

1. Gather the materials.
2. Draw a pattern.
3. Trace the pattern on the wood.
4. Cut out the pattern so that tracing line can still be seen.
5. File to the pattern line.
6. Sandpaper edge and surfaces.
7. Paint the object.
8. Sand lightly.
9. Apply a second coat of paint.
10. Varnish.

B

1. Plan the job.
   A. Gather materials.
   B. Draw a pattern.
   C. Trace the pattern on wood.
2. Cut out the pattern.
   A. Saw so the tracing line can be seen.
   B. File to the pattern line.
   C. Sandpaper edge and surface.
3. Finish the object.
   A. Paint.
   B. Sand lightly.
   C. Apply a second coat of paint.
   D. Varnish.

Although both sets of directions are essentially the same, the inclusion of the arbitrary headings in *B* enables us to visualize the process as having three steps instead of ten. As a result, most people would tend to remember the second set of directions more easily than the first. Most processes will provide an opportunity for such an arbitrary grouping. The "plan–do–finish" organization cited above is a common type of grouping for explaining how to make something. A little thought on the best way of grouping similar steps will pay dividends in audience understanding and recall.

Our example also illustrates the major kind of organization for most process speeches. Both sets of directions represent a *time order* organization: each point is a step of the process that must be accomplished before the next step is in order. Because a process does require a step-by-step procedure, a time order is a preferable organization. Occasionally, however, you will find your material falling into a *topic order*. In such cases, the subdivisions of each topic will usually be discussed in a time order. For instance, you might want to show that there are three ways of making spares in bowling. Your main points would be the three ways: spot bowling, line bowling, and sight bowling; then each of the methods would be explained in terms of the steps involved.

Visualization

Although it is possible to enable your audience to visualize a process through vivid word pictures—in fact, in your impromptu explanations in ordinary conversation, it is the only way you can proceed—when you have time to prepare, you will probably want to make full use of visual aids.

When the task is relatively simple, you may want to complete an actual demonstration. If so, you will want to practice the demonstration many times until you can do it smoothly and easily. Remember that, under the pressure of speaking before an audience, even an apparently easy task can become quite difficult. Since demonstrations often take longer than planned and since motor control will be a little more difficult in front of an audience than at home (did you ever try to thread a needle with 25 people watching you?), you may want to select an alternate method even though the process could be demonstrated within the time limit.

One alternative is the modified demonstration. Suppose you had worked at a florist's and you were impressed by how floral displays were made. Making some special floral display would be an excellent process for this speech. The following example illustrates how one speaker accomplished her goal with a modified demonstration. For her speech on flower arranging, she brought a bag containing all the necessary materials. Since her second step was to prepare the basic triangle to begin her floral arrangement, she began to put the parts together in their proper relationship. Rather than trying to get everything together perfectly in the few seconds she had available, she drew from a second bag a partially completed arrangement that illustrated the triangle. Her third point was to show how additional flowers and greenery could be added to bring about various effects. Again, she began to add flowers to give us the idea of how a florist proceeds, and then she drew from a third bag a completed arrangement illustrating one of the possible effects that could be made. Even though she did not complete either of the steps for us, we saw how a florist handles her materials. In effect, her use of visual aids was every bit as professional as the floral arrangement she showed us.

Technically, this would not be a demonstration, for she did not go through all the steps in their entirety. Since discretion is the better part of valor, however, with any complex subject it is probably better to have some of the steps completed beforehand.

Additional Considerations

Your speech will be even better if you keep the following pointers in mind as you prepare.

1. *Consider your materials.* The effectiveness of your explanation may depend upon the nature and the number of materials, parts, equipment, or ingredients you select to show. In your consideration, separate the essentials from the accessories. A bowler needs a ball, bowling shoes, and access to an alley. Wrist bands, thumb straps, finger grip, and fancy shirts are all accessories that may not be worth mentioning. For some speeches, you will want to bring all the materials for display; for other speeches, a list of materials may suffice.

2. *Speak slowly and repeat key ideas often.* In most speeches the audience need retain only the ideas behind the words. When you explain a process, it is important for an audience to retain considerably more detail. Don't rush. Especially, during the visualization steps, you want the audience to have a chance to formulate and to retain mental pictures. Give sufficient time for your words and your visual aids to "sink in." It is a good idea to repeat key ideas to make sure that the audience has command of the material.

3. *Work for audience participation.* We learn by doing. If you can simulate the process so that others can go through the steps with you, it will help to reinforce the ideas. If the process is a simple one, you may want to give materials for the audience to work with. For instance, in a speech on origami—Japanese paper folding—you may want to give your audience paper so that they can go through a simple process with you. You could explain the principles; then you could

pass out paper and have the audience participate in making a figure; finally, you could tell how these principles are used in more elaborate projects. Actual participation will increase interest and insure recall.

Assignment

Prepare a three- to six-minute speech in which you show how something is made, how something is done, or how something works. Outline required. Criteria for evaluation will include quality of topic, our belief in your knowledge and experience with the topic, your ability to group steps, and the visualization of the process.

**Outline: Speech Utilizing Visual Aids
(3–6 minutes)**

> *This outline needs one minor revision to strengthen its structure. Since the purpose of the speech is to explain the four parts of a piston stroke,* A, B, C, *and* D *under* II *are really the main points of the speech and should be labeled as* I, II, III, *and* IV. *The idea labeled as* I *is really orientation and should be included in the introduction. Otherwise, the outline meets the tests included on pages 50–53.*

Specific Purpose: To explain the four parts of a piston stroke.

Introduction

I. You can have a baby without knowing what's going on for nine months; you can speak without having very much knowledge of phonetics; you can drive without knowing what's going on under the hood. But it's a little more helpful if you do understand a little bit of what's going on behind the scenes.

II. I would like to give you a little bit better understanding of where the power comes from in your engine.

Body

I. Power is transferred from your gasoline to your back wheels through an instrument called a piston.
   A. The piston moves up and down in a cylinder.
   B. A six-cylinder car has six cylinders; an eight-cylinder car has eight.
   C. A valve opens and closes.

II. This piston stroke has four parts.
   A. The first part is intake.
      1. The gas valve opens.

    2. The piston makes a down stroke.

    3. Gas is sucked into the cylinder.

B. The second part is compression.

    1. The piston starts its upward stroke.

    2. The gasoline that's in the cylinder is mashed together.

C. The third part is ignition.

    1. The spark plug ignites the gas.

       a. It's the same as putting a match to the gas.

       b. The gasoline explodes.

    2. The valve is closed and there's no place for the gas to go.

    3. The expanding gas pushes the piston down giving the force to drive the car.

D. The final part is called exhaust.

    1. The exhaust valve opens.

    2. The piston moves upward.

    3. The stale gas is pushed out into the air.

Conclusion

I. The four parts are intake, compression, ignition, and exhaust.

Study the following speech transcribed in the inside column in terms of kinds and uses of visual aids, organization, and audience adaptation.[1] Read the speech through at least once aloud. After you have read and analyzed the speech, turn to the detailed analysis in the outside column.

The Automobile Piston Stroke

Speech

You can have a baby without knowing what the heck's going on for nine months. You can speak without having very much knowledge of phonetics. And in a similar manner you can drive a car without knowing what the heck's going on under the hood. But I think we'll all agree that it's a little more helpful if you do understand a little bit of what's going on behind the scenes. And don't get the wrong idea, I'm not going to try to make you all mechanics or something in five easy steps. But I would like to

Analysis

This informal, slightly humorous opening proved quite effective. By adapting to the majority of the class, in this case a largely female audience, the speaker gave a real reason for listening. Notice, he is not expecting the audience to gain a working knowledge, but only to have a familiarity with the central process involved in the gasoline engine. The first

---

[1] Speech given in Fundamentals of Speech class, University of Cincinnati. Printed by permission of Derek Dunn.

give you a little bit better understanding of where the power comes from in your engine.

Now first of all, power is transferred from your gasoline to your back wheels through an instrument that's called a piston. This is what a piston looks like—now this one came out of a motorcycle, but essentially it's the same as one in a car, except for a difference in size. This is a shank. The piston head moves up and down in a cylinder, a tube-shaped object. Hence a six-cylinder car has six cylinders with one piston in each; an eight-cylinder has eight pistons and so forth.

I have a little schematic drawing [Figure A], and it is schematic because this is not exactly the way it looks. But this would be the edge of your cylinder, this is your piston, and this is to denote a valve. In this position the valve is closed, when it's not sticking out into the cylinder, and in this position the valve would be considered open. This is essentially to say that if you put a hole in a bag you can let something come in or go out. Now, basically, the piston stroke has four parts.

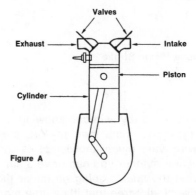

Figure A

The first part is intake [Figure B]. Your gas valve, I'll call it, opens up (we'll get our piston in the starting position)—the gas valve opens up and the piston makes a downward stroke. Since this is a closed system, and we've opened this part here, essentially what you do is you suck your gasoline into the cylinder.

---

sentence is well adapted to a young audience, the second sentence relates to a speech class, and the third sentence suggests the general nature of the topic. In effect, he got the audience's attention on the subject.

The speaker begins his orientation by showing an actual piston, giving us a realistic view. There's nothing wrong with using a motorcycle piston since, according to the speaker, it looks about the same. He would have been wiser to tell us which piston would be the larger. We assume the one in the automobile, but we don't know.

Here the speaker moves to his schematic drawing with movable parts. At this point, we begin to get the idea that we are actually going to see how the various parts work. He has completed the orientation; the audience is ready to follow the steps of the process. Notice that the speech contains the same minor weakness noted in the outline. The speaker thought of this section of orientation as the first main point of his speech, when in reality it is part of the introduction. Nevertheless, his wording at the end of this section leads us to believe that he knows the heart of the speech has to do with the four parts. The fault might not be so much failure to recognize which are the main points, as an uncertainty about how to represent the main points on paper.

The speaker states his first main point clearly. As he begins to talk about the first part, he notices that during the introduction he got his piston in the wrong position, so he takes a second to fix it. Although the speaker might have selected a better word than "suck" to describe the process, his phrasing certainly communicates what happens.

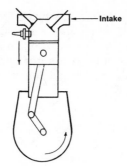

Figure B
Intake

Now, next, after that has occurred, you close your valve, which now makes a closed system and the piston starts its upward stroke, and this is called compression [Figure C]. Now, during compression, what you've done is you've taken the gas that's been in the cylinder and you've mashed it together in compression.

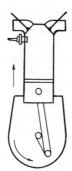

Figure C
Compression

"Now, next," serves as the transition to this second major part. Because of the way he leads into the step, a great deal of emphasis is lost. Perhaps he could have said, "After the first part of the stroke, intake, the piston starts its upward stroke. This second part is called compression." Whatever the wording, the speech would be slightly improved by some transition statement that let the audience know that compression is really the second part. Once more, the speaker uses a very graphic, if not particularly elegant expression, "mashed it together." Despite the questionable word choice, the idea is clear.

Now, at the peak of compression—this here is our spark plug—at the peak of compression, your spark plug ignites. This is done by letting the electrical charge jump across a gap. It's the same thing as putting a match into the gasoline. And what really happens is that it sets the gasoline on fire and causes an explosion [Figure D]. Notice our valve is

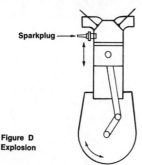

Sparkplug

Figure D
Explosion

The speaker gets into the third part with no transition at all. Notice that five sentences are spoken before the main point is suggested. This is a common fault when describing a process. The speaker tends to get so involved with the flow of the process that he forgets to itemize the main points. And since he made a point of saying in the introduction that there are four distinct parts, he should be careful to elucidate these parts as he comes to them. Nevertheless, his excellent use of visual aids during the speech gave a visual clarity to the process where verbal clarity was lacking. The comparison between a spark plug igniting fuel and putting

closed, so there's not a place for the gas to push
out except through this movable part, the piston.
And what we have then is our power stroke or our
ignition. And thus as the gas expands and pushes
our piston down, we get the force that drives the
car [Figure E].

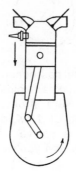

Figure E
Power

Our next and final stroke is called exhaust. And
what essentially happens in exhaust is that our
exhaust valve opens, the piston makes an upward
movement and pushes all that stale gas out into the
air and gives you smog and makes you cough and
everything like that. Now, then, this valve closes
and our gas valve opens, and essentially what we
do is start the process over again [Figure F].

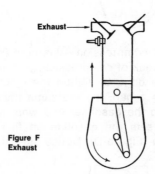

Figure F
Exhaust

So, you can see there are four parts here seen all at one time [Figure G]. You start out with intake— we suck the gas into the cylinder. Our second stroke, the piston moves upward and compresses the gas. The third stroke, we have our spark plug setting off our power stroke ignition. And our fourth stroke begins our smog through our exhaust pipe. Now, hopefully, this little demonstration will give you a little bit better idea of where the power comes from in your car, so the next time you go to the garage, and the mechanic says, "Uh, you don't have compression," you don't have to say, "Is that something like having hiccups?" You will have a little bit better idea of what's going on. Thank you.

For the conclusion, the speaker did show a single visual aid with each of the steps drawn separately. Notice that the conclusion is rather long, but the reiteration contributed to the probability that the audience would remember the steps better. Again, the last sentence returns to the light touch that was apparent in the opening and carried throughout the speech. In this instance, the final "Thank you," was really unnecessary, the audience was visibly impressed by the speech. There's no doubt that better grammar and more careful word choice would make the speech sound better. Nevertheless, the spontaneous quality, the excellent use of visual aids, and the fine audience adaptation far outweighed the speech's weaknesses.

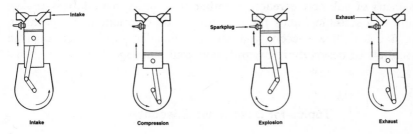

Intake   Compression   Explosion   Exhaust

Figure G

Descriptive Speeches

11

Because description may be so important in achieving clarity and vividness in your speeches, a descriptive speech assignment provides an excellent opportunity for emphasizing language skill. The goal of the descriptive speaker is to give an accurate informative description of an object, a structure, or a place. Although animals and people may seem like obvious subjects, the tendency to describe them in terms of subjective reaction rather than objective analysis makes them less suitable topics for informative description. In preparation for a descriptive speech, you should consider topic selection, the essentials of description, organization, and language.

Topics for Descriptive Speeches

Although the first things that come to mind may be the pencil sharpener on the wall, the statuette on the shelf, or your favorite chair, you should select your topic by using the methods and applying the tests outlined in Chapter 3. If you discover that your original lists do not include any subjects that would be appropriate for description, continue the brainstorming process until you have compiled several possibilities to choose from. For instance, if your hobby is "camping," you might list "turtleback campers," "campsite," "kerosene lantern," "tent trailers," "tents," "sleeping bags," and other topics associated with camping. If your major is medieval history, you might list "moats," "castles," "jousting spear," "coat of mail," or "crossbows."

In evaluating your topic selection, remember that it must meet the principal test of informative speeches—the potential for new information. Description itself is, and must be, subordinate to informative intent. You want to describe what the object, place, or building looks like, but your intent must be informative rather than poetic. You want to create an accurate, vivid, verbal picture of what you are describing.

Essentials of Description

You achieve your goal in descriptive speaking by providing word pictures for your audience. In order for the auditor to reconstruct a mental image that corresponds with your perception, an amount of essential data is required. If the object is simple and familiar (a light bulb, a rocking chair), the description need not be very detailed; if the object is complex and unfamiliar (a sextant, a nuclear reactor), the description must be more detailed. Even common objects must be described vividly if you want to differentiate them from the standard. Description is, of course, made considerably easier with visual aids. Since the purpose of this assignment is the development of verbal facility, your description should be clear enough and vivid enough to create a mental picture without visual aids. The essentials of description are size, shape, weight, color, composition, age and condition, and location of subordinate items.

Size

Size is described subjectively by "large" or "small" and objectively by dimensions. Ordinarily a meaningful description of size will contain a comparison. For instance, neither "The book is a large one," nor "The book is 9 inches by 6 inches," by itself creates an image. On the other hand, "The book, 9 inches by 6 inches by 3 inches, is a large one, the same length and width but twice the thickness of your textbook" would be descriptive.

Shape

Shape is described in terms of common geometric forms. "Round," "triangular," "oblong," "spherical," "conical," "cylindrical," and "rectangular" are all descriptive. A complex object is best described as a series of simple shapes. Since most objects do not conform to perfect shapes, you can usually get by with approximations and with comparisons to familiar objects: "The lake is round," "The lot is pie shaped," or "The car looks like a rectangular box," all give reasonably accurate impressions. Shape is further clarified by such adjectives as "jagged," "smooth," or "indented."

Weight

Weight is described subjectively as "heavy" or "light" and objectively by pounds and ounces. As with size, descriptions of weight are clarified by comparisons. Thus, "The suitcase weighed about 70 pounds, that's about twice the weight of a normally packed suitcase" would be descriptive.

Color

Color, an obvious necessity of description, is difficult to describe accurately. Although most people can visualize black and white, the primary colors (red, yellow, and blue), and their complements (green, purple, and orange), very few objects are these colors. Perhaps the best way to describe a color is to couple it with a common referent. For instance, "lime green," "lemon yellow," "brick red," "green as a grape," "banana yellow," or "blue as the sky" give rather accurate approximations. Just be careful with how far you carry the comparisons. Paint companies, fabric dealers, and cosmetics manufacturers stretch our imagination to the breaking point at times with such labels as "blimey blue" or "giddy green."

Composition

The composition of an object helps us to visualize it. A ball of aluminum does not look the same as a ball of yarn. A pile of rocks gives a different impression than that of a pile of straw. A brick building looks different from a steel, wood, or glass building. Sometimes you will refer to what the object seems like rather than what it is. An object can appear metallic even if it is not made of metal. Spun glass can have a woolly texture. Nylon can be soft and smooth as in stockings or hard and sharp as in toothbrush bristles.

Age and Condition

Whether an object is new or old can make a difference in its appearance. Since age by itself may not be descriptive, it is often discussed in terms of condition. Although condition is difficult to describe objectively, it can be very important to an accurate description. The value of coins, for instance, varies tremendously depending on whether they are uncirculated or their condition is good or only fair. A 1915 Lincoln penny in fair condition may be worth two cents, whereas an uncirculated 1960 penny may be worth five cents. Books become ragged and tattered, buildings become run down and dilapidated, land is subject to erosion. Age and condition together often prove especially valuable in developing informative descriptions.

Location of Subordinate Items

If your object for description is complex, the parts must be fitted into their proper relationship before a mental picture emerges. Remember the story of the three blind men who described an elephant in terms of what each felt? The one who felt the trunk said the elephant was like a snake; the one who felt a leg said the elephant was like a tree; and the one who felt the body said the elephant was like a wall. Not only must we visualize size, shape, weight, color, composition, age, and condition, but also we must understand how the parts fit together.

Since the ultimate test of description is that it enables the audience to visualize, the speaker probably should include too much detail rather than not enough. Moreover, if some particular aspect is discussed in two or three different ways, everyone might get the mental image, whereas a single description might make the image vivid to only a few. Begin your practice sessions with more material than you could possibly get into the time limits for your speech. As you gain a mastery of the material in practice, you can begin to delete until you get the speech down to a workable length. Keep in mind, however, that with the descriptive speech perhaps more than any other you will have to resist the desire to memorize.

Organization of Description

Since at least one of the goals of a descriptive speech is to leave with the audience a visual image of your subject, arrangement of main points by space order will often prove the most workable. A description of a jet-powered racing car might go from back to front, front to back, outside to inside, or inside to outside. A description of a painting might go from foreground to background, background to foreground, left to right, or top to bottom.

Although space order organization should be used most often, when you are describing a class of objects you might use a topic order with a space order of subdivisions. For instance, in a description of your campus, you might want to speak on the topics of buildings, the walk system, and the wooded park areas. Or, in a description of Yellowstone Park, you might talk about Old Faithful geyser and the Fountain Paint Pot as the two main topics. Each of the main topics would in turn be developed with a space order arrangement of subordinate detail.

A significant benefit of a space order organization is that your decision about placement of main points is simplified. Once you determine that you will go from left to right, top to bottom, or inside to outside, every key feature that the eye encounters will become either a main point or an important subdivision of a main point.

Language

Although a descriptive speech has several goals, it derives its major benefit as a language exercise. With this assignment you can concentrate on *clarity, vividness, emphasis,* and *appropriateness,* fundamental qualities of style we discussed in Chapter 5. You want to make your description so vivid that the audience will be able to visualize your subject accurately.

As you consider your wording of the speech remember the function of description. You want your speech to be informative, not poetic. Be on the lookout for florid description, emotive words, and excessive adjectives and adverbs. A description, speech should not sound like a page from a literary magazine. By keeping the emphasis on the informative nature of the topic and not the beauty, by keeping the emphasis on the functional nature of the language and not the poetic, you should be able to make your speech clear, vivid, emphatic, and appropriate without being affected or artificial.

Earlier you were cautioned about not memorizing this speech. Since there are unlimited ways that you can describe in any part of your speech, in each practice keep the essentials in mind, and try to use slightly different wordings to express your descriptions. By adapting to your audience and by having a true spontaneity, you will be able to avoid memorization.

Assignment

Prepare a two- to four-minute speech describing an object, a building, or a place. Outline required. Criteria for evaluation will include clarity, vividness, emphasis, and appropriateness of the description.

**Outline: Descriptive Speech
(2–4 minutes)**

Notice that the outline follows a space order going from outside to inside. Main point II, the inside, is further developed by means of the space order method.

Specific Purpose: To describe the Munich Hofbrau House.

Introduction
I. This past summer I accomplished in one night what I couldn't accomplish in three years in college—I enjoyed drinking beer.
II. I think the success has more to do with the hall than with the beer.

Body
I. The Munich Hofbrau House is the largest and best-known beer hall in Munich.
   A. Especially on Saturday evening, all traffic seems to lead to the Hofbrau House.
   B. You are led into the Hofbrau House through two large hand-carved doors.
      1. The wood is very old and heavy.
      2. The carvings are typically German.
II. The inside is an enormous structure with a very high ceiling.
   A. There are no windows.
   B. A small band plays German songs in the front left-hand corner of the hall.
   C. Off to your right as you walk in are numerous rows of tables and benches.
      1. The tables are long.
      2. They are completely occupied with people of all ages.
   D. On both sides of the room the walls are covered with shelves filled with various knickknacks, cuckoo clocks, and beer steins.

E. A high ceiling is covered with beautiful wooden beams.

F. At the rear of the room are two large doors.

  1. They are smaller than the ones through which you enter.

  2. These lead to the upper floor where much of the same is found.

  3. These also lead to the often frequented restrooms.

Conclusion

I. Everything looks the same after two litres.

II. You might as well be in the Mug Club in Cincinnati.

As you read the speech transcribed in the inside column, analyze the descriptions of size, shape, weight, color, composition, age, condition, and location of subordinate items.[1] Which descriptions are vivid? Which need more detail? After you have read the speech at least once aloud, read the analysis in the outside column.

The Munich Hofbrau House

Analysis

Speech

Although Miss Paul leads into her topic quite well, her statement, "I'm not drinking beer right now," should be reworded. We get the idea that she's not drinking beer while she's talking, but she means that she has not become a beer drinker.

This past summer I accomplished in one night in a Munich beer hall what I couldn't accomplish in three years in college, and that was I actually enjoyed drinking beer. I think that the beer hall had more to do with it than the beer because I'm not drinking beer right now. I'd like to describe the beer hall to you. The Munich beer hall or better known as the Hofbrau House is the largest beer hall. And in order to find it all you really have to do is follow any crowd coming from any direction. And especially if it's a Saturday night, the crowd will probably deposit you right in front of the beer hall.

We probably need a little better description of the outside of the hall. Although we "see" the size of the two large, old, heavy wooden doors, we don't have a visual image of the carvings or the rest of the outside of the hall.

As you are standing in front of the beer hall, you'll walk through two large doors, each about 8 feet high and nearly 4 feet wide. The wood these beautiful doors are made out of is very old and heavy, and the hand carvings on them belongs in Munich.

[1] Speech given in Fundamentals of Speech class, University of Cincinnati. Printed by permission of Toni Paul.

The hall itself is just an enormous structure, that must be nearly the size of the Topper Club, with a very high ceiling. Along the ceiling are wooden beams that run from one wall to the other, and also from the ceiling to the floor. As you enter the beer hall, off to the left in the fronthand corner of the room is an old-fashioned band playing German beer music from a bandstand. Benches and tables, which look very much like picnic tables but they're much larger, are located in a line along the right-hand side of the room and the left-hand side. These tables, covered with the traditional red-checked table-cloths, are overflowing with people who are over-flowing with beer. And very rarely can you find a place to sit. And that just doesn't seem to bother people because they're also sitting on top of the tables. But it makes for a very merry evening. Along the walls on both the right side of the room and the left side of the room you'll see very large shelves that are covered with cuckoo clocks that range in size. They don't cuckoo. But if they did, I doubt if anybody would hear them.

Here Miss Paul shows size by comparing the hall to a dance hall that Cincinnati students could visualize. The order of Miss Paul's description is quite clear throughout this main point. Probably the strength of this speech is her creation of atmosphere. In addition to seeing the hall and its parts, we can imagine the sound, the activity, the gaiety. For instance, her statement about cuckoo clocks, "But if they did [cuckoo], I doubt if anybody would hear them," allows us to sense the degree of noise.

Also located on these shelves on the walls are steins of various designs, colors, and shapes. Now, their beer mugs are not like ours. When you order a mug of beer, you are ordering a liter, which in essence is a quart of beer. And it doesn't come any smaller. And people seem to drink them like we drink our mugs of beer. On the rear of the hall you'll find another large door that empties to a large staircase that can either take you upstairs to a room similar to the one downstairs, or to the rest-rooms. Now, this door's frequented quite often in the beer hall.

This is a good description of the size of the beer stein.

This allusion to the frequency of use of the door leading to the restrooms adds a light touch to the speech.

But after one or two liters of beer, you forget that you are in the Munich beer hall, and you can just assume you are in the Varsity Mug Club on Calhoun Avenue.

The conclusion, alluding to a favorite spot near the Cincinnati campus, is satisfactory. The descriptive speech may be one of the most difficult of informative speeches. You must be very observant in order to describe accurately. In addition, you must think creatively in order to make the description vivid. Although this is not an exceptional speech, it does a good job of describing size and atmosphere.

Speeches of Definition

12

Every time we use a dictionary, we are reminded that our working vocabularies are relatively small compared to the total number of words in the English language. Moreover, anyone who has attempted to answer small children's constant refrain "What does that mean?" is well aware that even those words we use every day are often difficult to explain. As a result of our problems with vocabulary, our attempts at relating to others often fail—sometimes because we don't know the meaning of a word and sometimes because we accept one meaning when the communicator intended another. Yet, since we cannot solve problems, learn, or even think without meaningful definitions, the ability to define clearly and vividly is essential for the effective communicator. Since Plato first attacked the Sophists for their inability to define and to classify, rhetoricians have seen definition as a primary tool of effective speaking. In fact, Richard Weaver, representing the view of many modern scholars, has placed definition as the most valuable of all lines of development.[1] In this chapter, we are studying definition in an informative speaking context; you will find, however, that you will be applying the principles of sound definition to any and all kinds of speeches.

How Words Are Defined

Although individuals have used numerous methods to define words for their audiences, you can improve your communication by mastering the following four.

[1] Richard Weaver, "Language Is Sermonic," from Richard L. Johannesen (ed.), *Contemporary Theories of Rhetoric: Selected Readings.* New York: Harper & Row, 1971, pp. 170–171.

Classification and Differentiation

When you define by classification and differentiation, you give the boundaries of the particular word and focus on the single feature that gives the word a different meaning from similar words. For instance, a dog may be defined as a carnivorous, domesticated mammal of the family Canidae. "Carnivorous," "mammal," and "family Canidae" limit the boundaries to dogs, jackals, foxes, and wolves. "Domesticated" differentiates dogs from the other three. Most dictionary definitions are of the classification-differentiation variety.

Synonym and Antonym

Synonyms are words that have the same or nearly the same meanings; antonyms are words that have opposite meanings. When you use synonym or antonym, you are defining by comparison or contrast. For instance, synonyms for "sure" are "certain," "confident," "positive." An antonym would be "doubtful." Some synonyms for "prolix" would be "long," "wordy," or "of tedious length." Antonyms would be "short" and "concise." Synonyms and antonyms are often the shortest, quickest, and easiest ways to clarify the meaning of a new word. Of course, the use of synonym and antonym presupposes that the audience is familiar with the synonyms and antonyms selected.

Etymology and Historical Example

Etymology is the derivation or an account of the history of a particular word. Depending upon the word being defined, etymology may or may not be a fruitful method of definition. Since words change over a period of time, origin may reveal very little about modern meaning. In many instances, however, the history of a word reveals additional insight that will help the audience remember the meaning a little better. Consider the following definition: "A sophist is an individual who is more concerned with ingenuity and specious effectiveness than he is with soundness of argument." In this case, the following explanation of the history of the word adds considerable insight to the rather barren classification definition:

> In ancient Greece there were professional teachers who distinguished themselves for their teaching of practical politics, language, and speech. These men became some of the most renowned men in Greece. Although most of them were dedicated, intelligent, and

valuable contributors to their cultures, some of them became so entranced with their powers of persuasion that they regarded belief as more important than truth. Plato was so incensed by the power of these men who could "make the worse case appear the better" that he devoted large segments of many of his dialogues to destroying the reputation of the sophists. He was so successful that today when we refer to someone as a sophist, we do not mean an excellent teacher of practical politics; instead we mean a rather slippery individual who is more interested in effectiveness than in truth.

Under certain circumstances, etymology and historical example can give an excellent assist in the definition of a word.

Uses and Functions

A fourth way to define is to explain the use or the function of a particular object. Thus when you say, "A plane is a hand-powered tool that is used to smooth the edges of boards," you are defining the tool by indicating its use. Since the use or function of an object may be more important than its classification, this is often an excellent method of definition.

Regardless of the kind of definition you select, it should always differentiate, meet all circumstances, include all that is necessary, and, perhaps most important, be understandable.

Developing a Speech of Definition

Definition can be applied to your speeches in at least two basic ways: either as a form of support or as the framework for the speech itself. Since this chapter is concerned with an assignment of a speech of definition, we need to see how such a speech may be developed. One method is to adopt a standard definition found in a dictionary or other authoritative source and expand it. The other method is to develop an original definition.

Adopting a Standard Definition

Webster's Seventh New Collegiate Dictionary defines "jazz" as "American music characterized by improvisation, syncopated rhythms, contrapuntal ensemble playing, and special melodic features peculiar to the individual interpretation of the player." Like most dictionary definitions, this is of the classification-differentiation variety that requires an understanding of the various terms used within the definition. Before its meaning would be clear, most people would have to look up "improvisation," "syncopation," "contrapuntal" (which refers to "counterpoint"), and "ensemble." Nevertheless, such a dictionary definition makes for a very good purpose sentence for a speech. By utilizing each aspect as a prospective topical development of the speech, a potentially sound organizational structure is provided with very little effort on your part. Assuming that you had the background to attest to the accuracy of the definition and to understand the various topics mentioned, your structural outline would look like this:

Specific Purpose: To explain the four major characteristics of jazz.

I. Jazz is characterized by improvisation.

II. Jazz is characterized by syncopated rhythms.

III. Jazz is characterized by contrapuntal ensemble playing.

IV. Jazz is characterized by special melodic features peculiar to the individual interpretation of the player.

With this method, then, the organization is suggested by the definition itself. The inventive process determines how you enlarge upon each aspect of the definition. Your selection and use of examples, illustrations, comparisons, personal experiences, and observations would give the speech original distinctive flavor. Furthermore, you would have the option of utilizing other methods of definition to reinforce various parts of the speech.

Developing a Definition

The second procedure, to evolve a definition, allows for a slightly different methodology. A purpose sentence, instead of utilizing an existing definition, is evolved from the various existing definitions and from individual analysis of the subject. Suppose you wished to define or clarify the concept "a responsible citizen." A dictionary would indicate that "responsible" means "accountable" and "citizen" means a "legal inhabitant who enjoys certain freedoms and privileges." But this definition does not really tell what a "responsible citizen" is. As you think about citizenship in relation to responsibilities, you might begin to list such categories as social, civic, financial, and political. From this analysis, you could evolve the following subjective definition: "A responsible citizen is one who meets his social, civic, and financial obligations." Once you are satisfied with the soundness of your definition, you may proceed in much the same way as the person who has adopted a dictionary definition. Your organization, developed topically, would look like this:

Specific Purpose: To show that a responsible citizen is one who meets his social, civic, and financial obligations.

   I. A responsible citizen meets his social responsibilities.

  II. A responsible citizen meets his civic responsibilities.

 III. A responsible citizen meets his financial responsibilities.

This second method allows you to talk about concepts that have connotative or subjective meanings that are not usually found in dictionaries.

For the following assignment you are of course not restricted to either of these procedures. Your goal is to give the clearest, most meaningful definition possible, utilizing any of the methods of definition suggested above.

Assignment

Prepare a two- to four-minute speech of definition. Outline required. Select a word or concept that is not readily definable by most members of the class. Criteria for evaluation will include the clarity of the definition, organization of main points, and quality of the developmental material.

Outline: Speech of Definition (2–4 minutes)

Notice the clear statement of purpose and clear elucidation of the three main points, insuring a clearly organized speech. Also notice that each main point is an essential of the definition. This 170-word outline is within the recommended limits for a two- to four-minute speech.

Specific Purpose: To discuss the three major points in the definition of the word "fossil."

Introduction

I. Haven't we all at some time picked up an object and thought it was a fossil?

II. The common concept of a fossil is not clear.

III. Any fossil must possess three qualities.

Body

I. A fossil must be the remains of a plant or animal.
   A. This rules out all objects that never lived.
      1. Examples of commonly mistaken objects.
   B. This aspect of the definition would still seem to include recently living animals and plants.
      1. Recently living animals and plants are rejected as fossils because of the second aspect of the definition.

II. The remains must be preserved in rock by natural means.
   A. Imprints are not natural means.
   B. Chemical replacement is the chief natural means.
      1. Examples and/or comparisons.

III. The remains must be old.
   A. Our usual definitions of old aren't very useful.
      1. Anecdote.
   B. A fossil implies a degree of antiquity older than historic times.

Conclusion

I. Thus, a fossil can be described as the remains of a plant or animal, preserved in rock by natural means, and having a degree of antiquity older than historic times.

Study the following speech in the inside column in terms of organization, clarity of definition, and means of developing the aspects of the definition.[2] Before you attempt to evaluate, read the speech at least once aloud. After you have read and analyzed the speech, turn to the detailed analysis in the outside column.

A Definition of Fossils

Speech

Analysis

Haven't we all at some time picked up an object of some sort and thought it was a fossil? Perhaps you

The speaker begins with a question that states a reasonable

---

[2] Speech given in Fundamentals of Speech class, University of Cincinnati. Printed by permission of Frank Ettensohn.

assumption. With the very first sentence he has been able to get audience agreement. He continues to adapt to the class by alluding to objects that they might have thought were fossils. With his allusion to the professors as fossils, the speaker got the laugh he wanted without detracting from the subject matter. Well-used humor that grows from the content will usually contribute to a speech. His forecast of the organization at the end of the introduction is a good idea. It prepares the audience to listen for each of the three main points.

found an old arrowhead or a petrified cow's horn and thought it was a fossil. Then you've got some people who like to refer to teachers or professors as fossils. So as you can see there is a great diversity as to what people commonly think fossils are. But there are three basic qualities which all fossils must possess.

This first main point is clearly stated. Enumeration is a satisfactory transitional device, for it lets the audience know what point is being considered. The phrasing "all things that never lived, such as people..." illustrates the kind of grammatical problem that often creeps into extemporaneous speaking. Throughout this section and the rest of the speech, the speaker tends to overuse "well." Extraneous words of this kind seldom serve any useful purpose. In the speaker's favor, notice that throughout most of the speech his word choice is specific and concrete.

First, they must be preserved remains of a plant or animal. Well, this right away will cast out all things that never have lived, such as people finding Indian arrowheads, pretty stones, or crystals. Some people think these things are fossils but they aren't. What about the animals that die in the woods and their bones are left lying around, aren't they preserved? Well, to a certain extent they are, but this example I think we'll find will be cast out by the next part of the definition which is that the fossil must be preserved in rock by natural means.

Notice that even though the second main point was introduced at the end of the first section, some of the emphasis is lost. Perhaps part of the problem is the abandonment of the enumeration. Speakers, especially beginners, tend to begin series with such statements as "the first..." The device is self-defeating, however, if "one" is never followed by "two," "three," and "four." In this case, for purposes of consistency as well as clarity, it would have been better for him to introduce the second part by saying: "The second characteristic of a fossil is that it must be preserved in rock by natural means." "Now,

Well, now, I can go and stick my foot or drop a leaf in some concrete and get a nice print. Fine. I can put my hand in some mud and make a nice imprint and watch it fill over. And, sure, maybe after the concrete or the mud hardens you might think you have a fossil, but you don't because it wasn't preserved by natural means. Now, what is natural means in relation to fossils? Well, specifically it's chemical replacement, and I can draw a rough contrast to chemical replacement by what happens to this class after it leaves out. Now, I call it student replacement. As soon as the bell rings, some of us are kinda slow, we take our time getting our books together, and some of us get out very quickly. Well, as we go out, other students come in and take our places—gradually the whole class is replaced. And if I were standing up here,

I would see the exact same arrangement of chairs, but the composition would be different. There'd be different people, their clothes would be different colors. So we have the same exact shapes, but we have a different composition. And this is what happens with fossils when they're replaced. The animals die or fall into the sea. The compounds within the shell are very unstable. So we have another compound that comes in and replaces them. And one by one we get a completely new object in the same shape but different composition.

what is natural means . . ." represents a very good use of rhetorical question. Well-phrased and well-presented questions interspersed throughout the speech encourage the audience to think along with the speaker. His explanation of chemical replacement is a very interesting invented comparison. Since it explains the most difficult concept in the speech and since it is clear, vivid, and easy to follow, it is perhaps the most effective part of the speech. It certainly represents excellent use of originality and audience adaptation.

Now the last criterion, one that's sort of a new point in geology, is how old is the fossil. Well, they have to be extremely old. I once heard a little story that says if it stinks, it belongs to zoology; if it doesn't, it belongs to the study of fossils. Well, most geologists will concede that a fossil must have a degree of antiquity older than historic time, and this will roughly go back to, say, 7000 B.C. or something like this. It's ah, they're not quite sure when.

Unlike the introduction of the second main point, this transition and statement of the main point are quite good. Notice, however, that the speaker has given up his enumeration. The story about the difference between zoology and geology is a good one. Although something may well stop "stinking" within a few months, the story adds another touch of humor to the speech. The final two sentences in this section are rather weak. It would have been better for the speaker to state his material more authoritatively.

So, grouping all these things together, we can say that a fossil is the remains of a plant or animal, preserved by natural means in rock, and possessing a degree of antiquity older than historic times. Thank you.

A good summary. At the end of the speech, however, the "thank you" is unnecessary. If the speech was good, the audience will be appreciative anyway; if the speech was not good, the "thank you" has no real effect on the quality of the speech. During the speech, the speaker mentioned the three aspects in the introduction, discussed each in detail during the body, and drew the definition together in the conclusion. Despite some questionable word selection and a few grammatical lapses, this is a worthy model for a speech of definition.

Expository Speeches

13

Throughout history man has had an insatiable need to know. Unanswered questions stimulate research; research yields facts; and facts, when properly ordered and developed, yield understanding. Oral communication of the understanding of these questions is made through expository speaking.

Although any speech of explanation is in a sense an expository speech, for purposes of this assignment an expository speech is defined as one that places emphasis on the understanding of an idea and that requires outside source material to give the speech depth. For example, "the causes of juvenile delinquency," "the practice of religion in ancient Egypt," "the nature of a guaranteed annual income," "the history of the struggle for women's suffrage," and "the origin and classifications of nursery rhymes" are all examples of topics for expository speaking. Under this definition, a descriptive or demonstrative speech or a speech that can be given using only personal knowledge or observation would not be acceptable. In explanation of this assignment, we will consider some of the types of expository topics, research, and creative development of resource material.

The Types of Expository Topics

In order to stimulate your thinking about topics and to help you anticipate and solve some of the problems associated with major types of expository speeches, let's consider, as separate categories, exposition of political, economic, and social issues; exposition of historical events and forces; exposition of a theory, principle, or concept; and exposition of critical appraisal.

Exposition of Political, Economic, and Social Issues

Before you can hope to solve a problem, you must know something about it. Now, as perhaps never before, the ordinary citizen needs all kinds of information to help him cope with his environment. Take our battle with air pollution as an example. Although we may believe that something should be done about it, many of us don't know enough about the complexity of the causes and we have little knowledge about existing or proposed solutions. As an expository speaker, you have the opportunity and perhaps the obligation to make us aware of the various factors that should be considered before a decision can be made. You are not charged with the responsibility of proving the harm of an existing problem, nor do you attempt to move us to a particular action—these are all within the province of the persuasive speaker. You, as an expository reporter, provide the facts about some phase of the problem. Your goal is understanding.

One of the special problems met in dealing with contemporary issues is objectivity. You cannot hope to speak objectively (to discuss your topic in a detached manner) unless you are also objective in your analysis of the problem. For instance, you should not begin your research with the thought "I'm going to prove to them that we've got to put more money into the solving of this problem now" or "I'm going to show them why gas-fueled transportation should be banned." What you can do is decide what aspect of the contemporary issue needs to be discussed, then go ahead and find the material that will yield understanding of that aspect. For instance, if after reading a few articles, you decide that the experts see the elimination of the internal combustion engine for automobiles as an answer to air pollution, you can speculate about alternative automotive power plants. Further research might show that the present thrust in automotive engineering is directed toward battery-driven and steam-driven automobiles. As an expository speaker, then, you may talk about why experts are considering the elimination of the internal combustion engine, or you may talk about one or both of the alternative systems. You would not attempt to prove that we should abandon the gasoline engine, nor should you attempt to convince us that either of the two alternatives is superior. So, objectivity is insured by reading widely on the topic, selecting an aspect of the topic, then presenting the information as an addition to our knowledge and not as proof of a position.

Arousing audience interest may be even more difficult than maintaining objectivity. Psychologically, you may face at least two problems: antipathy toward matters of importance and audience saturation. The first of these, antipathy, might be called the spinach syndrome. Just as some people rebel at eating spinach because it is "good for them," they also rebel at listening to speeches that will be "good for them." Since an understanding of contemporary issues is obviously important, you must think of ways to make these important topics interesting. The second related problem is our tendency to "turn off" when we reach a saturation point; at various times, all of us just get tired of hearing about riots, Southeast Asia, inflation and other crises. The answer to the saturation problem is to consider some aspects of a contemporary issue that will be new to the audience. Although a speech on the causes of the women's liberation movement may get a deaf ear, a speech on the emerging role of women in politics may arouse audience interest. Instead of giving the impression that you are going to give another one of the innumerable talks about a "common" problem, select some aspect that is fresh. In summary, new information presented in a fresh manner may counter both antipathy and saturation.

Although your topics should always grow from your brainstorming sheet, here and in each of the following sections several subject areas will be listed to help stimulate your thinking.

Topics for Consideration

Methods of solving air pollution	Pesticides and wildlife
Modernization of police forces	Effects of marijuana
Progress on research on cancer	Cable television
Extent of mercury in fish	Women's liberation
School financing	Effects of TV on children
Urban renewal	Nuclear power
Mass media	Inflation

Exposition of Historical Events and Forces

It has been said that men who don't understand history are forced to repeat it. History can be fascinating for its own sake; moreover, through historical analysis we learn to appreciate the causal relationships that can help to explain or at least to illuminate contemporary society. Whether you talk about the strategy of war, mathematics, wrestling, or air pollution, you can find historical information to give an insight into the subject matter that is impossible to get in any other way.

Through thinking historically, you can uncover fascinating topics relatively quickly. For example, let's assume for a moment that you have an interest in machines, mechanics, building, construction, or related areas. As a result, you may be fascinated by the knowledge of all that is involved in creating a skyscraper or a bridge or a high-rise apartment. Let your mind wander a bit. Think of some of the famous constructions of the past—of the Great Wall of China, Stonehenge, or the Pyramids. In ancient times, man did not have such equipment as cranes, steamshovels, and bulldozers. How were these remarkable structures built? Why were they built? What materials were used? Why have they lasted? These are just examples. Every area of study is replete with topics of historical interest that are worth exploring. Because history is a mirror of life, it may be dull or exciting.

History can be made lively and interesting when you select examples, illustrations, and experiences that vivify your ideas. Recreation of actual events, actions, and description all will help add interest to historical analysis. If you've noticed, many people who say they don't like history enjoy historical fiction. Why? Because the history is made vivid and exciting.

Relevancy is a second major problem of historical analysis. Since your audience may not share your immediate or automatic interest, you must show a relevancy to contemporary times. Building pyramids may be related to modern construction problems, medieval jousts may be related to one or more modern sports, battle strategy may be related to modern warfare. As an expository speaker, you must seek out the tie between historical knowledge and our interests. Notice, I say seek out the tie. If the material has any intrinsic value or merit, it can be related to audience knowledge and needs.

Topics for Consideration

Pyramids	Oriental use of gunpowder
Greek drama	One-room schoolhouse
Roman chariots	Pirates
Circus Maximus	Establishing trade routes
Roman roads	Exploration
Genghis Khan	Napoleonic wars
Castles	Inventions
Chivalry	Battle strategy
Stonehenge	Witches

Exposition of a Theory, Principle, or Law

The way we live is determined by natural laws, physical principles, and man-made theories. Yet as important as these are to us, many of us do not understand the laws, principles, and theories, either in themselves or in how they affect us. Take gravity, for example. We know that when we drop something it goes "down." We know that all of us stand upright on earth and that "up" to people on opposite sides of the earth happens to be opposite directions. Some of us may even remember that all heavier-than-air objects drop at the same rate of speed regardless of size or weight; or that, although speed remains the same, their momentum (weight times speed) differs. When astronauts reach a given height, they experience weightlessness. If you have an interest in physical laws, perhaps you could explain these and other phenomena having to do with gravity. Or you may be able to discuss applications of this law to other phases of our lives—applications that would be of tremendous informative and interest value to your audience. Because we are really so naïve about the forces around us, theories, principles, and laws make excellent expository topics.

The exposition of a theory, principle, or law brings about at least one problem that is peculiar to this kind of speech: the tendency to overuse or become dependent upon scientific terminology, formulas, and jargon. This dependence is one reason why some engineers, mathematicians, economists, and behavioral scientists find it very difficult to talk with people outside their professions. Your problem, then, is to explain scientific terms in a language that can be understood. Popularizers such as Vance Packard, Margaret Mead, and Isaac Asimov, have earned reputations for their ability to bridge the gap between the specialists and the common man. A good expository speaker must be such a popularizer. He must understand the subject, and he must be able to discuss that understanding in an intelligible manner. An effective tool of the popularizer is the example. Any theory, principle, or law can be explained by using one or more examples. The more closely the example relates to the frame of reference of the listener, the more easily it can be understood. For instance, when you learned πr^2, the formula for the area of a circle, you probably needed one or more examples to give you a mastery of the formula. When your teacher wrote $22/7 \times 7 \times 7 = 154$ on the board, you saw how the formula worked. After she wrote $22/7 \times 10 \times 10 = 2200/7 = 314\frac{2}{7}$, you may have said, "I understand." The two examples then allowed you to put the formula into practice. You can help your audience gain a mastery by using examples to put the law, theory, or principle into practice. Furthermore, you can let the use of examples help you avoid a dependence upon jargon.

As with historical exposition, relevance is also a problem with theories, laws, and principles; however, one of their most exciting aspects is *how* they relate to us. The fact that plastic has the property of being molded into almost any form and the capacity for retaining that form under many stresses allows us to make many uses of plastic. The law that force is equal to mass times acceleration allows us to make jet engines. The "law" of supply and demand allows us to understand many modern business practices. And the formula $E = mc^2$ holds the key to our possible salvation or ultimate destruction. To assure your success you must show us what a particular law, theory, or principle means to us—with good topics, the challenge shouldn't be difficult.

A third problem is to avoid misleading an audience. We hypothesize about many things in this world. From our hypotheses we formulate theories. Be sure that you know whether your topic is a theory or a fact. The formula πr^2 will give us the area of a circle, pure water boils at 212° Fahrenheit at sea level, and gravity can be measured. Relativity, evolution, and multiplier effect are theories that may or may not be valid. If you keep this differentiation in mind, you can avoid confusing yourself or your audience.

Topics for Consideration

Binomial theory	Colors—complement and contrast
Boyle's law	Condensation
Archimedes' law	Light refraction
Binary number system	X-rays
Einstein's theory of relativity	Multiplier effect
Harmonics	Magnetism

Exposition of Critical Appraisal

Probably every university in the country offers courses in film, art, and music appreciation. The purpose of these and similar courses is to give insight into the standards of criticism. To appreciate means to understand *why* we respond the way we do. Because much of our pleasure and satisfaction is based upon our evaluation of paintings, musical composition, books, films, speeches, and other art forms, the exposition of critical appraisal is worth considering for your exposition speech.

A major problem with this kind of assignment is recognizing the difference between objective evaluation and persuasive intent. We should, of course, be well aware that anything we say in a speech may have a kind of persuasive appeal for an audience. The difference, however, between a persuasive speech and an informative one is the intent of the speaker. A speech in which you tried to prove to the audience that Van Gogh's "Starry Night" is a great painting or is overrated, would be persuasive. In contrast, a speech on the characteristics of the painting that help to make it popular or a study of the painting in terms of Van Gogh's mental state would be informative.

In addition, as a critic you must have an accepted critical base from which to work. You should be familiar enough with the subject area to have some confidence in your knowledge and ability to explain and not just list. For instance, in appraisal of "Starry Night," you could comment on the use of heavy brush strokes. Although this fact in itself may be interesting, it would be better for you to explain what this kind of a stroke does to or for the painting and to show what kinds of effects are possible as a result. In other words, you must be prepared to go beyond superficial analysis and to give real insight into the work.

A third and a very real problem in a short speech is to give the audience enough orientation. With a speech on a Van Gogh painting, this can be done by showing a color reproduction of the painting itself; within a few seconds, an audience can get as much knowledge as it needs about the work being analyzed. If, however, you discuss a book, a film, or a speech, you may have to familiarize your audience with the work itself before you can go into a critical appraisal. The following guidelines will help you decide how much orientation will be necessary. If you select as a subject something that can be grasped by observation, you have no major problems. If you have a subject that is well known (for example, Lincoln's Gettysburg Address), you can assume an audience understanding. If the subject cannot be grasped on observance or is not familiar, you must make sure that you can explain it in no more than two minutes. If you cannot explain it in that time, it probably is not a good topic for this class and these time limits.

Subject Areas for Consideration

Painting:
Picasso
Van Gogh
Rembrandt
Rockwell

Speeches:
Inaugural addresses
Courtroom speaking
Legislative speeches

Film:
Silent movies
Foreign movies

Literature:
Poetry
Novels
Short stories
Science fiction

Music:
Jazz
Folk rock
Symphony
Concerto

Research

Ensuring Comprehension

Quality research is a requirement of good exposition. Quality research will make your speech comprehensive. By comprehensive we mean covering the areas that need to be covered in order to satisfy your purposes. Or, put in another way, comprehensive means researching the best available material on the subject. Although comprehensive research on any expository subject could take a team of researchers weeks or more—for a class assignment, we would expect the speech to be comprehensive "within reason," which might be defined as utilizing at least four or more sources of information. A review of sources of information (including the interview—perhaps one of the best sources for topics on contemporary issues) in Chapter 3 should help you get the best bibliography. My advice would be to check out or look into at least eight or ten different sources.

As you gather the sources, which will be included in your bibliography, you may find that you have discovered more material than you can possibly read completely. In order to locate and record the best material, you should develop a system of evaluation that will enable you to review the greatest amount of information in the shortest period of time. Most students find that with a little practice they can increase their efficiency by skip reading. If you are appraising a magazine article, spend a minute or two finding out what it covers. Does it really present information on the phase of the topic you are exploring? Does it contain any documented statistics, examples, or quotable opinions? Is the author qualified to draw meaningful conclusions? If you are appraising a book, read the table of contents carefully, look at the index, and skip read pertinent chapters asking the same questions you would for a magazine article. During this skip-reading period, you will decide which sources should be read in full, which should be read in part, and which should be abandoned. Every minute spent in evaluation will save you from unlimited amounts of useless reading.

Insuring Accuracy and Objectivity

In addition to yielding comprehensiveness of analysis, a wide variety of sources are needed to insure accuracy and objectivity. Because your goal is to find the facts regardless of what they may prove, you will need to get material on all sides of the topic being explored. Your material may reveal some contradictory aspects; your speech should reflect the nature of the conflict.

Any source that you read will be a representation of fact and opinion. A fact is anything that is verifiable; an opinion is an expressed view on any subject. That apples have seeds is a fact; that apples taste good is an opinion. Some opinions are related to, based upon, or extended from facts—some are not. Before you build your lines of development, you need to test the accuracy of the "facts" you've discovered and the objectivity of opinions. Determining accuracy of every item in a source can be a long and tedious and perhaps even an impossible job. In most cases accuracy can be reasonably assured by checking the fact against the original, or primary, source. If your source states that, according to the most recent Department of Labor statistics, unemployment went down 0.2 percent in December, you should look for those most recent Department of Labor statistics. If your history book footnotes the original source of an important quotation, you should go to that original source. Although checking sources in this way may appear to be an unnecessary task, you will be surprised at the number of errors that occur in using data from other sources.

If the original or primary source is not available, the best way of verifying a fact is to check it against the facts in a second source on the subject. Although two or more sources may on some occasion get their "facts" from the same faulty source, when two or more sources state the same fact or similar facts, the chances of verification are considerably better.

A second and equally important test is to determine the objectivity of an opinion. Facts by themselves aren't nearly as important as the conclusions drawn from them. Since conclusions are more often than not opinions, they have to be weighed very carefully before they can be accepted. Researchers find that a good procedure is to study a variety of sources to see what they say about the same set of facts; then the researcher draws his own conclusion from the facts. His conclusion may duplicate one source, or may draw from several sources, or occasionally may differ from the sources. But only after you have examined many sources, are you in a position to make the kind of value judgment that a thinking speaker needs to make. In your research you may be surprised how many times two sources will appear to contradict each other on the interpretation of a set of facts. Whether the issue is the cause of the Great War, the effect of use of "the pill" on women, or the importance of free trade to a nation's economic position, what the source says may depend on the biases of the author, the availability or selection of material, or care in evaluation of material. As a result, the expository speaker must assure himself that he is not communicating a distorted, biased, or hastily stated opinion as fact.

Citing Source Material

A special problem of a research speech is how you can cite source material in your speech. In presenting any speech in which you are using ideas that are not your own personal knowledge, you should attempt to work the source of your material into the context of the speech. Such efforts to include sources not only will help the audience in their evaluation of the content but also will add to your credibility as a speaker. In a written report, ideas taken from other sources are designated by footnotes. In a speech, these notations must be included within the context of your statement of the material. In addition, since an expository speech is supposed to reflect a depth of research, citing the various sources of information will give concrete evidence of your research. Your citation need not be a complete representation of all the bibliographical information. In most instances, the following kinds of phrasing are appropriate:

According to an article by Senator Muskie in last week's *Life* magazine . . .

In the latest Gallup poll cited in last week's issue of *Newsweek* . . .

One conservative point of view was well summed up by Barry Goldwater in his book *Conscience of a Conservative.* In the opening chapter, Goldwater wrote . . .

But in order to get a complete picture we have to look at the statistics. According to the *Statistical Abstract*, the level of production for underdeveloped countries rose from . . .

In a speech before the National Association of Manufacturers given just last fall, Governor Rockefeller said . . .

Although you don't want to clutter your speech with bibliographical citations, you do want to make sure that you have properly reflected the sources of your key information. If you will practice these and similar short prefatory comments, you will find that they will soon come naturally.

Creativity and Originality
in Expository Speaking

If you have selected a worthwhile topic and have gathered sufficient reliable material, your speech should have the necessary depth. Because you are engaging your audience in a learning process, you also want to do what you can to make your ideas interesting. By thinking creatively you can add originality to your speeches. An original speech is new; it is not copied, imitated, or reproduced. To you, the expository speaker, this means that your speech must be a product of, but entirely different from, the sources you used. You find material, you put it in a usable form, then you inject your insights and your personality into the speech.

Originality is a product of the creative process. Some people have the mistaken idea that creativity is a natural by-product of a special "creative individual." Actually, we all have the potential for thinking creatively—some of us just haven't given ourselves a chance to try.

To be creative, you must give yourself enough time to allow the creative process to work. Creative thinking is roughly analogous to cooking. You just can't rush it. Have you ever tried to make a good spaghetti sauce? It takes hours and hours of simmering the tomatoes, herbs, and spices. A good cook knows that success with the best ingredients and the best recipes is dependent upon allowing the proper length of time. So it is with speechmaking. Once you have prepared yourself fully (when you have completed your outline), you need two or three days for your mind to reflect upon what you have gathered. Let's take the practice period as an example of the result of giving the creative process time to work. You may find that the morning after a few uninspiring practices you suddenly have two or three fresh ideas for lines of development. While you were sleeping, your mind was still going over the material. When you awoke, the product of unconscious or subconscious thought reached the level of consciousness. Had there been no intervening time between practice sessions and delivery, your mind would not have had the time to work through the material.

But time alone is not enough. You must be receptive to new ideas, and you must develop the capacity to evaluate comparable ideas. Too often we are content with the first thought that comes to mind. Suppose, for your speech on plastics, you thought you would begin the speech with "Years ago when you learned that something was made out of plastic you often rejected it as an inferior product. Today you wouldn't give it a second thought. Let's examine some of the ways plastics have been developed to strengthen their quality." Now there's probably nothing wrong with such an opening. But is it the best you can do? There's no way for you to know until you have tried other ways. Here is where you can usefully employ the brainstorming method for a goal other than selecting topics. Try to start your speech in two, three, or even five different ways. Although several attempts will be similar, the effort to try new ways will stretch your mind, and chances are good that one or two of the ways will be far superior and much more imaginative than any of the others.

Being receptive also means taking note of ideas that come to you regardless of the circumstances. Did you ever notice how ideas will come to you at strange times? Perhaps while you're washing dishes, or shining your shoes, or watching a television program, or waiting for your date, or waiting for a stop light to change. Also, have you often noticed that when you try to recall those ideas they have slipped away? Many speakers, writers, and composers carry a pencil and a piece of paper with them at all times; and when an idea comes, they take the time to write it down. They don't try to evaluate it, they only try to get the details on paper. Not all of these inspirations are the flashes of insight that are characteristic of creativity, of course, but some of them are. If you don't make note of yours, if you are not receptive to them, you will never know.

The greatest value of the creative process is to enable you to work out alternative methods of presenting factual material. In addition to methods already discussed, familiarity with possible lines of development will help guide your creative thinking. From a body of factual material, an infinite number of lines of development are possible. In any one speech, you may wish to use a single line of development or a combination of lines of development, depending upon the scope of the speech, the number of points you wish to make, and the time available to you. To illustrate the inventive process fully, let's suppose you are planning to give a speech on climate in the United States, and in your research you came across the data in Table 13–1.

Now what we want to show is how this data can be used in a variety of ways to help yield an understanding of climatic conditions. The difference between this discussion and the one in Chapter 3 is that here we are going beyond finding materials; now we are talking about creating alternate lines of development using the same set of facts.

Development by Statistics

A statistical line of development is one in which a compilation of details, usually in numerical or percentage form, is used to illustrate the point. By examining the climatic data in Table 13–1, we could create a statistical way of showing the material. For instance:

Table 13–1

City	Temperature Jan. Max.	Min.	Year High	Low	Extremes		Precipitation July	Annual
Cincinnati	41	26	96	2	109	−17	3.3	39
Chicago	32	12	93	−6	103	−39	3.4	33
Denver	42	15	100	−5	105	−30	1.5	14
Los Angeles	65	47	88	39	110	28	T	14
Miami	76	58	96	44	100	28	6.8	59
Minneapolis	22	2	96	−21	108	−34	3.5	24
New Orleans	64	45	98	23	102	7	6.7	59
New York	40	27	97	11	106	−15	3.7	42
Phoenix	64	35	114	27	118	16	T	7
Portland, Me.	32	12	93	−6	103	−39		42
St. Louis	40	24	97	2	115	−23	3.3	35
San Francisco	55	42	86	33	106	20	T	18
Seattle	44	33	91	15	99	0	.6	38

Statement: Normal high temperatures in American cities vary far less than normal low temperatures.

Development: Whereas, of the thirteen cities selected, ten of them (77%) had normal highs between 90° and 100°, three cities (23%) had normal lows above freezing; six of them (46%) had normal lows between zero and 32°, and four of them (30%) had low temperatures ten below zero or colder.

Development by Example

Development by example occurs when a single instance or a group of instances is used to illustrate the statement:

Statement: It hardly ever rains in California in the summer.

Development (single instance): The average rainfall during the whole month of July in San Francisco is less than one half of one inch.

Statement: It hardly ever rains on the West Coast in the summer.

Development (several instances): The average rainfall in July in Los Angeles and in San Francisco is less than one half of one inch. In Seattle, a city thought to be rather rainy, the average rainfall in July is only six tenths of an inch.

Development by Illustration

Development by illustration occurs when a single instance or example is presented in such a way that it becomes a story rather than an instance.

Statement: It hardly ever rains in California in the summer. (Same as the one above under *example*.)

Development: I had a chance to vacation in San Francisco for a couple of weeks last summer. And like most people, I was concerned about whether I'd get good weather. During the first few days, the sky was crystal blue all day long. On about the fourth day some clouds swept in and a few drops of rain fell. For the rest of the stay some clouds blew in late in the afternoons, but we didn't have another drop of rain. Naturally, I thought I had really been lucky— two whole weeks and only a few drops of rain. For the fun of it I looked up the average rainfall in my almanac. Much to my surprise, I learned that my experience wasn't as unusual as I had thought. During the entire month of July, normal rainfall in San Francisco is less than one half of one inch.

Development by Comparison and/or Contrast

A comparative line of development places the emphasis on the similarities or on the differences involved. By and large, one of the best ways of giving meaning to figures and to abstract ideas is through comparison.

Statement: Whereas last year's high temperatures in major cities were much the same, low temperatures varied by more than 60°.

Development: Cincinnati, Miami, Chicago, and New York all had high temperatures of 96° or 97°; in contrast the lowest temperature for Miami was 44°, whereas the lowest temperatures for Cincinnati, Chicago, and New York were 2°, −10°, and 11° respectively.

Development by Analogy

An analogy is a special kind of comparative development in which a point is made about an unknown quality by showing its similarities to a known quantity.

Statement: If you like the weather in St. Louis, you'll probably like the weather in Cincinnati.

Development: Normal high and normal low temperatures for St. Louis and Cincinnati are about the same; both cities have about the same amount of average rainfall per month; and both cities have rather hot and humid summers and rather mild winters.

Assignment

Prepare a four- to seven-minute expository speech. Outline and bibliography (at least three outside sources) required. Criteria for evaluation will include quality of the content, the use of source material in the speech, and the originality and creativity shown in the presentation. The speech should be informative and interesting. A question period of one to three minutes will follow (optional).

Alternate Assignment

Prepare a four- to seven-minute report on some aspects of the topic you have been given. Outline and bibliography are required. Focus on the status or progress of a problem, organization, or movement. Criteria for evaluation will include (1) how well you have limited the topic, (2) how substantial is your resource material, (3) how well you have introduced bibliographical citations, and (4) how interesting you have made the development. Here follow sample speeches for each of the assignments described above.

**Outline: Expository Speech—Historical
(4–6 minutes)**

The following is a clear and well-organized outline:

Specific Purpose: To explain four major classifications of nursery rhymes.

Introduction
I. "Hey diddle diddle, the cat and the fiddle, the cow jumped over the moon. The little dog laughed to see such sport, and the dish ran away with the spoon."

II. Did you know that there are four major classifications of nursery rhymes?—ditties, teaching rhymes, historically based, and modern use.

Body
I. Ditties are nursery rhymes with a prophetic purpose.
   A. A fortune-telling rhyme is told while counting the white spots on the fingernails.
   B. Just as in *Poor Richard's Almanack*, by Benjamin Franklin, Mother Goose had her merry wise sayings.
   C. Traditionally, a rhyme on the topic of love fidelity is said while plucking the petals of a daisy.

II. Some nursery rhymes were used as teaching aids.
   A. "Hickory Dickory Dock" is an example of onomatopoeia, which is an attempt to capture in words a specific sound.

B. Song rhymes helped the children with their coordination.
   1. Historical background.
   2. Children's usage.
C. Numbers in nursery rhymes obviously retain the traces of the stages by which prehistoric man first learned to count.

III. Many nursery rhymes have historical significance.
   A. Religious problems entered into the nursery rhymes with "Jack Sprat."
   B. It became a tradition in England that some of these country rhymes may have been relics of formulas used by the druids in choosing a human sacrifice for their pagan gods.
   C. Cannibalism is quite prevalent in nursery rhymes.

IV. A modern classification of the nursery rhyme is the parody.
   A. The famous prayer "Now I lay me down..." was first published in 1737, but has now been parodied.
   B. A joke has been created out of "Mary and Her Lamb."

Conclusion

I. Every song, ballad, hymn, carol, tale, singing game, dance tune, or dramatic dialogue that comes from an unwritten, unpublished word-by-the-mouth source contributes to the future culture of our nation.

II. Remember that with your next cute saying, teaching aid in the form of a rhyme, reference to our history, or modern use of the nursery rhymes, you may become the next Mother Goose.

Bibliography

Baring-Gould, William S., and Cecil Baring-Gould, *The Annotated Mother Goose* (New York: Clarkson A. Potter, 1962).

Bett, Henry, *Nursery Rhymes and Tales—Their Origins and History* (New York: Henry Holt and Co., 1924).

Ken, John Bellenden, *An Essay on the Archaeology of Popular Phrases and Nursery Rhymes* (London: Longman, Rees, Orme, Brown, Green, and Co., 1837).

Mother Goose, *Mother Goose and the Nursery Rhymes* (London: Frederick Warne and Co., 1895).

Read the transcription of the speech in the inside column at least once aloud.[1] Examine the speech to see how information is made clear and interesting. After you have studied the speech, read the analysis in the outside column.

---

[1] Speech given in Fundamentals of Speech class, University of Cincinnati. Printed by permission of Susan Woistmann.

Classifications of Nursery Rhymes

Analysis

Speech

Miss Woistmann uses a common rhyme to capture our attention. After noting our certain recognition, she anticipates our reaction toward nursery rhymes. Her next sentence is an attempt both to indicate that there's more to these rhymes than we might anticipate and to forecast that there will be four classifications covered in the speech.

"Hey diddle diddle, the cat and the fiddle, the cow jumped over the moon, the little dog laughed to see such sport and the dish ran away with the spoon." You recognize this as a nursery rhyme, and perhaps you always considered these nursery rhymes as types of nonsense poetry with little if any meaning. As we look at the four classifications of nursery rhymes, I think that you'll see as I did that there's more to nursery rhymes than meets the ear.

She begins the body of the speech by identifying the first classification. The next sentence gives us the three subdivisions of the major classification. The commendable part of this and all sections of the speech is the use of the specific examples to illustrate the various types and subtypes. As far as real information is concerned, this main point doesn't go much beyond labeling and classifying our own knowledge. The last part is of some interest in that it shows the evolution of wording.

One of the major classifications of nursery rhymes is ditties. Ditties are fortune-tellings, little wise sayings, or little poems on love fidelity, and they are the most popular form of nursery rhyme. There are various ways of telling your fortune through ditties. One is saying, "A gift, a ghost, a friend, a foe; letter to come and a journey to go." And while you say this little ditty, this fortune-telling, you count the little white spots on your fingernails. Or you can say, "Rich man, poor man, beggarman, thief, doctor, lawyer, merchant, chief," and count your buttons. Whichever button you end up on is the type of guy you are going to marry. Another kind of ditty is the wise saying. Just as in *Poor Richard's Almanack* by Benjamin Franklin, Mother Goose had her own little sayings. She said, "A pullet in the pen is worth a hundred in the fen," which today we say as "A bird in the hand is worth two in the bush." Love fidelity, the third kind of ditty, can be proven while plucking the petals off a daisy. "Love her, hate her, this year, next year, sometime, never." But today's usage has brought it up to "Love me, love me not, love me, love me not."

Again the main point is clearly stated. She begins this section with an interesting look at a common rhyme. Once more, an excellent use of specifics to illustrate the point she is making. Although speech language should be informal it should not be imprecise. Notice that the antecedent for "he" in "he's trying to show the tick-

Another classification of nursery rhymes is those used as teaching aids, such as in the saying "Hickory dickory dock." This is the use of onomatopoeia, which is trying to develop a sound from the use of words. In this case, he's trying to show the ticking of a clock. London Bridge, although it has some historical background, is used for teaching children coordination, such as running around the circle raising their hands up and jumping back down. Similarly, in the ancient times, man made up rhymes in order to make things easier for him to remember, such as in the saying, "one, two, buckle my shoe; three, four, close the door." And as time went on, he eventually found out that he could use the fingers and toes to count. This is where "This little piggy went to market and this little piggy stayed home" originated.

Also, did you know that nursery rhymes have historical background? The third classification of nursery rhymes are those of historical significance. In the Middle Ages, which is when most nursery rhymes were formed, the saying, "Jack Sprat could eat no fat, his wife could eat no lean; and so betwixt the two of them, they licked the platter clean," refers to the Catholic Church and the government of the old Roman Empire. This is when the Catholic Church was blessing tithes, and wiping the country clean. The government came in and collected the taxes; and between the two of them, the country had no wealth and no money. The Druids, in their relics of old formulas for selecting human sacrifices, used the "eeny meeny, miny, moe." And cannibalism is quite prevalent in almost all the nursery rhymes. Such as in "Jack and the Beanstalk," the big giant eater, and "Fee, Fi, Foe, Fum, I smell the blood of an Englishman. Be he alive or be he dead, I'm going to use him to make my bread." This also came up again in Shakespeare with *King Lear* and *Midsummer Night's Dream.* "Little Jack Horner" is about a man named Jack Horner, who was steward of the abbot of Glastonberry. And in 1542, he was sent by this abbot to King Henry VIII of England with a pie. And in this pie were documents which were the documents of the ownership of land around the Abbey of Glastonberry, in Somersetshire. And on his way to the king, he stuck in his thumb and pulled out a document to the ownership of Meld, which he kept to himself. And until this day, over in Somersetshire, the Manor of Meld belongs to the Horner family.

The fourth classification of the nursery rhyme is the modern use, parodies and jokes, such as in "Mary had a little lamb, its fleece was white as snow," today the kids go around saying, "Mary had a little

ing" is unclear. You should be careful to avoid these common grammatical errors. This section of the speech illustrates how information can sometimes be communicated in such an interesting way that we aren't even aware that we have learned anything.

Again Miss Woistmann moves smoothly into the statement of the main point. As far as the quality of information is concerned, this is probably the best section of the speech. Because it seems to be the best part of the speech, it should probably be placed as the last point in the speech. Since there is an equally logical reason for placement of her last point, her violation of the placement principle may be necessary. Notice that she continues to use her examples and illustrations very well.

Of all the single examples in the speech, this is probably the best. To Miss Woistmann's credit it is given excellent placement within the main point and represents excellent proportion.

Once more we are aware of the statement of a main point. Miss Woistmann returns to classifying and labeling information that as an audience we have in our possession.

From the foregoing criticism it can be seen that the speech is very clear, extremely interesting, and informative enough to meet the criteria for expository speaking. Two possibilities for strengthening the speech are worth considering. Since the third main point is so informative, it might have been better for the speaker to limit the entire speech to this particular subject. She could have mentioned the other three classifications. In the introduction, then told us why she would focus on historical significance. The advantage of such a revision would of course be that the information level of the speech would have been better. Secondly, since the bibliography accompanying the outline shows the amount of research, she should have taken better advantage of the research by including some of the scholarly methodology involved. She could have told us where the scholars uncovered their information. She could have told us which aspects of the analysis were fact and which were theory. As it is, the speech is a good one. It could have been perhaps equally as interesting and just a little more informative.

lamb and was the doctor ever surprised." Or else they tend to make parodies of these nursery rhymes. Such as the famous little prayer, "Now I lay me down to sleep. I pray the Lord my soul to keep. If I should die before I wake, I pray the Lord my soul to take." It was first published in 1737, so you can see the age of this prayer. But, nowadays, the children say in joke, "Now I lay me down to sleep with a bag of peanuts at my feet. If I should die before I wake, you'll know I died of a stomach ache."

This conclusion ties the speech together pretty well. The wording of the summary gives the conclusion a necessary lift.

So every song, ballad, hymn, carol, tale, dance rhythm, or any cute little saying that you might come up with may contribute to the future culture of our nation. So remember, the next time you start spouting wise sayings, using rhymes as a teaching aid, referring to our history, or when you start making jokes of the traditional nursery rhymes, who knows, you might be the next Mother Goose.

**Outline: Research Report
(4–7 minutes)**

Specific Purpose: To familiarize the audience with the intoxicant called marijuana and its immediate and long term effects.

Introduction

I. What is marijuana?

II. What are its effects upon us?

III. As the use of marijuana continues to grow and as all of us realize that we may come in contact with this drug, we should ask ourselves these questions and many more.

IV. I would like to answer some of these questions tonight.

Body

I. What is marijuana?
  A. The botanical name of the marijuana plant is *Cannabis sativa.*
  B. Marijuana belongs to the hemp family.
  C. The upper leaves contain the largest amounts of the plant's intoxicating ingredient THC (tetrahydra cannabinol).

II. What happens when a person gets high?
  A. Intoxicating effects vary with personalities and moods and are related to whether the user is experienced or not.
  B. Regular smokers get high more easily than novice smokers.
  C. The two most noticeable immediate physical effects are dilation of the red blood vessels of the eyes and increased heart rate.
  D. Use can result in bad experiences.

III. What are the long-term effects of marijuana?
  A. All authorities agree that marijuana is not physically addictive.
  B. As with any intoxicant, marijuana can be psychologically addictive to some users.
  C. Some researchers indicate that a buildup of THC in the fatty tissue of the body accounts for the experienced user's easy high.
  D. Other reports led to the theory that THC does not make you high; but, rather, it is a degenerated by-product form of the drug broken down by the liver. The increase in efficiency of the liver with continued use increases the user's ability to get high.
  E. Although the drug is not addictive, it may create a craving for harder drugs.

Conclusion

I. Much of the data on marijuana is inconclusive, and we really do not know enough to make valid conclusions about particular aspects of the drug's effects.

II. The most evident danger to objective research is ignorance and biased conclusions based on half-truths and incomplete evidence.

III. We should be concerned with the issues but we should look at the issues with a third eye, try to be objective, and base our opinions on fact.

Bibliography

Aaronson, Bernard, and Humphry Osmond, *Psychedelics* (New York: Doubleday & Co., 1970).

Bloomquist, E. R., *Marijuana* (Toronto, Canada: Glencoe Press, 1968).

Geller, Allen, and Maxwell Boas, *The Drug Beat* (New York: Cowles Book Co., 1969).

"Marijuana: Is It Time for a Change in Our Laws?" *Newsweek* (September 7, 1970), pp. 20–32.

Oursler, Will, *Marijuana, The Facts, The Truth* (New York: Paul S. Eriksson, 1968).

"Pot: Safer than Alcohol?" *Time* (April 19, 1968), pp. 52–53.

Snyder, Solomon H., "Work with Marijuana: I. Effects, II. Sensations," *Psychology Today* (May 1971), pp. 37–44.

"The Effects of Marijuana," *Time* (December 20, 1968), p. 48, p. 53.

The Effects of Marijuana

Analysis

Speech[2]

Mr. Armstrong was given the topic "the effects of marijuana" as a research assignment. He begins the speech with a personal reference question. The opening proved to be a good attention getting device. Furthermore the three questions forecast the three areas he will cover in the speech: definition, short term, and long term effects.

If someone in class has given a speech that relates to your topic, it's a good idea to refer to it as a means of adaptation.

Here Mr. Armstrong showed a picture of the marijuana plant. Although this particular fact wouldn't require documentation

What is this drug that we call marijuana? What does it do to us? What are its effects upon us? Everybody knows these answers, right? Wrong. We must ask ourselves some of these questions, because as Mr. Menninger pointed out last week, the use of marijuana is very widespread and it is growing. So the chances of each and every one of us coming in contact with the drug itself or with someone who uses it is increasing. Here I have a picture of a marijuana plant—this is what marijuana looks like. The botanical name is *Cannabis sativa*. It is a member of the hemp family. And as E. R. Bloomquist, in his book entitled *Marijuana,* pointed out, it is the upper leaves that contain the most of the intoxicating element found in marijuana, and that is tetrahydra cannabinol or THC. These leaves are then cultivated, dried, and either smoked or eaten to produce the intoxicating effects.

[2] Speech given in Effective Speaking class, University of Cincinnati. Printed by permission of Robert Armstrong.

The next question that we might ask ourselves is—
What exactly does marijuana do to me? What are
the immediate effects? Marijuana gives us what is
known as a high—a kind of euphoria that produces
temporary changes in perception of time, of humor,
of sense experiences such as eating, sex, and
listening to music. These marijuana highs vary from
individual to individual. They're dependent upon a
person's personality; they're dependent upon the
mood of the person. They're also dependent upon
other variables. As the May 1971 *Psychology Today*
points out, experienced users can get high easier
and on smaller amounts of marijuana than people
who have never taken the drug before.

—it is generally well known
and generally accepted as
fact—his introduction of the
source illustrates acceptable
procedure. Mr. Armstrong continues the question method of
introducing main points. The
method clarifies the points and
helps increase audience involvement.

Mr. Armstrong's pattern is to
go from general points that
we're aware of to specifics that
are less well known.

Are there any harmful immediate effects? Its use
can result in bad experiences. Dr. Ana Farnsworth
says, "The drug is especially apt to trigger such
reactions in people with unstable personalities or
emotional difficulties." In some cases a smoker
shows signs of temporary derangement. However,
Dr. Andrew Wiel of the University of Boston School
of Medicine states that almost all "psychotic reactions are in fact very severe panics by those who
interpret physical or psychological effects of the
drug to mean that they are dying or losing their
minds." This panic usually subsides. In addition,
toxic overdoses can produce hallucinations, para-
noia, disorganization of thought that may last for
days. However, most overdoses have been reported
in cases where someone has eaten the stuff—not
smoked it.

After he gives descriptive information he describes some
of the harmful effects.

Notice that throughout the
speech Mr. Armstrong introduces his sources smoothly and
with no apparent difficulty.

Mr. Armstrong relies on explanation, quotation, and specific
enumeration. Some of his points
could have been made more
vividly with illustration or
anecdote.

Now this leads us into the question that is at the
focal point of the controversy over marijuana—
What are the long-term effects? Well, this experienced user's reverse tolerance has led into' research as to whether or not THC actually builds
up in the body. While some research does indicate
that marijuana has been known to last in the body
in excess of three days, this leads us to believe that
there are some trace amounts to be found later on,
and these can be built up in the fatty tissues of the
body. However, there are conflicting reports on this.
Andrew Wiel has this to say about it: they have
theorized—now this is all based on inconclusive
evidence—they have theorized that it is not actually
the THC that makes a person high. It is a by-
product of the THC which is formed by the liver

Again, we see a smooth transition between main points and
again Mr. Armstrong introduces
his point with a question.

Here is one of the most informative and most interesting
parts of the speech. Notice how
Mr. Armstrong maintains his
objectivity throughout the
speech. This is especially noteworthy on the topic of marijuana. There's a temptation to
insert a little personal opinion—
but Mr. Armstrong sticks to the
facts. When his point is theory—
not fact—he lets us know.

acting upon the drug to break it down. Now this is the natural function of the liver in the body—to break down drugs when they enter the body. So as a person uses the drug, and continues to use the drug, the liver's ability to break the drug down into by-products increases. Well, if the by-product makes us high and the liver gets more efficient in producing this by-product, then it stands to reason that experienced users would be able to get high easier and easier and on smaller amounts.

What else do we know about the long-range effects? We know that it is not physically addictive; however, as Mr. Menninger pointed out, it can be psychologically addictive, as any intoxicant has been found to be.

And, of course, many people believe that even though it doesn't create a physical craving for harder drugs, it does kindle a fascination that leads users to experiment with more dangerous stuff. In one survey reported in the September 7, 1970 issue of *Newsweek,* of 200 chronic smokers, 49 percent had tried LSD, 43 percent an amphetamine, and 24 percent a barbiturate. Still some authorities argue that this is not the case for ordinary smokers.

In conclusion, we must continue to search for the facts. Although we know a lot about the drug, there are a great many questions still unanswered. Is marijuana really a relatively harmless euphoric? Or is it a dangerous drug that has many harmful side effects? We still can't be sure.

As you go back through the speech you notice that Mr. Armstrong has worked in a great deal of information, and he has stated it clearly and objectively.

**Persuasive
Speaking**

Five

Principles of
Persuasive Speaking

14

In the previous unit, our focus was on informative speechmaking. Now let us consider the second major type of speaking, persuasive. You will recall that the sole intent of informative speeches is to enhance the audience's understanding of the subject you select for your speech. In persuasive speaking, however, your concern goes further than achieving an understanding of ideas or procedures. Now you must affect audience attitudes *about* ideas or procedures. By definition then, a persuasive speech is one that is intended to strengthen an audience attitude, change an audience attitude, or move an audience to action.

Perhaps one of the first points we should make about persuasive speaking is that all the principles we have discussed about information reception, understanding, and retention are important for persuasion as well. The idea that should guide you in your approach to persuasion is that, rather than being a different category, it is an extension of informative speaking. For instance, a description of your apartment may be an important step in motivating a person to move there; an explanation of Thor Heyerdahl's theory is probably a necessary aspect of convincing an audience that his theory is the best one; and a discussion of scientists' progress on finding means of predicting earthquakes is probably necessary before you can convince an audience that more money should be spent to support their work.

So, recognizing that persuasion may well begin from an informative base, you can begin to think of the means at your disposal for affecting audience attitudes about the information. Although you have considerable procedural leeway—there is no one formula for a persuasive speech—your means are not limited. Perhaps the most important limiting factor that you face is your ethical responsibility. You could perhaps achieve your speech purpose through lies and distortion—

certainly some speakers have done so in the past and others will continue to do so in the future—but the study of effective speaking is by definition a study of ethical speaking. We must always be aware that the means we use to achieve success are equally important as the end we desire. Lying to an audience or distorting the truth may have short-term advantage for the individual, but no society based upon lies and deceit can long endure. If an idea has value, a speaker can demonstrate it through ethical means, and we will be considering ethical responsibility as we go along. For now, however, we want to introduce the basic logical and psychological principles that should be considered in the preparation of any persuasive speech.

1. *Persuasion is more likely to be achieved when the goal sought is not too far from the focus of audience belief.* Beliefs can be changed, but to expect 180° shifts of opinion as a result of a single speech is unrealistic and probably fruitless. William Brigance, one of the great speech teachers of this century, used to speak of "planting the seeds of persuasion." If we present a modest proposal seeking a slight change of belief, we may be able to get an audience to think about what we are saying. Then later when the idea begins to grow, we can ask for greater change. If your audience believes that taxes are too high, you are unlikely to make them believe that they are not. However, you may be able to influence them to see that taxes are not really as high as they originally thought or not as high as other goods and services.

2. *Persuasion is more likely to be achieved when an audience likes, trusts, and has confidence in the speaker.* As we discuss this more fully later, we will see that many writers regard this as the most important factor in persuasion. For instance, if a teacher you like asks you for your assistance, you are more likely to help him than if a teacher you don't like asks you. If you are not prepared to earn your audience's friendship and respect, your degree of success as a persuader will be severely limited.

3. *Persuasion is more likely to be achieved when the speaker shows a conviction in his subject.* A speaker's delivery is often regarded as a sign of the intensity of speaker conviction. Your points may be logical, well developed, and in the best interests of the audience; however, if the audience doesn't perceive some visual or auditory sign of that conviction, what you say is likely to be suspect. Of course, if you really have a strong conviction, there's a good chance that your voice and bodily action will reflect it.

4. *Persuasion is more likely to be achieved when you can show an audience that it has a personal stake in the outcome.* Psychologically, it is true that we become more and more concerned with

problems, events, and situations as we become more involved in them. We get concerned about the path of a new highway when it is intended to come through our property; we become concerned about conditions in schools when our children reach school age; and we get concerned about the cost of food when we do the shopping. If members of an audience don't see how a proposal affects them, they are unlikely to be concerned. Whether you are talking about taxes, the food shortage in India, or space exploration, you have to get your listeners involved before you can expect them to care.

5. *Persuasion is more likely to be achieved when you can show the audience the reasonableness of the proposition.* Most audiences won't be particularly interested in long logical developments of points; and they are equally unlikely to pay attention when the plan sounds far fetched, impractical, or just highly improbable. Just as it is much more likely that you can convince your roommate to take his umbrella when it's cloudy than when it's sunny, you'll find it more likely to win an audience's approval when it can see that the plan is reasonable.

In this brief chapter, we have attempted only an overview of persuasive methods. In the next three chapters, we will explore logical development of persuasion, refutation, and psychological factors of persuasion in more detail, as we consider assignments in these three areas.

Logic in Persuasion:
A Speech of Reasons

15

Persuasion may be achieved in many ways, some unethical—bribery, extortion, lying—and others ethical. We regard an ethical persuasion as one in which a speaker provides a rationale for what he wants us to believe or to do. A speech of reasons assignment—a straightforward presentation of a rationale in support of a proposition—offers you an excellent opportunity for gaining a mastery of the logical basis for persuasive speaking.

Preparing a Speech of Reasons

A speech of reasons is an attempt to present a clear proposition, clear reasons, and support for the reasons. Your goal is to achieve your persuasion by proving the value of your proposition. Let's examine each of the components of such a speech: a clear proposition, clear reasons, and support for the reasons.

Determining the Specific Purpose

Whereas the informative specific purpose indicates the boundaries of the information to be communicated, the persuasive purpose, often called a proposition, indicates what you want your audience to do or to believe. Whether you are preparing a speech of reasons or attempting to persuade in some other way, you must begin your preparation with a clear, well-worded proposition.

Ordinarily, the proposition is phrased to reinforce a belief held by an audience, to change a belief held by an audience, or to move the audience to act. "Every eligible citizen should vote" and "America is a great nation" are examples of propositions for speeches to reinforce beliefs. In both instances, the speaker would try to strengthen an attitude that prevailed in the majority of his audience. "That all states should adopt a 'no-fault' automobile insurance program" and "Kareem Jabbar is the best basketball player in the National Basketball Association" would have purposes of changing the beliefs of the audience. Even though some classmates would already favor them, these two propositions are in opposition to current belief. "Watch the 'Hallmark Hall of Fame' tonight" and "Write your congressman to find alternative support to finance public schools" are both phrased to gain immediate action. In these instances, the speaker wants more than intellectual agreement—he wants us to act. These three types of propositions are not always clearly divisible, nor are they meant to be. The important matter is not that you know what kind of proposition you are presenting but that you have a clear, specific proposition to work with.

The Function of the Main Points

The main points of a persuasive speech of reasons supply the justification for the desired belief or action. When someone says, "You ought to watch the special on TV tonight," you would probably ask "Why?" You would want some justification for watching. The statements that answer *why* a proposition is justified are called *reasons*. If the reasons given to justify your watching a particular television show satisfied you, you would probably watch—if they didn't, you wouldn't. In the following examples, notice how the main points, the reasons, provide a justification for each proposition:

Proposition: You should read labels on products carefully before you use them. (Why?)

I. Taking time to read labels saves time in the long run.

II. Taking time to read labels may save money.

III. Taking time to read labels prevents errors.

Proposition: Kareem Jabber is the best player in the National Basketball Association. (Why?)

I. He is one of the leading scorers in the league.

II. He is an outstanding playmaker.

III. He is an excellent defender.

Proposition: The federal government should guarantee a minimum annual cash income to all its citizens. (Why?)

   I. A minimum cash income would eliminate the present poverty conditions that breed social unrest.

  II. A minimum cash income would eliminate the need for all the overlapping state and federal welfare agencies.

III. A minimum cash income would go directly to the people in need.

Reasons, of course, are not enough to prove the truth of a proposition; they, in turn, must be supported with examples, quotations, statistics, and other supporting material.

If the reasons given to justify the proposition are sound, then the attempted persuasion is logical; if the reasons satisfy the audience, then the reasons are persuasive. Thus, in developing a speech of reasons, you have two goals in mind: (1) to select reasons that prove the proposition and (2) to limit the speech to the reasons that are likely to be most persuasive—the reasons that are likely to have the greatest impact on your audience.

How do you determine reasons? As with the main points for any kind of speech, reasons may either be discovered or invented. If you are trying to discover reasons, look for the reasons that writers suggest in their particular works. If, in an article on capital punishment, an author uses statistics to indicate that capital punishment does not seem to deter potential criminals, the statement "capital punishment is not a deterrent to crime" should be written down and considered as one of the possible reasons to be used in your speech. If, in that or a different article, you read that rich people are less likely to be executed than poor people and that white people are less likely to be executed than people from minority groups, then "capital punishment is not just" would be another reason you would want to note. A reading of four or five articles or parts of books would probably yield several reasons to choose from.

But you are not limited to reasons discovered from your readings. Especially for domestic, campus, and other familiar areas, your observations or your experience itself may well suggest one or more reasons that are worth considering. Suppose you wanted to persuade the audience to eat at a particular restaurant. From your experience in eating at the restaurant, you may have noted that the waitresses always take your order with a smile, that the waitresses are always willing to do a little extra to make your meal a special occasion, that the atmosphere is particularly enjoyable, that the prices are reasonable, that the tables are arranged in such a way that you have some elbow room, and that the food is always served piping hot. These are reasons for eating at that restaurant, and each should be considered as potential support for the proposition.

After you have a list of five or more reasons, you can select the best ones on the basis of which are most adaptable to your audience. You may discard some reasons on your list because you do not have and cannot get material. From those that are left, you can determine which will probably have the greatest effect on your specific audience. For most speeches, you need at least two and probably not more than four of the best, most applicable reasons.

Idea Development

In an informative speech, idea development clarifies or elaborates the main points. In a persuasive speech, the idea development helps to establish the climate of persuasion that affects audience attitudes. Because an assignment for a speech of reasons stresses the logic of development, the examples, statistics, and quotations you use will be in support of or will prove the validity of the reasons you have stated.

Basically, all supporting material may be reduced to two kinds of statements: *fact* and *opinion*. For instance, in one of our examples, it was stated that Kareem Jabbar is the best player in the National Basketball Association because he is one of the leading scorers in the league. If this statement were supported by quotations from other players, sports' journalists, and fans, the support would be opinion. On the other hand, if we checked the records and found him second in scoring this year, first last year, and third the year before, our support would be fact.

The best support for any reason is fact. Facts are statements that are verifiable. That metal is heavier than air, that World War II ended in 1945, and that marijuana is a mild hallucinatory drug are all facts. If you say, "It's warm outside; it's 60°," and if the thermometer registers 60°, then your support is factual.

Although factual support is the best there are times when the facts are not available or when the facts are inconclusive. In these situations, you will have to support your conclusions with opinion. The quality of opinion is dependent upon whether the source is expert or inexpert. If your gasoline attendant says it is likely that there is life on other planets, the opinion is not expert—his expertise lies in other areas; if on the other hand, an esteemed space biologist says there is a likelihood of life on other planets, his opinion is expert. Both statements are only opinions, not facts, but some opinions are more authoritative than others. Opinions are also more trustworthy when they are accompanied by factual data. If it is an automotive engineer's opinion that a low-cost electric car is feasible, his opinion is valuable, since automotive engineering is his area of expertise. If accompanying his opinion, he shows us the advances in technology that are leading to a low-cost battery of medium size that can run for more than 200 hours without being recharged, his opinion is worth even more.

Testing the Logic of Your Development

Since a speech of reasons is an exercise in logical development, you must assure yourself that the speech development is sound.

Testing the Logic of Structure

The logic of structure of a speech is tested by use of the speech outline. Thus, in slightly abbreviated form, an outline on the direct election of the President might look like this:

Proposition: To prove that the United States should determine the President by direct election.

Introduction
I. In 1968, we barely avoided the electoral catastrophe of selecting the President in the House of Representatives.

II. The time to reform the electoral system is now.

III. Direct election of the President offers the best alternative to the electoral college.

Body
I. Direct election of the President is fair.
   A. It follows the one-man, one-vote policy laid down by the Supreme Court.
   B. It allows every vote to count equally, regardless of where it is cast.
   C. It eliminates the possibility of the election of a candidate who receives a lesser number of popular votes.

II. Direct election of the President is certain.
   A. The identity of the new President would be public knowledge once the votes were counted.

   B. The election of the President would not be subject to political maneuvers.

III. Direct election of the President is a popular plan.

   A. A recent Gallup poll showed that the majority of people favor direct election.

   B. Many political leaders have voiced their approval of this plan.

Conclusion

 I. The time to anticipate possible catastrophe is now.

II. Support direct election of the President.

With such an outline, you can test the clarity of the proposition, the clarity of the reasons, and the support for each of the reasons. If you have an outline that looks like this abbreviated one, you are reasonably certain to have a speech of reasons that *sounds* logical.

Although the outline illustrates idea relationships, it does not describe the reasoning process nor does it test the logic. If you are familiar with formal logic, you know tests that you can apply to your thinking. If you have not taken formal logic, however, you may still plot your arguments in a way that will allow you to describe the reasoning you have done and test the logic of the arguments used. The suggested framework is based upon the Toulmin model of argumentation.[1]

Testing the Logic of Argument

A workable test is based upon the assumption that any argument is reducible to three basic requirements. These requirements are called the *data,* the *conclusion,* and the *warrant.* An understanding of these words will enable you to construct and analyze the simplest or the most complex arguments. "Data" means the evidence, assumption, or assertion that provides the basis for a conclusion; "conclusion" means the end product of a specific argument; "warrant" is the description of the reasoning process, the justification for the conclusion. The warrant, which denotes the substantive relationship between data and conclusion is the key term of this model, the one that provides the essential test, and the only one of the essentials that is not included in the structural outlines.

To illustrate the three essentials, let's put a simple argument into

---

[1] See Stephen Toulmin, *The Uses of Argument* (Cambridge, England: Cambridge University Press, 1958).

its layout form. Suppose that the temperature today reads 38°, the wind is blowing, and a hard rain is falling. As you come into the classroom, you might say to your neighbor, "It's a crummy day, isn't it?" Using (D) for data, stated or observed; (C) for conclusion; (W) for warrant; and an arrow to show the direction of an argument, the argument could be laid out schematically:

(D) Temperature 38°
    Wind blowing   ⟶   (C) It's a crummy day.
    Rain falling

        (W) (Low temperature, wind and rain are three
                major characteristics of a crummy day.)

How did we get from (D) to (C)? The warrant, written in parentheses because it is implied in the argument and not actually stated, describes the thinking process. Thus, the statement, "low temperature, wind, and rain are three major characteristics of a 'crummy' day," bridges the gap between (D) and (C).

The tests we apply to this argument are twofold. First we test the data. For a logical conclusion to follow, the data must be sufficient in quantity and quality. If either no data or insufficient data are presented, you must supply more; if the data are inaccurate, biased, or from a questionable source, the conclusion will be suspect. If you are satisfied that "temperature 38°," "wind blowing," and "rain falling" are accurate, you can examine the logic of the descriptive warrant. The warrant is tested by casting it as a "Yes or No" question: "Is it true that low temperature, wind, and rain are the major characteristics of a 'crummy' day?" If the answer is Yes, the reasoning is sound; if the answer is No, the reasoning process is fallacious.

Now let's apply our testing procedure to the speech on direct election of the President. In schematic form, the speech in its entirety would look like this:

(D) Direct election is fair.   (C) The United States should
(D) Direct election is certain.   ⟶   determine the President
(D) Direct election is popular.   by direct election.

        (W) (Fairness, certainty, and popularity are the
                three major criteria for determining how a
                President should be elected.)

To test this warrant, we ask, Is it true that fairness, certainty, and popularity are the criteria for selecting a method of election? If experience, observation, and source material indicate that these three are of fundamental importance, the speech is logical. If, on the other hand, source material indicates that some other criterion is more important, or that two or three others are of equal importance, then the warrant does not meet the test of logic and the argument should be reconsidered.

Assuming that this warrant does meet the test of logic, we can be assured that the over-all structure of the speech is logical. But what of the individual units that make up the speech? Each of the three items of data listed above is in itself a conclusion of an argument that must be tested. Let's make a schematic examination of the first of those statements: "Direct election is fair":

(D) Direct election follows the one-man, one-vote policy .

(D) Direct election allows every vote to count equally.

(D) Direct election eliminates the possibility of the election of a candidate who receives a lesser number of popular votes.

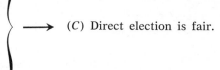

(C) Direct election is fair.

(W) (Fairness of election procedure requires that all votes must count equally and that the majority rules.)

First, we should test the data. Since we are working with an abbreviated outline (probably only half as detailed as an outline you would be working with), for purposes of this analysis, we will assume our data are representative and accurate. Next, we would test the warrant by asking, Is it true that election method fairness requires that all votes must count equally and that majority rules? If we find from experience, observation, and source material that election system fairness does require these, then the argument is logical. But if election fairness is determined by criteria apart from those included as data, the warrant is faulty and the argument would need to be revised.

Analyzing the argument schematically in the data, conclusion, warrant framework does not insure the infallibility of the logic. But if you take the time to write the arguments out in this manner and ask whether the warrant is supported by research, the chances of discovering illogical arguments are increased considerably.

Although warrants could be phrased in many ways for any given unit of argument and literally hundreds of variations are possible in the kinds of arguments, most arguments will fall into one of the five major categories. Since these categories do supply so many warrants, you should familiarize yourself with them. The tests following the warrants indicate under what circumstances the warrants are reasonable.

Generalization

A generalization warrant says that what is true in some instances is true in all instances. Generalization warrants are the basis for polls, predictions about how some individual or some team will perform, and numerous other common kinds of situations. The following illustrates the kind of generalization you might make about a course you are taking.

(D) Tom studied and got an A.
Jack studied and got an A.   ⟶   (C) Anyone who studied will
Bill studied and got an A.   get an A.

(W) (What is true in representative instances will
be true in all instances.)

A generalization warrant may be tested by these questions:

Were enough instances cited?
Were the instances typical?
Were the instances representative?

Causation

In causation, a special kind of generalization, we assume that one single circumstance always produces a predictable effect or set of effects. The following illustration exemplifies a causative argument:

(D) The temperature has
dropped to 10°.   ⟶   (C) My car won't start in
the morning.

(W) (Whenever the temperature drops below 20°,
the coldness causes the battery to be so weak
that my car won't start.)

A causation warrant may be tested by these questions:

Are the data alone important enough to bring about the particular conclusion?

Do some other data that accompany the data cited really cause the effect?

If we eliminate the data, would we eliminate the effect?

Analogy

Analogy is another special kind of generalization. In reasoning by analogy, you are attempting to show that similar circumstances produce similar conclusions. A warrant in the form of an analogy would be stated, "What is true or will work in one set of circumstances is true or will work in another comparable set of circumstances." Perhaps you have used this form of reasoning in situations like this:

(D) Joe was accepted as   ⟶   (C) I'll be accepted
     a member last year.   this year.

     (W) (Since Joe had certain qualifications and was
          accepted, I will be accepted because I have
          the same [or similar] qualifications.)

An analogy warrant may be tested by these questions:

Are the subjects capable of being compared?

Are the subjects being compared really similar in all important ways?

Are any of the ways that the subjects are dissimilar important?

Definition

A definition is a kind of verbal generalization. A definition warrant is usually stated, "when a situation has all the characteristics that are usually associated with a term, then we can use that term to describe the product of those characteristics." The warrants on pages 180 and 181 are both slight variations of the definition warrant. The following is a typical example of a definition warrant that may be familiar to you:

(D) He takes charge.
He uses good judgment.
His goals are in the best
interests of the group.

$\longrightarrow$ (C) He is a leader.

(W) (Taking charge, showing good judgment, and
considering the best interests of the group
are the characteristics most often associated
with leadership.)

A definition warrant may be tested by these questions:

Are the characteristics mentioned the most important ones in determining the definition?

Is an important aspect of the definition omitted in the statement of the characteristics?

Are those characteristics best described by some other term?

Deduction

With all the warrants so far, you have been examining one item or a series of items and drawing a generalized conclusion about those or similar items. In using deduction, you examine a classification and make some judgment about one member of that classification. A deductive warrant is usually stated, "what is true about a classification of circumstances will be true about a member of that classification." On the first day of a new course you might have used the following argument:

(D) Professors who read lecture
notes are boring lecturers.
Professor X is reading his
notes.

$\longrightarrow$ (C) Professor X will be a
boring lecturer.

(W) (What is true about a classification [professors who read lecture notes are boring lecturers] will be true about a member of the classification.)

A deduction warrant may be tested by these questions:

Does the generalization being used as the data approach certainty?

Is the subject being judged really a member of the classification?

The above are some of the common warrants. As you are testing your arguments, you may find that the description you use to explain your reasoning does not fall into one of these classifications. Nevertheless, by describing the reasoning verbally, you can determine some of the necessary tests that will help you judge the soundness of your logic.

Assignment

Prepare a three- to six-minute speech of reasons. Outline required. Criteria for evaluation will include the clarity of the proposition, the clarity and quality of the reasons, the quality of the data used to support the reasons, and the logic of the units of argument presented.

Outline: Speech of Reasons
(3–6 minutes)

Because this is the first complete persuasive speech outline and will as a result stand as a model for persuasive speech outlining, it will be analyzed in detail.

Outline

Analysis

Proposition (Specific purpose): To prove that the listeners should purchase insurance while they are young.

The purpose sentence for a persuasive speech that indicates specifically what you want your audience to believe or to do.

Introduction

I. Insurance in my mind was always a form of savings for older people.

II. There are four reasons for young people to buy life insurance.

As with the informative speech outline, the material included in the introduction should allow you to gain attention and lead into the body of the speech.

Body

I. Buying insurance while you are young provides a financial savings and gain.

Main point *I* is a clear reason. If you ask, "Why should people buy insurance while they're young?" the reason "because it provides financial savings and gain" answers the question.

The logic of main point *I* is described as follows:

Data: Between 21 and 25, rates per thousand are lower than they would be at older ages.

Between 21 and 25, dividends per thousand are higher than at older ages.

Conclusion: Buying insurance while you are young provides a financial savings and gain.

Warrant: (By definition, paying lower rates means making a financial saving and accumulating higher dividends means making a financial gain.)

Main point *II* is a clear reason. If you ask, "Why should people buy insurance while they are young?" the reason, "because it provides a systematic, compulsory savings" answers the question. Technically, this point includes two separate but related reasons: systematic and compulsory. Ordinarily it is better to limit each main point to one idea. Since they do overlap, handling them together in this case is acceptable.

The logic of main point *II* is described as follows:

Data: Periodic reminders of premiums due are sent to you.

Money invested in insurance cannot be withdrawn.

Conclusion: Buying insurance provides a systematic, compulsory savings.

Warrant: (By definition, if payments are made at fixed intervals, they are systematic; and if payments must be made and cannot be withdrawn, they are compulsory.)

Main point *III* is a clear reason. If you ask, "Why should people buy insurance while they are young?" the reason "because it enables you to have an in-

A. Between the ages of 21 and 25, the rates per thousand are low.
   1. Age 25—about $16 per thousand.
   2. Age 35—about $23 per thousand.
   3. Age 45—about $33 per thousand.
B. In addition to lower rates the dividends are higher.
   1. Dividends left to accumulate between ages 25 and 65 amount to $777 per thousand.
   2. Dividends left to accumulate between ages 35 and 65 amount to $432 per thousand.
   3. Dividends left to accumulate between ages 45 and 65 amount to $250 per thousand.

II. Buying insurance while you are young provides a systematic, compulsory savings.
   A. Each month, quarter, or year a reminder is sent to you of your premium's being due.
      1. This service is not provided by a bank, building and loan, or the stock market.
   B. Once money is invested it is saved.
      1. There is no put and take with insurance.

III. Buying insurance while you are young enables you to have an insurability clause put into the contract.
   A. This means that from the age of 21 to 40 you can reinvest the same amount up to $15-

000 every three years at the standard rate for your age.

B. By this I mean that your premium doesn't go up due to medical reasons or a job considered dangerous provided you are in good health and in a safe job at age 25.

surability clause put into the contract" answers the question.

The logic of main point *III* is described as follows:

Data: From age 21 to 40 you can reinvest the same amount every three years at the standard rate for your age.

Premiums do not go up due to medical reasons if you are in good health.

Conclusion: Buying insurance while young enables you to have an insurability clause put into the contract.

Warrant: ?
In this case, there doesn't seem to be a clear relationship between the data and the conclusion. The data explain what an insurability clause is. The explanation is important to the speech. But in order for the conclusion stated to follow, the data must include proof that an insurability rider can be put in "while you are young." This part of the outline needs some repair.

IV. Buying insurance while you are young enables you to protect your personal financial value.

A. Your background and future are monetarily valuable.

B. Your family is dependent on this value for their support.

1. At age 25 your value may be $400,000.

2. If you die uninsured at the age of 27, your family is unprotected with a loss of $380,-000.

3. Insurance provides the money if you die.

Main point *IV* is a clear reason. If you ask, "Why should people buy insurance while they are young?" the reason "because it protects your personal financial value" answers the question.

The logic of main point *IV* is described as follows:

Data: You have a lifetime of earning power.

Your family is dependent upon your potential life's earnings.

Conclusion: Buying insurance enables you to protect your potential earnings.

Warrant: (If an insurance plan provides the same money that you would have made if you had worked, then by definition the insurance plan protects your financial value.)

Conclusion

This conclusion, a summary, is satisfactory for a speech of reasons.

Now let's describe and test the logic of the entire outline:

Data: **Insurance while young provides financial savings.**

Insurance provides systematic, compulsory saving.

Insurance while young enables you to attach an insurability rider.

Insurance while young enables you to protect your financial value.

Conclusion: **You should buy insurance while you are young.**

Warrant: **(Financial saving, compulsory saving, having an insurability rider, and financial protection are major criteria for determining whether and when you should buy insurance.)**

Because these criteria are for the most part the key criteria, the outline is logical.

I. You should buy insurance while you are young because it provides a financial savings; it provides a systematic, compulsory savings; it enables you to attach an insurability rider; and it protects your financial value.

As you analyze the following speech of reasons in the inside column, judge whether each of the reasons is clearly stated in the speech and whether the developmental material supports the reasons clearly, completely, and interestingly.[2] After you have made your analysis, study the analysis in the outside column.

Buying Insurance While You Are Young

Analysis

Speech

Miss Horan begins with a sentence that establishes a point of audience agreement from

I'm sure you're all familiar with the value of insurance for older people. However, the more I learned about it the more I realized it's wise to buy

---

[2] Speech given in Fundamentals of Speech class, University of Cincinnati. Printed by permission of Elaine Horan.

it while you're young. And what I'd like to do this morning is give you four reasons why we should invest in life insurance while we're young. It's a financial saving; it's a method of compulsory saving; you can have an insurability rider put into your contract; and it is wise to secure your own personal financial value.

First, the financial saving. When you are young, the rates are lowest. For instance, at age twenty-one, insurance is about 16 dollars per thousand. Purchased at age thirty-five, it's 23 per thousand, and at the age of forty-five, it's 33 per thousand. This is an indication that while you're young your rates are lowest. In addition to saving money while buying while you're young, you also gain a higher dividend. For instance, if your money is invested in insurance, and it remains from the age of twenty-five to sixty-five, your dividend is 727 dollars per thousand. At the ages of between thirty-five to sixty-five, the dividend is 432 dollars per thousand and if it's left to remain between forty-five and sixty-five, your dividend is about 250 dollars per thousand. So you see there is an increase of about 500 dollars if your money is left to remain from between the ages of twenty-five to sixty-five rather than forty-five to sixty-five. This is all done by the process called compound interest.

Compound interest leads me into the second reason why it's wise to buy life insurance at a young age, that is, it is a method of compulsory savings. After each month, or quarter, or each year, your life insurance company will send to you a reminder that your premium is due. This is a service not rendered by a bank, a building and loan or mutual fund. In addition, when you invest in life insurance, your money remains there; it cannot be withdrawn such as in a bank account, where you might be tempted to withdraw it for various reasons. Instead, it remains until your policy is redeemed and compounds interest for you. Of course it's not wise to invest all your money in life insurance because you do want some money available to purchase a house or car. Nevertheless, it is good to put your money in a safe place where you cannot touch it. There's no put and take in life insurance.

The third reason why you should invest in life insurance at a young age is rather complicated but

which she can begin her argument. The next sentence shows that the speaker approached the topic with an open mind and suggests that the audience should do likewise. Since the speech of reasons calls for direct presentation, her preview of major reasons is appropriate.

Since it is usually not a good idea to state main points as labels, her first sentence would be better stated, "First, buying insurance now, while you're young, means a financial saving to you." The data showing costs per thousand provide the necessary specifics. Incidentally, the statement of those statistics would be improved by using the verb "costs" rather than "is." Active verbs are preferable to "is," "are," "was," and "were." Her developmental material indicates that the financial saving will come in the areas of "costs of insurance" and "increased dividends." The reason is a good one; the support is clear and logical.

Miss Horan uses a good transition to lead her to her well-stated second reason. Her whole idea grows from the assumption that we want to save money, but that most plans do not provide the necessary motivation. Notice that she does not say that insurance savings would be greater than bank savings. By staying with the subject of motivation she adds strength to her argument. The subpoints which show that we are obligated to pay premiums at regular intervals and that we can't withdraw the money are clear and logical.

Although we know *when* Miss Horan begins her third reason,

a very rigid reason. That is, you can have an insurability rider put into your policy contract. Now, an insurability rider allows you to purchase the same amount of insurance every three years until the age of forty, based on standard rates for your age. And, you ask, what does this mean? Well, it means that if you are in good health, between the ages of twenty-one and twenty-five and you have a safe secure job, your rates are at the standard rates. However, if you should contract an ulcer, or accept a dangerous job such as piloting an aircraft or even a spacecraft, the premiums are going to go up, unless you have this insurability rider. So with an insurability rider it means you pay only the standard rate for a person of your age every three years between the ages of twenty-five and forty and you may purchase the same amount of life insurance up to 15,000 during this period.

The fourth reason why it is wise to invest in life insurance at a young age is to secure your own personal financial value. Now, this means that your parents, or yourself, have invested a lot of money in your education and in the attainment of a certain social status. With your background you are capable and have the potential of securing a high paying job which increases your own personal value. Now, take, for example, a man twenty-five. Upon graduation from college, he receives a job paying 10,000 a year. Assuming that he maintains this at the same salary, his own personal financial value is worth 400,000 dollars, which will be used to support his family. Now, in case this man should die at the age of twenty-seven, the family not only loses him, but his potential earnings of 380,000. For this reason, a man must protect his own personal financial value in order to secure the support for his family. A woman too has a personal financial value. As the housekeeper and mother she has certain duties. However, upon her death a maid or housekeeper must be brought in to assist and assume these duties for her. For this reason, a woman, too, has her own personal financial value, which must be protected.

So what I have tried to do this morning is to give to you four reasons to buy life insurance while you're young. First, there is a financial savings, second, it is a method of compulsory saving, third, you can have an insurability rider put into your contract, and, fourth, it is wise to secure your own personal financial value.

when they are coupled with an appeal, an example, or an anecdote that will leave the audience with a little more vivid impression of the specific purpose.

This is a good example of a speech of reasons. The proposition is clearly stated, three of the four reasons are clearly presented, and each reason is clearly supported. The speech would have been improved with the addition of sources for some of the statistics, better examples to illustrate some points, and more direct audience adaptation.

Speeches
of Refutation

16

For every assignment suggested in this textbook so far, you have been concerned with preparing a speech, delivering it to the audience, and then retiring to your seat to listen to either another speech or an evaluation of your speech. Although your professor may provide question or discussion periods for some speeches, he probably has not asked you to defend or attack any position taken. A useful assignment in a persuasive speaking unit is one that provides an opportunity for direct confrontation of ideas, a speech of refutation. In order to make the best use of your potential in social, legislative, vocational, and other decision-making bodies, you must develop some confidence in your abilities to reply.

Specifically, refutation means disproving, denying, or invalidating an idea that was presented. A speech of refutation assignment gives an experience with confrontation without all the trappings of formal debate. Such an assignment has at least three parts: a speech advocating a debatable proposition, a speech by an opponent refuting the advocate's speech, and a second speech by the advocate refuting the opponent's speech. The speech of reasons discussed in Chapter 15 provides the framework for the advocate's first speech. Our discussion that follows is concerned with how the opponent can refute that speech and how the advocate can refute the speech of the opponent. We will focus on what can be refuted and how refutation is prepared and presented.

What Can Be Refuted

Refutation, like all other aspects of speechmaking, can and should be handled systematically. A speech of refutation begins with anticipation of what the opponent will say. If you research your opponent's side of the proposition as carefully as you research your own, you will seldom be surprised by his arguments. The second step of refutation is to take careful notes on your opponent's speech. The key words, phrases, and ideas should be recorded accurately and as nearly in his actual words as possible. You don't want to run the risk of being accused of distorting what your opponent really said. Divide your note paper in half vertically and outline your opponent's speech in the left-hand column. The right-hand column will be used for noting your line of refutation on each of the particular points.

At this stage you will have anticipated your opponent's preparation and you will have a reasonably accurate account of all that was said. Now, how are you going to reply to his speech? You will present refutation based upon the quantity of the data, the quality of the data, and the reasoning from the data.

Quantity of Data

Human beings are notorious for asserting opinions. "It always rains on my birthday," is an assertion, a statement with no visible support. Assertions are not necessarily false. It's just that from an assertion alone, an audience has no way of testing the validity of the reasoning. A speaker is obligated to substantiate his statements. If he asserts with no substantiation, no data, you have the opportunity to refute his argument on that basis alone.

Likewise, you can refute an argument if you think that the total data were insufficient. For instance, if a person says, "Food prices are terrible, the price of a dozen eggs has gone up ten cents in the last week," you could question whether the price of eggs is indicative of other products. Perhaps last week eggs were on sale at ten cents below normal prices. Perhaps other food products have actually gone down in price. A single item of data is seldom enough to support a major conclusion.

Attacking quantity of data is the easiest form of refutation. Although students who understand argumentative speaking should not make the mistakes of asserting or using too few data, you may still find the opportunity to refute a speech on that basis.

Quality of Data

A better method of refutation is to attack the quality of the data presented. Quality refers to the substance of the data. Cicero, the great Roman speaker and writer, said, "In my own case when I am collecting arguments . . . I make it my practice not so much to count them as to weigh them."[1] Data are weighed by judging source, recency, and relevancy.

Source of the Data   On a topic of the President's role in determining foreign policy, a statement by a political scientist who has studied executive power would be worth far more than several opinions from athletes, musicians, or politicians who have not studied the subject. Nevertheless, even a qualified source may be biased. For instance, an economist with a conservative view of economic trends might not be expected to give an objective analysis of a new liberal theory. If data come from a poor source, an unreliable source, or a biased source, no reliable conclusion can be drawn, and you should refute the argument on the basis of the dubious quality of those data.

Recency of the Data   In our age as never before, products, ideas and other data become obsolete almost as soon as they are produced. You should be very much aware of *when* the particular data were true and *when* they were stated to be true. Five-year-old data may not be true today. In scientific or technological circles, two-year-old data may be obsolete. Furthermore, an article in last month's *Time* may still be using five-year-old data. If all the data used to establish the claim are "old," attack the argument on that ground.

Relevancy of the Data   You may find that the data are true and come from a desirable source but have little to do with the point being presented. This question of relevancy may well lead you into the reasoning process itself.

Reasoning from the Data

What makes argumentative speaking so exciting is the opportunity for exercising the intellect. Even after individuals have learned to use data to support conclusions and to test the quality of those data, they find that reasoning can still be faulty. Reasoning, the process we use to get from data to conclusion is the source of the greatest number of errors in argumentative speaking. A line of argument on a recent intercollegiate debate proposition illustrates how faulty reasoning can come from useful data. The speaker was trying to prove that "20 percent of all Americans cannot obtain adequate

---

[1] Cicero, *De Oratore*, Vol. II, trans. by E. W. Sutton and H. Rackham (Cambridge, Mass.: Harvard University Press, 1959), p. 435.

food and shelter." He said, "The federal government has set the threshold of poverty for a family of four at $3,100." This statement was well documented. He continued by saying, "By definition, then, 20 percent of all American citizens are living in poverty." This is sound reasoning from the data. But when he said, "So that proves that 20 percent of all Americans cannot obtain adequate food and shelter", he was making a conclusion that could not be drawn from the data presented. Nothing in the argument showed that an income of less than $3,100 meant a family could not obtain adequate food and shelter. More relevant data would be needed in order to draw this conclusion.

To prepare yourself to judge the reasoning, go back to the explanation of warrants in the last chapter. For practice, get in the habit of framing warrants for all the arguments you hear. As you listen to your opponent, write your wording of the warrants for all the arguments presented by him in the right-hand column of your note sheet. Remember, it is unlikely that your opponent will state his warrant. It's up to you to record a warrant and test its logic. Although attacking the reasoning process is difficult, it is by far the best method of refutation. Quantity of data can be increased; quality of data can be upgraded; faulty reasoning cannot be readily repaired.

How to Refute

Since this assignment is an exercise in direct refutation, your goal is to examine what your opponent has said, then to deal with each part in a clear direct manner. Although you don't have as long to consider exactly what you are going to say, your refutation must be organized nearly as well as your planned informative and persuasive speaking assignments. If you will think of refutation in terms of units of argument, each of which is organized by following four definite steps, you will learn to prepare and to present refutation effectively:

1. State the argument you are going to refute clearly and concisely. (Or as the advocate replying to refutation, state the argument you are going to rebuild.)

2. State what you will prove; you must tell the audience how you plan to proceed so that they will be able to follow your thinking.

3. Present the proof completely with documentation.

4. Draw a conclusion; don't rely upon the audience to draw the proper conclusion for you. And never go on to another argument before you have drawn your conclusion.

In order to illustrate the process of refutation, let's examine both a small portion of a typical note outline sheet (based upon Miss Horan's speech of reasons presented in Chapter 15) and a short unit of refutation directed to one of her arguments.

Comments	Outline
(Thoughts recorded by the opponent as he listens to advocate's speech)	(Including one point of advocate's speech)
True, but are these necessarily beneficial?	II. Buying insurance provides a systematic, compulsory savings.
True, but what if you miss a payment?	A. Each month you get a notice. (Banks, etc., don't provide service.)
True, but what if you need money? You can borrow, but you have to pay interest on your own money! Cash settlement results in loss of money benefits.	B. Once money is invested, it is saved. (You can't get it out at your discretion.)

In the following abbreviated statement, notice how the four steps of refutation (stating the argument, stating what you will prove, presenting proof, and drawing a conclusion) are incorporated. For purposes of analysis, each of the four steps is enumerated:

(1) Miss Horan has said that buying insurance provides a systematic, compulsory savings. (2) Her assumption is that "systematic, compulsory savings" is a *benefit* of buying insurance while you are young. But I believe that just the opposite is true—I believe that there are at least two serious disadvantages resulting from this. (3) First, the system is *so* compulsory that if you miss a payment you stand to lose your entire savings and all benefits. Most insurance contracts include a clause giving you a thirty-day grace period, after which the policy is canceled . . . (evidence). Second, if you need money desperately, you have to take a loan on your policy. The end result of such a loan is that you have to pay interest in order to borrow your own money . . . (evidence). (4) From this analysis, I think you can see that the "systematic, compulsory saving" is more a disadvantage than an advantage for young people who are trying to save money.

Assignment

Working with a classmate, select a debatable proposition and clear the wording with your professor. Phrase the proposition so that the first speaker is in favor of the proposal. Advocate's first speech—four minutes; opponent's speech—five minutes; advocate's second speech—two minutes.

The advocate's four-minute speech should be prepared as a speech of reasons. The opponent has two choices for the presentation of his speech: (1) he may spend his entire time in direct refutation of the reasons presented; or (2) he may wish to spend a couple of minutes stating and proving his own negative reasons and then spending the rest of his time in direct refutation. The advocate's second speech will be direct refutation for the purpose of analyzing the flaws in his opponent's reasons (if any were given) or to rebuild his original set of reasons. Criteria for evaluation will include soundness of argument and skill in refutation.

**Outline: Speech of Refutation
(advocate's first speech)**

Proposition: (specific purpose): To prove that a voluntary army should replace the Selective Service System.

Introduction
I. A voluntary army should replace the Selective Service System.

Body
I. A voluntary army would end the injustices of conscription.
  A. Controversies over deferments and equity would be eliminated.
      1. *Time* magazine states that volunteer army appeals to those who see the injustice of the draft.
  B. Selective Service boards, local boards that contribute to this inequity, would be eliminated.

II. A voluntary army would allow the individual to determine his own destiny.
  A. Abolition of conscription would allow young men to decide whether they wanted to serve.
  B. Selective Service compels the individual to give up his private life.

III. A voluntary army would make a highly professionalized army possible.
  A. It would attract and maintain the skilled manpower we need.
  B. Unskilled combat soldiers could be replaced by the skilled specialists.

1. At end of World War II combat soldiers accounted for 23.6 percent of enlisted personnel.
2. In 1962 the figure was 14.5 percent.
3. In the future it will be even less.

Conclusion

I. A voluntary army should be adopted because it would end the injustices of conscription, it would allow young men to decide for themselves what they wanted to do, and it would make a highly professional army possible.

The following section includes Miss McClure's four-minute speech advocating a voluntary army, Mr. Steltenkamp's five-minute speech refuting Miss McClure's speech, and Miss McClure's two-minute speech refuting Mr. Steltenkamp's speech.[2] As you study the speeches, pay special attention to the key arguments and how they are refuted. After you have analyzed the three speeches, read the analysis in the outside column.

Miss McClure's Speech in Favor of a Voluntary Army

Analysis

Speech

"This morning we're going to talk about" is not a good introduction. Even for a speech of refutation assignment, the opening words should capture the interest of the audience. The first reason, "ending injustice of conscription," is clearly stated. These quotations could be introduced more interestingly and could be related to the main reason and to each other a little better. Miss McClure has presented enough data to establish the reason.

This morning we're going to talk about the proposition "Resolved: that a voluntary army should replace the Selective Service System."

A voluntary army would, number one, end the injustices of conscription. Controversies over deferments and equity would thus be eliminated. An essay which appeared in the January 10, 1969, issue of *Time* magazine states that "the idea of a voluntary army appeals to all those who have become increasingly aware that the draft weighs unfairly upon the poor and the black, the drop-out and the kid who does not get to college." John Medrison, who is former research associate for the Institute for Policy Studies, in an article which appeared in *Current History,* August, 1968, points out that the problem of equity exists because the armed forces do not need all the men between the

---

[2] Speeches given in Argumentation and Debate class at the University of Cincinnati. Printed by permission of Kathy McClure and Gerald Steltenkamp.

ages of eighteen and twenty-five who make up the draft pool. The Selective Service policy of autonomy for local boards increases the inequity of the draft. There are no national deferment standards. A man deferred in one jurisdiction may be drafted in another. An editorial entitled, "Should There Be a Draft" appearing in the March 20, 1967 issue of *The Nation,* stated: "The surest way for a young man sound in mind and in limb to avoid going to war is to stay in school." Automatically then, the poor, and especially Negroes, who cannot aspire to higher education, do a disproportionate part of the fighting and dying. A voluntary army would, number one, end the injustices of conscription.

Although this repetition of the first reason may not be necessary for the short speech, it does emphasize the structure.

A voluntary army would, number two, allow young men to decide for themselves what they wanted to do. An article entitled "The Pros and Cons of a Voluntary Army," appeared in *Current History,* August, 1968. It stated that the abolition of conscription would give young men greater personal freedom. It would allow them to decide whether they wanted to serve. The rhetoric of a free society, which allows men to make their own decisions, would become a reality. Dr. John M. Stromley, Jr., who is a professor of ethics and religion at St. Paul's School of Theology in Kansas City, states "For the most part, conscription means postponing or interrupting boys' plans for a job or for marriage or college, and an abupt severance of the home and family relationship that under normal conditions are only gradually relinquished in our society. It compels the individual to give up his private life to train and to perform acts which in other contexts would be recognized as morally wrong and demeaning."

This second reason is also clearly stated. Notice how Miss McClure documents each source clearly and completely. For debate speeches, it's usually a good idea to establish the quality of the data. Yet, a more artistic statement of the documentation would create a little more audience interest.

Here the movement from point to point is very abrupt. Some kind of transition is needed.

A voluntary army would, number three, make a highly professionalized army possible. It would attract and maintain the skilled manpower which we need. Proponents of a voluntary force feel it would help resolve the armed forces' present inability to attract and retain the skilled manpower. The advances in military technology since the end of World War II have changed the armed forces' manpower needs. The development of ballistic missiles, nuclear submarines, and electronic computers has meant the replacement of the unskilled specialist. It would also place emphasis on technical skill. At the end of World War II, combat soldiers accounted

Miss McClure continues to state her main points clearly and concisely. Under this reason, she has included the necessary data. Notice, however, that she needs to show idea relationships a little better.

Although Miss McClure shows that a highly skilled force is desirable, her data do not indicate whether a voluntary army plan would be able to provide such a force.

In this section, the statistics are left hanging. We need to see *how* these figures support the third reason.

for 23.6 percent of enlisted personnel. In 1962, the figure was 14.5 percent. During the same period, the ratio of electronic specialists increased from 6 to 13.8 percent and the ratio of technicians and mechanics rose from 28 to 32 percent.

This summary statement provides a satisfactory conclusion.

In summary, a voluntary army should be adopted because number one, it ends the injustices of conscription; number two, it would allow young men to decide for themselves what they wanted to do; and number three, it would make a highly professionalized army possible.

Mr. Steltenkamp's Speech Opposing a Voluntary Army

Analysis

Speech

Mr. Steltenkamp begins his speech with a personal reference. Even though he is going to try to refute Miss McClure's ideas, he wants to gain a little good will from the audience. He continues his introduction by giving his overall point of view toward the topic.

Well, first of all, I must say that I'm highly impressed with the amount of research my opponent has done. But, so far as the proposition is concerned, I don't think we have to do away completely with conscription. I think the problem is in the way it operates and not in the system itself.

Although this is not a complete statement of his opponent's first reason, it's good enough for us to see what he will be attacking. Notice that he follows the statement of the opponent's argument with the statement of his position on this issue. His entire refutation is centered on the reasoning behind the argument. He shows that the change would not yield a change in the composition of the army.

Now, in saying that a volunteer army would end the injustices of conscription, my opponent mentioned that the Negroes of today do a disproportionate share of the amount of fighting and dying. Yet, I think a volunteer army, unless our society is completely revamped, will still have a large proportion of Negroes in it. Labor leader Gus Tyler, who has written extensively on problems of minority groups, has said, "A volunteer army would be low income and ultimately, and overwhelmingly, Negro." One of the benefits, supposedly, that a volunteer army would bring is that it would raise the wage level to that of a policeman. In other words, Negroes would be attracted into this field because they would be able to get three square meals a day and have some sort of status.

This second unit of refutation attacking the underlying assumptions of Miss McClure's case would be strengthened by showing its relationship to her case better. He might have said: "Miss

As far as ending the draft is concerned, I think that this is inconceivable in our time. The volunteer army was tried in some way between 1947 and 1948 when the selective system didn't operate at all. In other words, hardly any men were drafted at all.

And it was shown that, during this time, manpower needs were not met. Five years ago, the Department of Defense did a study concerning a volunteer army and proved to the department's satisfaction that it would not work. As far as the foreign policy implications go, America has a leading role in the world; and whether we like it or not, America is the peace keeper. Hanson W. Baldwin, who is a military editor for the *New York Times,* has stated, "The elimination of the draft would have international, political, and psychological implications that would be adverse to the image of a strong and determined America." As far as the draft is concerned, such men as George Marshall, Harry Truman, and Dwight Eisenhower have all favored the Selective Service Act.

Now, my opponent has said that having a volunteer army would allow young men to decide for themselves their choice in life and would give them more personal freedom. I'd just like a little show of hands from the men in the audience how many men here would volunteer to go into the army. Well, this points out one of the problems of a volunteer army. It's obvious that since no man in this room raised his hand that a voluntary army isn't going to get in the kind of men that my opponent says will make it a highly professionalized and skilled army.

I'd just like to sum up by saying that, right at this time now, a voluntary army is not feasible because of the great needs that the United States has in the world today as far as keeping the peace. The draft should be reorganized, but it doesn't have to be necessarily done away with. I feel that by destroying some of the inequalities in our draft, we'll be able to better meet the challenges that the world offers us today.

McClure has given us three reasons for adopting a voluntary army. Although she hasn't said so, her argument implies that a voluntary army would be workable. I don't think it would." Then, he could continue his refutation as stated.

Mr. Steltenkamp's clear statement of the argument he will refute exemplifies accepted method. Although his in-class survey provides for audience adaptation, it doesn't prove anything. Whether the men of the class would volunteer to go into the army right then has nothing to do with the total argument. It *sounds* good on the surface, but it is fallacious.

Rather than asserting again that the draft should be reorganized, Mr. Steltenkamp should have restated what he had refuted.

Miss McClure's Second Speech

Speech

First, my opponent brought up the point that a voluntary army would naturally have more Negroes and low-income people in it. President Nixon, for one,

Analysis

Although Miss McClure states the argument to be refuted clearly, her single testimonial from President Nixon doesn't really refute the argument made by Mr. Steltenkamp.

has thrown this argument aside and said that the money which is appealing to a black man is just as appealing to a white man. And if you pay enough you'll get men who want to serve in the armed forces.

Here Miss McClure has the makings of a very good refutation of Mr. Steltenkamp's attack on workability. She examines the same study used by her opponent and shows why the results were questionable. Had she followed the four steps of refutation more carefully, her unit of refutation would be clarified considerably.

The study that was done by the Department of Defense five years ago, which my opponent mentioned, was simply not valid. Walter, Oig, Altman, and Fetcher—these are all people who worked in the Department of Defense on the study of the draft —feel that a voluntary army force is possible. Their conclusions result at least in part from the material gathered from the Department of Defense—material which was not released. In the first place, the questions asked sixteen-to-nineteen-year-olds were not specific enough. It was assumed when these questions were asked that the respondents knew that the salary for the first year enlistee was less than $100 per month and the minimum amount that veterans receive for schooling is $1,200 a year. Nothing was explained to these people before they asked them the questions. These assumptions are open to question.

This unit of refutation is more speculation then logical argument. Although we may hope she's right, her material does not really refute the point.

When my opponent mentioned that since the United States is the world's peace keeper, we would need more people to go to these remote parts of the world and take care of our friends. Yet, after Vietnam, the possibility might be a little lower that the United States will engage in this kind of activity.

Refutation is the most difficult kind of speaking. These examples point out common mistakes as well as effective methods of refutation. Although you, too, will find it difficult to prepare and present spur-of-the-moment refutation clearly and concisely, if you will study the suggested procedure and practice with care, you will be able to improve your ability to refute considerably.

So because a volunteer army would end the injustices of conscription, allow the young man to decide his own future, and make a highly professionalized army possible, I think we should support it.

Psychology in Persuasion: Speeches of Motivation

17

Whereas the speech-of-reasons assignment gave us an opportunity to study the logical base of persuasive speaking, the speech of motivation gives us the opportunity to study the psychological base. It is the use of psychological means that makes a speech persuasive. Let's examine some of these psychological means.

Consider the Persuasive Effect of Credibility

Who's your favorite teacher? What is it about him or her that impresses you so much? Did you know you'd like him before the course began? Was your reaction a result of a first impression? Is your reaction being constantly reinforced? As you analyze your experience with a teacher, you may well find that your belief or trust in him is so great that you accept what he says solely because *he* says it. The Greeks had a word for this quality—they called it *ethos*. We call it image, personality, or as we will refer to it in this textbook, credibility. Whatever you call it, almost all studies confirm that speaker credibility has a major effect in the production of audience belief and attitude change.[1]

The number of aspects of credibility differs somewhat in every analysis of that quality. Yet all analyses include the importance of competence, consideration, character, and personality. *Competence* is

---

[1] Kenneth E. Andersen and Theodore Clevenger, Jr., "A Summary of Experimental Research in Ethos," *Speech Monographs*, Vol. 30 (1963), pp. 59–78.

our respect for what a person knows. It may well be that your attraction toward your favorite professor is based upon competence. Although all professors are supposed to know what they are talking about, some are better able to project this quality in their speaking. As a rule-of-thumb, we believe that a person is competent when we believe he knows far more than what he is telling us now. For instance, when a student interrupts with a question, the competent professor has no difficulty in discussing the particular point in more detail—perhaps by giving another example, perhaps by telling a story, perhaps by referring the student to additional reading on the subject. Often our judgment of competence is based upon a past record. If we discover that what a person has told us in the past has proven to be true, we will tend to believe what he tells us now.

A second important aspect of credibility is *consideration*—particularly consideration for other people. When a student interrupts our favorite professor with a question, we will expect that professor to provide an answer, even though it interrupts his flow of thought or prevents him from covering quite as much as he had hoped in the hour. To put this another way, we like and we respect a person who puts others' needs before his own. For instance, when a salesman tells you that of the two coats you like, the less expensive one looks better on you, you perceive him as putting your best interest above his commission—as a result, your estimation of his credibility goes up. With some people, however, perhaps because of their negative record, you are led to respond to an apparent act of generosity with the cynical question "What's in it for them?" A past record of consideration for others builds confidence in a speaker; a past record of selfishness makes us question the speaker's motives.

A third important aspect of credibility is *character*. Character is sometimes defined as what a man is made of. We believe in people who have a past record of honesty, industry, and trustworthiness. Notice, however, that now we are not asking whether our professor knows what he is talking about; instead, we are judging the professor as a person. Are we likely to ask his advice on a personal problem? Do we believe that he will prepare an exam that is a good test of our knowledge? Is he likely to grade us on what we do and not on extraneous factors? Judging another's character comes down to our basic respect for the individual.

The fourth important aspect of credibility is *personality*. Sometimes we have a strong "gut reaction" about a person based solely on a first impression. Some people strike us as being friendly, warm, nice to be around. Some would argue that personality or likeability is the most important of all aspects of credibility. The old sports saying that "nice guys finish last" is just not true in interpersonal relationships.

Whether we're talking about a public speaker or a person we meet at a party, we make a judgment about whether we like him. If we do, we are more likely to buy his ideas or his products. If we don't, we are likely to shun him.

Credibility is not something that you can gain overnight or turn off or on at your whim. Nevertheless, you can avoid damaging your credibility and perhaps even strengthen it somewhat during a speech or series of speeches. You will probably see the cumulative effect of credibility during this term. As your class proceeds from speech to speech, some individuals will grow in stature in your mind and others will diminish. Being ready to speak on time, approaching the assignment with a positive attitude, showing complete preparation for each speech, giving thoughtful evaluation of other's speeches and demonstrating sound thinking—all of these contribute to classroom credibility. Some people earn the right to speak and to be heard. Having once earned that right, they command the confidence of their listeners. Others never earn the right and nothing they do will have a very real, lasting effect on their audience. Think about how you are representing yourself to your audience. What kind of a person are you projecting to the class? Credibility is an important means of persuasion.

Although credibility takes time to build, there are some things that can be done during your speech. Personality and character are projections of what you are, but competence and consideration can be affected by what you say. How do you illustrate your competence and your consideration? You should try to establish your credentials during the speech. A few sentences of explanation of your point of view, your concern, or your understanding may make a big difference. For instance, if you were speaking on prison reform, you might say, "I had read articles about conditions in prisons, but before I came before you with any suggestions, I wanted to see for myself, so I spent two days observing at . . ." Assuming you had visited the prison, this short statement would help to increase your credibility with the audience. Or to show the amount of work you've done you might say, "I had intended to read a few articles to prepare for this speech, but once I began, I became fascinated with the subject. I hope word doesn't get around to my other teachers, but quite frankly this past week I've put everything else aside to try to find the most accurate information I could." Or a speaker might show his fairness by saying "It would be easy for me to say we could get by without new taxes—such a move might get me elected, but I just don't see any way out of new taxes."

The key to the effectiveness of these and similar statements is the honesty of your representation. Whereas an arrogant, know-it-all approach will often backfire, a short, honest statement of qualifications, experience, or ability may build your speaker credibility.

Relate Material to Basic Audience Needs

To be an effective speaker, you will have to recognize that an audience is composed of individuals whose responses to your words will be dictated by different motives for action operating within them. These motives that help each individual make the choices he faces are related to or grow from basic needs within all men. Abraham Maslow[2] classifies basic human needs in five categories:

1. Physiological needs
2. Safety needs
3. Belongingness and love needs
4. Esteem needs
5. Self-actualization needs

Notice that he places these needs in a hierarchy: One set of needs must be met or satisfied before the next set of needs emerge. Our physiological needs for food, drink, temperature are the most basic; they must be satisfied before the body is able to consider any of its other needs. The next level consists of safety needs—security, simple self-preservation, and the like; they emerge after basic needs have been met, and they hold a paramount place until they, too, have been met. The third level includes our belongingness or love needs; these involve the groups that we identify with, our friends, our loved ones, our family. In a world of increasing mobility and breakdown of the traditional family, however, it's becoming more and more difficult for individuals to satisfy this need. Nonetheless, once our belongingness needs are met, our esteem needs predominate; these involve our quest for material goods, recognition, and power or influence. The final level is called, by Maslow, the self-actualizing need; this involves developing one's self to meet its potential. When all other needs are met, this need is the one that drives man to his creative heights, that urges him to do "what he needs to do."

What is the value of this analysis to you as a speaker? First, it provides a framework for and suggests the kinds of needs you may appeal to in your speeches. Second, it allows you to understand why a line of development will work on one audience and fall flat with another. For instance, if our audience has great physiological needs— if they are hungry—an appeal to the satisfaction of good workman-

---

[2] Abraham H. Maslow, *Motivation and Personality*. New York: Harper & Row, 1954, pp. 80–92.

ship, no matter how well done, is unlikely to impress them. Third, and perhaps most crucial, when our proposition is going to come in conflict with an operating need, we will have to be prepared with a strong alternative in the same category or in a higher-level category. For instance, if our proposition is going to cost money—if it is going to take money in the form of taxes—we will have to show how the proposal satisfies some other comparable need.

Let's try to make this discussion even more specific by looking at some of the traditional motives for action. The few we will discuss are not meant to be exhaustive—they are meant to be suggestive of the kind of analysis you should be doing. You have a proposition; you've determined reasons for its acceptance. Now try to relate those reasons to basic needs and discover where you may be getting into difficulty by coming into conflict with other motives or other needs.

Wealth

Wealth, the acquisition of money and material goods, is a motive that grows out of an esteem need. People are concerned about making money, saving it, losing it, or finding it. People who don't have money may be motivated by a plan that will help them gain money, save money, or do more with what they have. People who already have money may be motivated by a plan that will enable them to enlarge it or to use it in a way that will indicate their wealth. For example, those who have little money could perhaps be motivated to buy a Toyota or a Volkswagen primarily because they are economical; on the other hand, those who have a great deal of money could perhaps be motivated to buy a Rolls-Royce or a Ferrari because they are prestigious. Does your proposition affect wealth or material goods in any way? If it does in a positive way, you may want to stress it. If your plan calls for giving up money, you will need to be prepared to cope with an audience's natural desire to resist giving up money— you will have to involve another motive from the same category (esteem) or from a higher category to override the loss of any money they have to give up.

Power

For many people, personal worth is dependent upon their power over their own destiny, the exercising of power over others, and the recognition and prestige that comes from such recognition or power. Recognition, power, and prestige are all related to man's identity to his need for esteem. If he controls things, if he is well known, these feelings of control and recognition will raise his self-esteem and make him feel important. Consider whether your speech allows the person, group, or community to exercise power; if it does, it may offer a strong motivation. On the other hand, if your speech proposition takes away power from part or all of the audience, you will need to provide strong compensation to be able to motivate them.

Conformity

Conformity is a major source of motivation for nearly everyone. It grows out of man's need for belongingness. People often respond in a given way because a friend, a neighbor, an acquaintance, or a person in the same age bracket has so responded. Although some will be more likely to do something if they can be the first one to do it or if it makes them appear distinctive, most people feel more secure, more comfortable when they are members of a group. The old saying "There's strength in numbers" certainly applies. If you can show that many favor your plan, that people in similar circumstances have responded favorably, that may well provide motivation.

Pleasure

When you give people a choice of actions, they will pick the one that gives them the greatest pleasure, enjoyment, or happiness. On at least one level, pleasure is a self-actualizing need—more often it is an esteem need. Pleasure sometimes results from doing things you are good at. If you are able to shoot a basketball through the basket a higher percentage of times than most others, you probably enjoy the experience. At other times pleasure is a result of accomplishing something that is difficult. Getting an *A* in a class you regard as difficult may give you more pleasure than getting an *A* in a class that you regard as easy—challenges will often give people pleasure. Just as you respond to things that are pleasurable, so will your classmates respond favorably when they see that your proposition will give them pleasure. If your speech relates to something that is novel, promises excitement, is fun to do, or offers a challenge, you can probably motivate your audience.

As we have already said, these are only a few of the possible motives for action. Sex appeal, responsibility, justice, and many others operate within each of us. In any event, we can and should determine at what level our reasons are operating. If we discover that we are not relating our material to basic audience needs, we probably need to revise our procedure.

Phrase Ideas to Appeal to Senses and to Emotions

Motivational language encourages personal responsiveness to the ideas. If language appeals to the senses and to the emotions, an audience is more likely to react. Through language, a listener becomes physically and emotionally involved.

We have already talked about the need for clear, vivid, emphatic, and appropriate language in Chapter 5. Rather than repeat the suggestions, let's just remind ourselves that each person in the audience is an individual, and it is up to each of us to determine how we can reach each person—how we can make him feel what we are saying. In the following example, notice how John Cunningham, author and historian, concluded his speech—a speech directed to an audience of farmers. Look not only at the four elements of style but also to see how he tried to individualize and personalize his message.

And in the context of tonight's meeting, why can't we honor the farmer as a man most deserving of our gratitude? I say this, and you know it, we can survive for a time at least without lawyers, politicians, economists, engineers, writers, poets, college professors, teachers, business executives, bankers, highway builders, and a thousand more professionals. Without the farmer, we are dead. Literally.

Somewhere, somehow, we ought to be picturing the farmer as a man of consequence, the giver of life, the sustainer of mankind. In simpler times, it was so. Poets wrote of the farmer. Textbooks lauded his work. Magazines devoted space to his deeds. Young people ought to learn that being a farmer is indeed a noble occupation. Yet I imagine as many farmers and farmers' wives encourage their sons to be doctors or lawyers as do business executives and shopkeepers. It just isn't the thing now in America to work. Thinking is in. We may think ourselves out of existence while work goes undone.

For those who do stay down on the farm, there are dividends. Come on, now, you dedicated farmers, admit it!

There is the dividend of doing something worthwhile. There is the dividend of watching the sun come up and the sun go down; rare is the lawyer or writer who does that. There is the dividend of seasons that have meaning, rather than nuisance value. There is the dividend of being in tune with natural forces. Hearing raindrops end a prolonged drought, to a farmer, is like hearing the greatest symphony to a musician.

And there are the intangibles.

If you have ever leaned on a farm fence at twilight and heard the spring peepers peep; if you have ever stopped while crossing a pasture to listen for a Bob White; if you have ever breathed fresh air on the high hill, or picked watercress by a cool spring or felt the warmth in the cow barn on a January morning, then you are a farmer in spirit as long as you live.

If you have eaten strawberries as you picked along a row or munched beans off the bush; if you have ever seen frost threaten to kill the peach blossoms and then lived through the night to know danger was past; if you have been pleased when a lady customer returns to say, "I have never had better eggs," then you deserve your life.

Then you are a farmer. We may not be able to keep you down on the farm—but if you leave, you'll dream evermore of someday going back. And, if you leave, God help the rest of us.[3]

In addition to heightening the sensual or emotional reaction to the ideas, language can be used to create an emotional atmosphere for your message. Let's consider three special language usages—yes-response, common ground, and suggestion—that are used by persuasive speakers to condition an audience response. Like most means of persuasion, they apply equally well to ethical and unethical persuasion. You should learn to use them ethically and to recognize their unethical use by other persuaders.

Yes-Response   A favorable climate for persuasion is built upon audience agreement. Psychologists have found that when an audience gets in the habit of saying Yes, they are likely to continue to say Yes. If you can phrase questions that establish areas of agreement early in your speech, the audience will be more likely to listen to you and perhaps to agree with you later. In contrast, if you create areas of disagreement earlier, you may not be able to get agreement later. For instance, an insurance salesman might phrase the following questions: "You want your family to be able to meet their needs, don't you? You want to be able to provide for them under all circumstances, don't you? You want your family to have the basic needs, don't you? Then of course you want to have an insurance program that meets all these criteria, don't you?" With this set of yes-responses, the potential client is led to a yes-response he might not have made

---

[3] John T. Cunningham, "How Are You Going to Keep Them Down on the Farm?" *Vital Speeches*, March 15, 1971, p. 349.

earlier; that is, he may well say Yes to the suggestion that he buy an insurance policy.

Common Ground   This motivational device is based on an establishment of the same type of response pattern as the yes-response, but the initiation of the response pattern follows a somewhat different route. Essentially, the over-all response sought is: "We agree, or have common ground, on so many variously important subjects; it is, therefore, not proper that we should have disagreement in a single area so insignificant when compared to the vast area of our agreement." The politician might say to his constituents:

> You know, I was born just a quarter-mile west of this very spot. And I went to school over there at Central High. You remember Mrs. Wilson, the history teacher? She sure gave me a rough time, too. But then we had plenty of good times—the dances, the picnics.... You got to know me and my ideas pretty well, and then you sent me down to the capital to represent you—a job I've been doing for you for thirteen years. Perhaps your son or daughter is now going to old Central High just like my boy is. And we know that the old schoolhouse just isn't big enough or modern enough for today's kind of education. Now, about that school appropriations bill that some of you have been asking me about ...

Suggestion   Suggestion involves planting an idea in the mind of the listener, rather than saying it directly. Much of the presentation of sex in commercials is by suggestion. If a handsome, virile young man or a beautiful, well-built young lady is seen driving an automobile, the suggestion is that the automobile is associated with sex appeal. In almost all instances of this kind, the use of suggestion is really unethical because it is misleading. The advertisers say indirectly something that the Federal Communications Commission could prosecute them for saying directly. Unfortunately, we as consumers accept the blatant use of suggestion because we enjoy the sexual association even when we know it is untrue.

As an ethical speaker, however, you will find your use of suggestion limited. One prevalent use of suggestion in speechmaking is the use of directive. Such expressions as "I think we will all agree," "As we all know," and "Now we come to a most important consideration" are forms of suggestion that will help you to direct audience thinking. Another use of suggestion is to associate the name of a prominent individual to add prestige to a proposal. Of course, ethical use of this method is limited to those individuals who have given their backing to that particular proposal. In contrast to saying that a proposal is favored by notable men, you can say that Senator *X*, who received an award for his work on air-pollution control, favors the proposal to curb air pollution. This kind of use helps the audience to make the association between the proposal and responsible public officials. A third way to use suggestion is by phrasing ideas in specific, vivid language. Audiences are drawn to favor proposals that are phrased in memorable language. In 1946, Winston Churchill regarded by many as the most effective speaker of the twentieth century, introduced the use of the term "iron curtain" in a speech at Fulton, Missouri. This term suggested an attitude about Russian ideology that has permeated western thinking for more than twenty years. Because the subtle, less obvious statement of an idea may be more easily accepted by an audience, suggestion is an aid to persuasive speaking.

Base Your Organization
on Expected Audience Reaction

Although you will find that most persuasive speeches follow some kind of a topical organization, there are many different frameworks that will assist you in meeting expected attitude reaction. Since much of your success will depend on the kind of audience you face for the particular speech, you must have an appraisal of whether the members favor your proposition and to what degree they favor it. Audience attitude may be distributed along a continuum from hostile to highly in favor:

Hostile	Opposed	Mildly Opposed	Neutral no opinion uninformed	Mildly in favor	In favor	Highly in favor

Even though any given audience may contain one or a few members on nearly every point of the distribution, audience attitude will tend to cluster at some point on the continuum.

Except for polling the audience, there is no way of being sure about your assessment. But by examining the data in the way described in Chapter 7, you will be able to make reasonably accurate estimates. For instance, skilled workers are likely to look at minimum wage proposals differently from business executives; men will look at women's liberation proposals differently from women; Protestants are likely to look at property tax levy for schools differently from Catholics. The more data you have about your audience and the more experience you have in analyzing audiences, the better your chances of judging their attitudes somewhat accurately. By and large, a very precise differentiation of opinion isn't necessary.

Audience Attitudes

Through a sample of attitude, an insight into audience behavior, or a good guess, you can place your audience in one of the following classifications: *no opinion*—either no information or no interest; *in favor*—already holding a particular belief; *opposed*—holding an opposite point of view. Although these classifications may overlap, since you will have neither the time nor the opportunity to present a line of development that would adapt to all possible attitudes within the audience, you should assess the prevailing attitude and knowledge and work from there.

No Opinion   With some topics, your audience will have no opinion. Often this lack of opinion results from a lack of knowledge on the subject. Suppose you wanted to persuade the class "that elementary schools should explore the feasibility of ungraded primary schools." Unless your class is composed of prospective elementary teachers, only a few will know what an ungraded primary school is. Even those who know the term may not have enough knowledge to formulate an opinion. In this instance, yours will be a problem of instruction before you can hope to create a favorable attitude. Since they lack preconceived biases, you can usually approach the uninformed audience directly. If you can show enough advantages to meet their requirements, you have a good chance of persuading them. Despite this advantage, you may have a burden of explanation that must precede argumentation. If you have only five minutes to speak and it takes that long to explain the program, you will have a very difficult time creating any attitudes.

A lack of audience opinion may also result from apathy. When apathy is the problem but knowledge does exist, you can spend your entire time in motivation. Although an apathetic audience is difficult to motivate, you will have nearly the entire speech time to create interest and commitment. An apathetic audience presents a challenge and an opportunity for the persuasive speaker. Since the challenge is getting the audience to act, an organization based on comparative advantages may allow you to place emphasis where it is needed.

In Favor   In your analysis, you may find that the audience is already favorably disposed toward the proposition. Although this sounds like an ideal situation, it carries with it many hazards. When an audience is already in favor, they are seldom interested in a rehash of familiar material and reasons. Because of an ill-considered approach, a favorable audience can become hostile or apathetic to you as a speaker—a result as undesirable as negative commitment. If your campus is typical, a common complaint is the lack of on-campus parking. As a result, the subject matter of a speech in favor of increased parking space would already be accepted. In situations of this kind, the best line of argument is to develop a specific course of action satisfying the felt need. A speech on the need for an underground garage or a highrise parking garage on a present site or a new system of determining priority would build upon the existing audience attitude. The presentation of a well-thought-out specific solution increases the potential for action. In summary, when you believe your audience is on your side, don't just echo their beliefs. Try to crystallize their attitudes, recommit them to their direction of thought, and bring the group to some meaningful action that will help to solve or alleviate the problem.

Opposed   With many of the kinds of propositions that call for a change in existing attitudes and procedures, your audience attitude may range from slightly negative to thoroughly hostile. These two degrees of negative attitude require a slightly different handling. For instance, with the proposition "The United States is spending too little on the race for space," most people will have an opinion. Since this is a debatable proposition, about half the audience will probably be at least slightly negative. Yet, the other half may even be slightly favorable to strongly favorable. Usually, the best way to proceed is with the generalization that the audience can be persuaded if you can give good reasons and if you can motivate them. A straightforward, logically sound speech may convince those who are only slightly negative and will not alienate those in favor. A problem-solution method provides a usable framework for these conditions.

However, suppose the topic were "The federal government should guarantee a minimum annual income to all its citizens." With this proposition, there is an excellent chance that the majority of the audience would be negative to hostile. Hostile audiences can seldom be persuaded with one speech. In fact, a hostile audience may well turn itself off when it hears the topic. To get this kind of an audience even to listen calls for a great deal of motivation. Because of its indirection, a criteria-satisfaction approach provides a usable framework for your material. If you have done a good job, you will be able to plant the seeds of persuasion. The next week, the next month, or even the next year, one or more of that audience might well come to your way of thinking—but don't expect too much to happen during the speech.

Methods of Organizing

Depending upon the nature of your topic, the nature of your audience, and your personal preference, you may find that you can utilize one of the following typical arrangements for your materials.

Statement of Reasons Method   The speech of reasons (Chapter 15) illustrated the straightforward topical statement of reasons and supports. This type of organization works best when your audience holds no opinion, is apathetic, or is perhaps only mildly in favor or opposed to the proposition. The idea is that reasonable people who hold no special biases can be motivated by reasonable development.

The Problem-Solution Method   If you are attempting to prove to the audience that a new kind of procedure is needed to remedy some major problem, the problem-solution method will provide you with the framework for clarifying the nature of the problem that needs to be solved and for illustrating why the new proposal is the best measure for accomplishing the purpose. When you follow the problem-solution method, your speech will always have three main points: (1) that there is a problem that requires a change in attitude or action, (2) that the proposal you have to offer will solve the problem, and (3) that your proposal is the best solution to the problem. For the proposition, "To persuade the audience that the federal government should guarantee a minimum annual cash income to all its citizens," you could state three reasons:

I. A high percentage of our citizens are living in a state of abject poverty.

II. A guaranteed cash income would eliminate poverty.

III. A guaranteed cash income would be the best way to solve the problem.

Comparative Advantages Method   In your proposed speech, you may not be trying to solve a grave problem as much as you are suggesting a superior alternative course of action. Under such circumstances, your concern is with superiority of your proposal over any others. Let's say that you want to persuade your audience to take their dry cleaning to a particular establishment. Since people are already taking their clothes to some dry cleaner, the problem of how the class should take care of their cleaning is already being solved. You are trying to persuade them that a particular cleaner has advantages over any of the places where they may already take their clothes. Your speech then is built with the advantages of your proposal over any other proposal. The advantages then become the main points of your outline.

Purpose: To persuade the audience to take their clothes to Ace Dry Cleaners.

I. Ace always does that little bit extra for no additional charge.

II. Ace gives students a 10 percent discount.

Criteria-Satisfaction Method   In some situations, particularly with hostile audiences, you may find it to your advantage to establish audience agreement—a yes-response—before you attempt to present the proposition and reasons. Although reasons are still the basis for the persuasion, the preliminary statement of criteria is essential to the method. If your proposition were "To persuade the audience to vote for Jones," you might organize your speech to show the criteria and how Jones meets them.

I. You want a man who meets certain criteria.
   A. He must be wise.
   B. He must have a plan of action.
   C. He must be fearless.

II. Jones meets these criteria.
   A. Jones is wise.
   B. Jones has a plan of action.
   C. Jones is fearless.

The Negative Method   Sometimes the only way of establishing one course of action is by proving that the alternatives won't work. What you are doing is proving a course of action with negative reasons. Of course, this system will work only when the audience must select one of the alternatives. Again, if your proposition were, "To persuade the audience to vote for Jones," you might organize your speech by evaluation of his opponents.

I. Smith does not have the proper qualifications.

II. Brown does not have the proper qualifications.

III. Martin does not have the proper qualifications.

IV. Jones does have the proper qualifications.

Live Up to Your Ethical Responsibilities

Like any doctor, lawyer, or other professional man, the public speaker has an ethical responsibility. Because this responsibility is established by each individual rather than by a professional organization, the speaker must understand the nature of this responsibility. Although this responsibility is in operation with any kind of a speech being presented, the most important questions of ethics arise in connection with motivational speaking.

In Chapter 3 we raised the question of topic selection. Remember that you have an ethical responsibility to advocate propositions that you believe are in the audience's best interests. Persuasive speaking is not primarily for self-gratification; instead, it is for the purpose of bringing about a situation or condition that would better the lives of the audience as "citizens" of a student body, a community, a state, a nation, or the world.

The most critical area of ethical responsibility is concerned with how far you should go with psychological appeals in motivating your audience to accept your proposition. One meaningful ethical guideline is that, regardless of what kind of emotional climate surrounds your topic, you must have a logical framework to support your proposition. Although your speech may not be a "one, two, three" statement and development of reasons, it should be logically conceived and logically based. You are not meeting the requirements of ethical persuasive speaking unless your speech meets these tests.

To discuss this guideline from another direction, let us say that psychological appeals should accompany and not supplant reasoning. The ethical limit is reached when a persuader attempts to influence our decisions on the basis of emotional reaction alone—when what it said is meant to take the place of rational process and when it is misleading or untrue. Suppose you were trying to sell toothpaste. Suppose that the toothpaste you were selling (1) cleaned teeth quite well, (2) helped fight tooth decay, perhaps even better than most, and (3) tasted good. Because a rationally conceived decision about what kind of toothpaste to buy would involve consideration of cleaning effects, decay-fighting power, and taste, in using these three reasons you could try to motivate your audience, as long as your motivation was related to one or more of those reasons. Suppose, however, in planning your sales campaign, you determined to use any appeal that would help sell the product. Suppose, then, you told the audience that the toothpaste would increase their sex appeal, regardless of whether you could prove that it did. In this circumstance, the use of motivation would be unethical on at least two counts: first, because it would be trying to substitute an appeal to the sex drive for a rational process of decision making; second, because the implication that the toothpaste would increase sex appeal would be misleading and probably untrue.

We are not talking about what kind of persuasion is successful. Unfortunately, unethical persuasion has proved so successful that many of our highest paid advertising agencies persist in unethical use of motivation. Unless we want a society in which anything goes as long as it sells, we must recognize and penalize unethical behavior. One way to combat unethical persuasion is to have an audience that understands such means of persuasion. An important benefit of this section is to prepare you to be a critical member of an audience, as well as to help you use ethical persuasion more effectively. As an ethical persuasive speaker your goal is to use motivation to get an audience to respond to rationally conceived ideas.

Assignment

Prepare a four- to seven-minute persuasive speech of motivation. Outline required. In addition to clarity of purpose and soundness of reasons, criteria for evaluation will include your credibility, your ability to satisfy needs, and your ability to determine an organization that meets audience attitude.

Outline

Specific Purpose: To prove that the class should abstain from alcoholic drink.

Introduction

I. It cost $20 billion; it lost jobs; and it caused the death of 35,000 Americans.

II. The problem is not Vietnam—it's alcohol.

Body

I. Alcohol causes a tremendous economic drain on this country.
   A. It costs industry over $4 billion a year for absenteeism and low production alone.
   B. It is the cause of poor executive decisions.
   C. The total loss to the economy is over $20 billion.
   D. For every dollar collected in tax revenue five dollars are spent in rehabilitation.
   E. We must increase jails, police, and medical services as a result.

II. Alcohol causes a tremendous health problem.
   A. It is the fourth major health problem.
      1. Ranks after only cancer, mental illness, and heart disease.
   B. One of the fourteen people who drink become alcoholics.
      1. Alcoholism is the leading cause of cirrhosis of the liver.
      2. Life span is shortened by 12 years.
      3. Instances of other diseases are very high.
   C. Even social drinkers are not immune.
      1. One to two drinks may make us tipsy.
      2. Two drinks can cause up to 10 thousand of our brain cells to be damaged.

III. Alcohol is a moral problem.
   A. The Bible asks us to abstain.
   B. Alcohol is associated with crime and immorality.
   C. Alcohol causes us to set a poor example for our children.

IV. Alcohol causes fatal driving accidents.
   A. 28,000 of the 35,000 that died last year from alcohol died in automobile accidents.
   B. Fifty percent of all traffic deaths are due to drinking.
      1. One-half of the accidents this Labor Day weekend will be alcohol related.
   C. The next accident caused by alcohol could be to you or to a loved one.

Conclusion

I. If you never take a drink, you'll never take one too many.

Read the following speech recorded in the inside column at least once aloud and analyze the use of motivation.[4] What motives is the speaker appealing to? What are his methods of heightening motivation? After you have analyzed the speech, read the analysis in the outside column.

---

[4] Speech given in Fundamentals of Speech class, University of Cincinnati. Printed by permission of Terry McMillian.

Abstaining from Alcohol

Analysis

Speech

Mr. McMillian had a difficult task in this speech. Although most people recognize the danger of alcohol, they visualize this danger in terms of the other person and not themselves. Yet by the end of the speech, Mr. McMillian had everyone in class totally involved.

It cost the U. S. $20 billion last year. It has lost more jobs and has caused more disintegration of moral standards than any other one item last year. It caused the death of over 35,000 Americans. No, I'm not talking about the Vietnam war, but it is a problem just as deadly. That problem is alcoholic drink. Imagine a city with a population of 35,000. The inhabitants are not only men, but women and children as well. Many innocent women and children. Now imagine an enemy attacking that city, killing every man, woman, and child and completely leveling the city. In effect, that is what alcoholic drink did to the U. S. last year.

Mr. McMillian captures our attention before he states the problem. Notice the good use of hypothetical situation to help the audience visualize the scope of the problem.

Our society is plagued with many kinds of problems. We can see the dangers of air and water pollution, inadequate education, and the current economic crisis. We are appalled at man's inhumanity to man as seen with poverty and in war. Mankind has applied the best and latest technology to many problems, but some problems go unnoticed. Man knows the high percentage of deaths attributed to heart failure and cancer. And he doubles his efforts to find a cure. But one of the worst killers received very little attention. We can avoid this inhumane killer by abstaining from it.

Even though this is a speech of motivation, solid reasons provide a base for emotional development. The first area— economics—is in itself a motive appeal. Remember, if something can be demonstrated to affect our pocketbook, we're likely to pay attention.

Notice the use of details, often ones we can identify with, throughout the speech.

Four areas provide the basis for abstinence. The first of these areas is the tremendous economic drain on this country. It costs industry over $4 billion a year just for absenteeism and low production due to alcohol. What happens when a person gets drunk? Well, not only the hangover the next day, but also more than likely he won't be there. And if he is, he is working under a severe handicap and producing much less than he normally would. Many executive decisions are also made under the influence. Those few drinks at dinner or at supper are a cause of many poor decisions that affect large corporations in this country much to their detriment. The total cost to the economy is well over $20 billion a year. The manufacturers of alcoholic drink point with pride that alcohol brings in a lot of tax dollars. Why don't they really tell it like it is . . . the drunk at a party, the hangover the next day, children deprived of necessary food and clothing because the families income was spent on alcohol? What about that other side of the coin? A major burden on the taxpayer comes from combating the problems caused by drinking. For every dollar collected in tax revenue and advertisement, $5 are spent in rehabilitation. We need more jails; we need more police because 1/3 of all crime is associated with drinking. We need more medical services because of the disease of alcohol. Do you read the Andy Capp comic strip? Some of them are too true to be funny. In one, Andy Capp is seen eyeing a washing machine that was marked "just bought." His wife comes over to him and says, "Andy, quit spoiling about thinking about how many pints you can buy." Yes, money spent on alcohol cannot be spent for household necessities.

> **Here development through examples heightens our emotional reaction to the economic problem.**
> **This Andy Capp example doesn't prove anything, but it adds to the total emotional reaction.**

A second area is a health problem. Alcoholism is one of the major health problems. It is the fourth major health problem along with cancer, mental illness, and heart disease. One in fourteen of the people that drink will become an alcoholic. That's too high a percentage for me. Isn't it you? Cirrhosis of the liver, of course, is the killer disease of alcohol. Over 80 million people in this country drink, while 30 million don't. Those 30 million will probably not have to worry about cirrhosis of the liver. What about the social drinker? The person that drinks one or two drinks and becomes a little tipsy. In our brain are from 10 to 15 billion brain cells. Those two drinks can cause up to 10 thousand of our brain cells to be damaged or destroyed. Abstainers take no chances. Dr. Vernon Went of the Wayne State University School of Medicine states that abstinence makes the heart grow stronger. In a survey that he conducted with the assistance of his college students, he had conclusive evidence that the abstainer from alcohol will have a much stronger heart than the one who drinks. An insurance company report shows that the average alcoholic's life span is shortened by at least 12 years. Low health ratios are brought out by the president of the National Council on Alcoholism. You have a 29 to 1 chance of getting cirrhosis of the liver, for instance, if you drink. You have a 3 to 1 chance of obtaining ulcers, diabetes, heart disease, if you drink. Now let's explore a myth of alcohol. That is, that alcohol is a stimulant. It was once thought to arouse you phys-

> **"Alcohol is a health problem" is a reason with emotional impact. Through the use of this reason, Mr. McMillian appeals to our need for self-preservation.**

> **Here, as in a few other places earlier in the speech, we would like to know the source of the figures.**

> **In this part of the speech, Mr. McMillian gives us his sources of information. Although statement of sources will not necessarily make your speech more persuasive, it does strengthen your ethical position.**

> **These are good points, but they are not related to the problem of health, the subject of this section, as well as they might be.**

ically, mentally, and emotionally and thought that a few drinks would give you added strength, courage, and quicker reflexes. But actually alcohol is a depressant. It releases inhibitions and causes you to do sometimes foolish, wicked, and even violent things. It slows your judgment, you can't talk right, walk right, you can't even think right. So alcohol is a health problem.

And in a third area it is also a moral problem. One of my favorite books, the Bible, admonishes us to abstain from all appearances of evil. What do you associate drinking with? Are the drinking establishments places you would like to take your relatives? Friends? Even children? Yes, alcohol is associated with crime, immorality, and riotous living. As the Bible tells us, we shall indeed reap what we sow. There is a story of a Moslem that committed an offense against the king. And, as big punishment, he was told he must curse Allah, murder his mother, or get drunk. Now all these were against his religious principles. But to him the last seemed less evil than all the others. So he got drunk. Then under the influence of alcohol he both cursed Allah and killed his own mother.

This area is the weakest part of the speech. Although the Moslem story is impressive, the moral issue doesn't seem nearly so important as the others. This entire point could have been omitted with no harm to effectiveness of the speech. At least its placement doesn't hurt the speech materially.

What about our example: What happens when others see us drinking? Or, what happens when they see us abstaining from alcohol? What type of example would you like to set?

Mr. McMillian's fourth point is his strongest. You will find it to your advantage to put your strongest point either first or last. In final position, it leaves a good final impression with the audience.

These impressive figures help Mr. McMillian develop his fear appeal.

The fourth and final area that provides a basis for abstinence is the drinking driver. We are all told that drinking and driving do not mix. Do they? 28,000 of the 35,000 that died last year from alcohol died in automobile accidents. And as this picture implies, a skeleton is driving a car—the dead man. There were 500,000 disabling injuries suffered in alcohol accidents or alcohol-related accidents. How many drinks do you need to make you alcohol or accident prone? All you need are two. Over 50 percent of all traffic deaths are due to drinking. The Allstate Insurance Company reports that the drinking driver raises your car insurance rates about 30 percent. Watch for the accidents this coming Labor Day weekend. Remember that over a half of them are alcohol related. Abstainers take no chances.

Here the audience is given a little jolt—the expected "good"

I can't make a speech about this without saying at least one good thing about alcohol. It is a good mathematician. It adds troubles to your lives, sub-tracts money from your pockets, multiplies your in-firmities, and divides your property. The total—a wrecked life.

What influence will alcohol have on your life? I sincerely hope it will not have any. Here's a story tracts money from your pockets, multiplies your in-bottle of liquor hidden away in his cupboard for special emergencies. On a particular night his daughter had been crowned queen of her high school. So, she and her date had gone out to celebrate. Later that night her father was called to the scene of a tragic automobile accident. In a ditch along side the road lay the dead body of his beautiful daughter. On the pavement beside lay a broken bottle and the fumes of alcohol permeated the air. The father was seen wringing his hands in anguish and was overheard to say "If I could only get my hands on the criminal that sold them that bottle, I would make him pay the rest of his life." When finally he returned home, he decided he needed a little shot to bolster his nerves and give him some added courage. In the cupboard where he always kept a bottle hidden away for emergencies, he reached for it. It was gone. In it's place was a note. "Dear Dad: We're going to celebrate, so we borrowed your bottle. I'm sure you won't mind." If you never take one drink, you will never take too many.

is another negative point. The method used in this case is attention getting and effective.

Up to this point, the speech has illustrated how logical materials can be presented in a very emotional context. As he ap-proaches the ending, Mr. McMillian takes advantage of his last opportunity to really "hit home." This dramatic story gives the speech emotional clout.

After such a story, anything else would be anticlimatic. Mr. McMillian wisely closes his speech with only one concluding sentence.

Small Group Discussion

Six

Group Discussion

18

The characteristic American response to problem solving is "Let's form a committee." Despite the many jokes about committees and the often justified impatience with them, the committee system and the group discussion it encourages can and should be an effective way of dealing with common problems. For our purposes, discussion will be defined as a systematic form of speech in which two or more persons meet face to face and interact orally to arrive at a common goal. The goal may be to solve a problem, it may be to gain understanding of a topic, it may be for the entertainment of the participants, and in some situations it may be for therapeutic purposes. In addition to competence in the use of fundamental speech principles, effective group discussion requires knowledge of the forms, the methods for preparation, and guidelines for participation in interacting discussion.

The Forms of Discussion

Practically speaking, group discussions are either public or private. Since these two basic forms influence goals and procedures, let's examine each to show their characteristics and some of their advantages and disadvantages as well.

Public Discussion

In a public discussion, the group is discussing for the information or enjoyment of a listening audience as much as they are for the satisfaction of the participating members. Two prevalent forms of public discussion are the symposium and the co-acting panel.

Symposium   A symposium is a discussion in which a limited number of participants (usually three to five) present individual speeches of approximately the same length dealing with the same subject area to an audience. After the planned speeches, the participants in the symposium may discuss their reactions with each other or respond to questions from the listening audience. Although the symposium is a common form of public discussion, participation in one is often a dull and frustrating experience. Despite the potential for interaction, a symposium is usually characterized by long, sometimes unrelated individual speeches. Moreover, the part designated for questions is often shortened or deleted because "our time is about up." Discussion implies interaction—a symposium often omits this vital aspect. If the participants make their prepared speeches short enough so that at least half of the available time can be spent on real interaction, a symposium can be interesting and stimulating. Because a good symposium is so much more difficult than it appears, it is usually better to encourage participants to engage in a panel discussion.

Panel Discussion   A panel discussion is one in which the participants, usually from four to eight, discuss a topic spontaneously, under the direction of a leader and following a planned agenda. After the formal discussion, the audience is often encouraged to question the participants. So the discussion can be seen and heard by the audience, the group is seated in a semicircle, with the chairman in the middle, where he can get a good view of the audience and the panelists. Since the discussion is for an audience, the panelists need to be sure that they meet the requirements of public speaking. Because a panel discussion encourages spontaneity and interaction, it can be very stimulating for both a listening audience and the participants themselves.

Private Discussion

Although your classroom assignment may be in the form of a panel, the majority of discussions that you participate in will be private. Private discussions are ones in which the participants meet to solve a problem or exchange ideas on a particular topic without the presence of an onlooking or participating audience. Committees convened for the purpose of formulating a recommendation to be submitted to the larger legislative body, to another committee, or to the various individuals or agencies authorized to consider such recommendations engage in private discussion. Likewise, individuals who meet informally for the purpose of sharing ideas on topics of mutual interest engage in private discussion. Private discussions are most productive when they are conducted in an atmosphere where all members of the group have equal prominence. The best seating arrangement is a full circle, so that each person can see and talk with everyone else. Sometimes, as a stimulant for study groups, a "resource" person sits in with the group to suggest ideas and to add needed information. Because of the proximity of the participants in private discussion, the group need not be so concerned with public speaking. Furthermore, since no audience is present, the group can adjust its time to meet the needs of the topic. If the question cannot be resolved in one sitting, the group can meet later.

Lately, a "new" kind of private discussion, the T-group, has attracted the attention of business and industry. This sensitivity training can be very valuable for gaining insight into self and fellowman. Since it relates more to psychotherapy than to public speaking, sensitivity training will not be discussed in this chapter.

Preparation for Interacting Discussion

For either public or private discussion, preparation requires a systematic procedure for determining topics, selecting main points, amplifying ideas, and outlining the development.

Topics for Discussion

Although topics for discussion may be drawn from any subject area, they should be (1) of interest to the group, (2) controversial, (3) capable of being discussed within the time available, and (4) written in question form. Participants' interest is a primary test of topic for all forms of speechmaking, including group discussion. Discussion, however, also requires that the topic should be controversial. If all discussants have about the same point of view or if the subject matter leaves little room for interpretation, there is really very little need for discussion. "How to make a book" may be a satisfactory topic for an informative speech; for a discussion, however, the topic would generate very little collective reaction. On the other hand, the topic "Should *Catcher in the Rye* be included on the required reading list for tenth-grade English?" would leave room for various viewpoints. Even if a topic is interesting and controversial, it should not be considered for discussion unless it can be discussed within the time available. In an informal social discussion, there is value in coping with a problem regardless of whether consensus can be reached. For most group discussions, however, the resolution of the topic is the reason for meeting, and until or unless a satisfactory conclusion is reached, the discussion is for nought. If the topic is so broad that discussion can only begin to scratch the surface, then a more limited aspect should be considered.

Finally, a discussion topic should be stated in question form. Questions elicit response. Since the goal of discussion is to stimulate group thinking, the topic itself and all of the subheadings are phrased as questions. In phrasing the question, make sure it considers only one subject, that it is impartial, and that the words used can be defined objectively. "Should the United States cut back the space program and the war on poverty?" considers two different questions; "Should the United States recognize those wretched Red Chinese?" would be neither impartial nor definable.

As you consider various phrasings, you will discover that changes in wording affect the kind of response you are seeking. In order to test whether your wording correlates with your intentions, you should understand the implications of questions of fact, questions of value, and questions of policy.

Questions of Fact   Such questions consider the truth or falsity of an assertion. Implied in the question is the theoretical possibility of measuring the truth of the answer on an objective scale. For instance, "What is the temperature today?" is a question of fact because the temperature can be recorded and read. "Is Jones guilty of murder?" is also a question of fact. Jones either committed the crime or he did not; and, on a theoretical level, whether he did or did not is verifiable. "What would Russia's reaction be to an American invasion of Cuba?" is also a question of fact. In this case, however, the question considers a future fact which would not be verifiable until and unless we did invade Cuba. Although questions of fact like the one on the temperature are poor for group discussion, many questions of fact make for excellent discussions. Each of the following is a discussable question of fact:

What are the goals of the "new left"?

What can be done to stop cheating in college classes?

Does the "pass-fail" system help to relieve the pressures of college life?

Questions of Value   These questions consider relative goodness or badness. They are characterized by the inclusion of some evaluative word like "good," "better," "best," "effective," or "worthy." The purpose of the question of value is to compare a subject with one or more members of the same class. For instance, "Who is the *best* basketball player in the National Basketball Association?" would be a question of value. Although we can set up criteria for "best" and measure our choice against those criteria, there is no way of verifying our findings—the answer is still a matter of judgment. Because questions of value encourage comparative analysis of the relative importance of values, they often lead to spirited discussions. Each of the following is a discussable question of value:

Was Eisenhower (Kennedy, Johnson, or whoever) an effective President?

What is the best way of studying for an essay exam?

Is the British style of debate better than the American style?

Questions of Policy   Such questions judge whether a future action should be taken. The question is phrased to arrive at a solution or to test a tentative solution to a problem or a felt need. "What should the United States do to lower the crime rate?" seeks a solution that would best solve the problem of the rise in crime. "Should Ohio abolish capital punishment?" provides a tentative solution to the problem of how criminals should be punished in the state of Ohio. The inclusion of the word "should" in all questions of policy makes them the easiest to recognize and the easiest to phrase of all discussion questions. Because most discussion groups are convened for the purpose of determining what action should be taken, questions of policy are the most prevalent type of discussion question. Each of the following is a discussable question of policy:

Should the United States recognize Red China?

What should the downtown merchants do to meet the competition of suburban stores?

Should *X* University abandon its system of required courses?

What should *X* University do to relieve its parking problem?

In addition to knowing the kind of question, you should also be aware of whether the discussion question is general or specific. Specific discussion questions include a single fact, a single value, or a single course of action to be discussed; general questions include the entire subject area. Specific questions are answered Yes or No; general questions are answered with a sentence. Let's contrast three sets of questions:

How will Russia respond if the United States invades Cuba? (General question of fact.)

Will Russia declare war on the United States if the U.S. invades Cuba? (Specific question of fact.)

Which Presidents of the United States were effective Presidents? (General question of value.)

Was Johnson an effective President? (Specific question of value.)

What should Cincinnati do to lower the crime rate? (General question of policy.)

Should Cincinnati hire more policemen in order to lower the crime rate in Cincinnati? (Specific question of policy.)

Because a specific question contains one item to be evaluated, the outlining procedure is less complicated and the resulting discussion is often much shorter, a desirable goal for groups with short time limits. Yet, because they tend to polarize opinion, specific questions often result in less objective discussions. Since with "Yes and No" questions there is little room for a middle ground and compromise, there is a much greater possibility that debate will result. When discussants begin to debate, the discussion process usually breaks down. Because general questions are open ended, allowing for differing points of view, they are characterized by a more cooperative procedure. Unless your time is severely restricted or unless the group is convened expressly to discuss a specific question, general questions are preferable for group discussion.

Main Points of Discussion

When we talked about informative speaking, we said that the main points are the complete-sentence statements that best developed the purpose sentence; when we talked about persuasive speaking, we said that the main points are complete-sentence justifications that answered the question "why" placed after the proposition. In discussion, main points are the key questions that must be answered in order to answer the topic question. Instead of explaining or proving the purpose sentence, in discussion the main points stimulate inquiry. To help you in determining the selection of main point questions, each of the three kinds of discussion questions suggests a line of development consistent with that type of question. Once you understand the lines of development, with a little practice you can phrase a short list of key questions for almost any discussion topic question.

Questions of Fact   Remember that with a question of fact, you are determining the truth or falsity of a statement. As a result, the major questions will deal with definition and classification. The definitions of key words lead to the classification. Sometimes the task is to discover the characteristics of the classification; sometimes the task is to select a choice from among various classifications. Consider the following examples:

What are the goals of the Republican Party?

What are goals? (Definition)

What is the Republican Party? (Definition)

What is one goal? What is another? Another? (Establishing classifications that meet definitions)

Is Jones guilty of murdering Smith?

How is "murder" defined? (Definition)

Did Jones cause the death of Smith?

Can the cause of death be classified as murder?

Questions of Value   Questions of value deal with relative goodness or relative badness. Whenever we judge comparative value, we need standards of judgment from which to work. Since a standard is discovered by establishing criteria for judgment, analysis then depends upon definitions of key terms, statement of the criteria for evaluation, and then a measuring of the object against those criteria. Consider the following examples:

Was Johnson an effective President?

What are the criteria for determining the effectiveness of the President?

How did Johnson's decisions, actions, policies, and the like conform to these criteria?

Did he meet the criteria well enough to be called effective?

What is the best method of curbing cheating in the classroom?

What are the criteria for determining a good method?

What are the available methods?

Which of these available methods best meets the criteria?

Questions of Policy   Because by their nature questions of policy deal with courses of action, they involve two necessary aspects: (1) the presence of a problem that needs to be solved and (2) a solution that meets the problem better than any other. For our analysis of a question of policy, we can draw from a modification of John Dewey's problem-solving method: becoming aware of the problem, defining the problem, discovering the possible solutions, and deciding upon the best solution. Consider the following examples:

What should be done to lower the crime rate in the U. S.?

What is the problem?

What are the symptoms of the problem?

What are the causes of the problem?

What criteria should be used to test the solutions?

What are some of the possible solutions?

What is the best solution?

How do each of the solutions meet the criteria?

Which solution best meets the criteria?

Should Ohio abolish capital punishment?

What is the problem that capital punishment is supposed to be solving?

What are symptoms of that problem?

What are the causes of the problem?

What criteria should be used to test the effectiveness of capital punishment?

Does capital punishment solve the problem?

Does capital punishment meet the criteria established?

These two examples further illustrate the difference between specific and general questions. Notice that although the discussion group considers the same kind of questions, the presence of the specific course of action abbreviates the analysis. Regardless of whether the question is one of fact, value, or policy, the group must still consider all the questions that are fundamental to the resolution of the topic question. With questions that are specific, however, the subordinate questions will also be more specific.

This entire section illustrates another of the major contrasts between group discussion and the informal social discussion. In a social discussion no order is expected and no order is necessary, because you aren't trying to come to a conclusion that meets the needs of the entire group. In group discussion, since you have a set goal, you must seek that goal in the most logical manner. The suggested methods of analysis discussed above give you a *modus operandi* to consider. Analysis is a key to the planning of a discussion. The areas deemed necessary for the resolution of the topic question will eventually serve as the main points in discussion itself.

Content and Idea Development in Discussion

Just as in informative and persuasive speaking, the content for discussion comes from personal experience, observation, and resource material. The combined pool of material eventually provides the basis for conclusions. Since valid conclusions can be chosen only from sound data, you should find the best material possible. Because the "information" in an informal social discussion is often little more than opinion, social discussions seldom yield more than enjoyable conversation. In group discussion, however, every member of the group is obligated to present the best material he can.

The Discussion Outline

A basic assumption of this textbook is that outlining is the best way of testing the soundness of speech preparation. For discussion as well as for public speaking, a sound outline is prerequisite to sound speaking. In contrast with public speaking, however, in discussion there are two kinds of outlines possible: the group outline and the individual discussant's outline. The group outline consists of the mainpoint questions that need to be answered in order to resolve the topic question. Although these outlines may be as brief as those used to illustrate the process of analysis, sometimes the discussion outline includes a more complete listing of all the subordinate questions that might be covered. How such a preliminary outline is obtained varies from group to group. If there is an appointed leader, he may assume the obligation to prepare the group outline. For rather simple questions that can be answered without research (for example, "What should be the arrangements for the annual picnic?"), the leader may give copies of the outline to the group at the beginning of the discussion. When the topic is more complex, requiring research, the leader will usually get the preliminary outline into the hands of the discussants well before discussion time. When no leader has been designated or when that leader does not wish or deem it advisable to write out an outline, the group usually meets to work out such pre-liminary considerations. If time is available, it is usually better if the entire group has an opportunity to share in the writing of the group outline.

The individual outline differs in purpose and scope. It corresponds to the outline prepared for any regular speech. For a simple question (for example, the annual picnic), the discussants would probably not need individual outlines. They could cope with the problems at the time of the discussion. For a question such as "Should the United States recognize Red China?" however, the individual would probably want to get some of his reading and thinking down on paper. In addi-tion, he would want to key the material he had to various parts of the outline so that during the discussion he would know what ma-terial was relevant. The following are examples of the group outline or agenda and a portion of an individual outline for the same discus-sion question:

Group Agenda

Discussion Question: What should be the criteria used by the United States in determining which countries receive economic aid?

I. What are the present criteria for economic aid?
   How is it determined?
   What aspects are emphasized?

II. What problems have resulted from the present policy?
   Are there economic problems?
   Are there social problems?
   Are there political problems?

III. What are alternative criteria?

IV. Which of these alternative criteria should be incorporated?
   Which will help solve the problems?
   Which are feasible?

Individual Outline

I. What are the present criteria for giving economic aid?
   A. Military criteria.

      1. Securing military bases for economic aid.

      2. Gaining mutual defense treaties for economic aid.

  B. Preventing spread of communism.

      1. The Marshall Plan provided food, fuel, and machinery to rebuild war torn countries after WWII.

      2. The Point Four Program provides technical, industrial, and scientific know-how to underdeveloped and backward areas of the world.

  C. Goodwill.

      1. Gifts without specific purpose.

  D. Humanitarian reasons.

      1. Aid to people of the world in disaster areas caused by floods, earthquakes, disease, etc.

II. What problems have resulted from present criteria?

  A. Endless bidding between ourselves and Russia to gain favor with other countries.

  B. The loss of prestige in some areas where American capital controls a large portion of another country's industry—example, South America.

  C. Waste.

      1. In the types of programs.

      2. In the administration of the program at home and abroad.

Participation in Interacting Discussion

Participation in group discussion involves two separate kinds of activities, content contribution and leadership. Ordinarily we think of an appointed or elected individual acting as leader and all others in the group acting as content contributors. Although that's the way it's often done, it doesn't have to be that way. A group can be so organized that everyone shares the burden of leadership. Thus, a group can have leadership whether it has a designated leader or not. In order to decide whether your group should vest leadership responsibilities in one person or not, you must understand the advantages and disadvantages of each kind of situation.

When someone is appointed or elected leader, the group looks to him for leadership. If he is a good leader, the group will benefit. Each participant can concentrate on considering the issues being raised, confident that the leader will guide the group justly. Disadvantages are related to inadequacy of the leader: when that person is unsure, the group may ramble about aimlessly; when the leader dominates, participants don't feel free to contribute spontaneously and the discussion follows a path predetermined by the leader; when the leader is unskilled, the group can become frustrated and short-tempered. Good leadership is a necessity. When the appointed leader can't provide it, the group suffers.

When the group is leaderless, everyone has the right and the obligation to show leadership. Ordinarily, leadership will emerge from one, two, or perhaps three members of the group. Since no one has been given the mantle of leadership, everyone is on equal footing, and the discussion can be more spontaneous. Disadvantages are seen in a group where either no one assumes leadership or where a few compete for leadership. In such situations, the discussion becomes "leadershipless." Depending upon the qualities of the participants, a leaderless discussion can arrive at truly group decisions or it can be a rambling, meaningless collage of fact and opinion. If you have only one round of discussion, I would suggest trying the method that the group would have most confidence in to begin with.

Regardless, however, of whether there is a clear division between leader and content contributors, good discussions must illustrate certain characteristics.

Discussants Should Have Equal Opportunity to Speak

Conclusions are valid only when they represent the thinking of the entire group. Yet, in discussions some people are more likely or more willing to express themselves than others. For instance, if a typical eight-man discussion group is left to its own devices, two or three may tend to speak as much as the other five or six together; furthermore, one or two members may contribute little if anything. At the beginning of a discussion, at least, you must operate under the assumption that every member of the group has something to contribute. To insure opportunity for equal participation, those who tend to dominate must be held somewhat in check, and those who are content to observe must be brought into the discussion more.

Accomplishing this ideal balance is a real test of leadership. If an ordinarily reluctant talker is embarrassed by another member of the group, he may become even more reluctant to participate. Likewise, if a talkative yet valuable member of the group is constantly restrained, he may lose his value.

Let's first consider the handling of the shy or reluctant speaker. Often, apparently reluctant speakers want to talk but can't get the floor. As leader you may solve this problem by clearing the road for that speaker when he gives visual and verbal clues of his desire to speak; he may come up on the edge of his seat, he may look as if he wants to talk, or he may even start to say something. Because the reluctant speaker in this posture may often relinquish his opportunity if another more aggressive person competes to be heard, you can help considerably with a comment such as "Just a second, Jim, I think Mary has something she wants to say here." Of course, the moment that Mary is sitting back in her chair with a somewhat vacant look is not the time for such a statement. A second method of drawing out the reluctant speaker is to phrase a question that is sure to elicit some answer and then perhaps some discussion. The most appropriate kind of question is one requiring an opinion rather than a fact. For instance, "Joe, what do you think of the validity of this approach to combatting crime?" is much better than "Joe, do you have anything to say here?" Not only is it specific, but also it requires more than a Yes or No answer. Furthermore, such an opinion question will not embarrass Joe if he has no factual material to contribute. Tactful handling of the shy or reluctant speaker can pay big dividends. You may get some information that could not have been brought out in any other way; moreover, when the shy person contributes a few times, it builds up his confidence, which in turn makes it easier for him to respond later when he has more to say. Of course, there are times when one or more members do not have anything worth saying, because they just are not prepared. Under such circumstances it is best for you to leave him alone.

As a leader you must also use tact with the overzealous speaker. Remember, the talkative person may be talkative because he has done his homework—he may have more information than any other member of the group. If you "turn him off" the group may suffer immensely. After he has finished talking, try statements such as: "Tom, that's a very valuable bit of material, let's see whether we can get some reactions from the other members of the group on this issue." Notice that a statement of this kind does not stop him; it suggests that he should hold off for a while. A difficult kind of participant to deal with is the one who must be heard regardless of whether he has anything to say or not. If subtle reminders are ineffective with this individual, you can forget about hurting his feelings; he probably doesn't have any. You may have to say, "Bob, I know you want to talk, but you're just not giving anyone else a chance. Would you wait until we've heard everyone else on this point?" Of course the person who may be the most difficult to control is the leader himself. Leaders often engage in little dialogues with each member of the group. They sometimes exercise so much control that participants believe that they can talk only in response to the leader.

There are three common patterns of group discussion (see illustration. in which the lines represent the flow of discussion among the eight participants). Discussion *A* represents a leader-dominated group. The lack of interaction often leads to a rigid, formal, and usually poor discussion. Discussion *B* represents a more spontaneous group. Since three people dominate and a few aren't heard, however, conclusions will not represent group thinking. Discussion *C* represents something closer to the ideal pattern. It illustrates a great deal of spontaneity, a total group representation, and theoretically at least the greatest possibility for reliable conclusions.

Discussion A   **Discussion B**   **Discussion C**

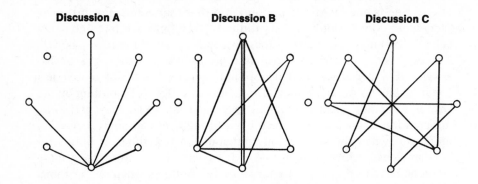

Discussants Should Contribute Responsibly

As we noted earlier, one of the greatest differences between a group discussion and an informal social discussion is in the quality of the developmental material included. Responsible discussion is characterized by documented factual material, careful analysis of every item of information, and sound conclusions and evaluations about and from the factual material. Let's examine each of these characteristics. Since you need documented factual material, your preparation should be extensive. The more material you have sampled, the better knowledge you will have of the subject and the more valuable your contributions will be. As a guideline to quantity of resource material, you should have access to considerably more than you could get into the discussion. It is not uncommon for discussants to be familiar with eight or ten sources. Since, of course, you can't predict all of the ideas that will be covered in the discussion or when you will be speaking, you can't prepare your actual contributions ahead of time. Nevertheless, you should be familiar enough with the material that you can find any item you need when you need it. Usually, you will bring your sources with you to the discussion. If you are disallowed the use of the actual sources by your professor, then make note cards containing all the material you are likely to need for the discussion.

A second characteristic of responsible contribution—careful analysis of every item of information—is shown by raising questions about and probing into contributions of others. Your obligation does not end with the reading into the record of items of information. Once an item of data has been submitted, it is the obligation of the membership to determine whether the item is accurate, typical, consistent, and otherwise valid. Suppose that in a discussion on reducing crime, a person mentioned that, according to *U.S. News & World Report*, crime had risen 33 percent in the past five years, the group should not leave this statement until they have explored it fully. What was the specific source of the data? On what were the data based? What years are being referred to? Is this consistent with other material? Is any counter material available? Now, the purpose of these questions is not to debate the data, but to test them. If these data are partly true, questionable, or relevant only to certain kinds of crime, a different conclusion or set of conclusions would be appropriate.

Sound conclusions about and from the factual material, a third characteristic of responsible contribution, refers to the real goal of the discussion itself. Discussants must pool information to provide a basis for conclusions about the topic question. Students sometimes blame the sterility of their discussion on the need to present information responsibly. Yet sterility is a result of poor discussants, not the format. You can still offer opinions, but unlike social sessions in which opinions substitute for data, in discussion, your opinions are based upon the previously tested materials.

Discussion Is Characterized by Objectivity

Discussion is a method of group inquiry. Unlike the debater who seeks to impose his opinions and who desires agreement, acquiescence, or approval, using only the data that will prove his point, discussants seek to ask questions, to share ideas, and to work together toward mutually satisfactory answers utilizing all the data at their disposal. Let's focus on two recommendations for insuring objectivity of approach. First, report data, don't associate yourself with it. If you reported that crime has risen 33 percent in the past five years, don't feel that because you presented the data that you must defend it. An excellent way of presenting data with a degree of disassociation is illustrated by the following: "According to *U.S. News & World Report*, crime has risen 33 percent in the past five years. That seems like a startling statistic. I wonder whether anyone else found either any substantiating or any contradictory data?" Presenting data in this way tells the group that you want discussion of the data and that, whether it is substantiated or disproven, you have no personal relationship with it. Contrast that disassociative approach with the following statement: "I think crime is going up at a fantastic rate. Why, I found that crime has gone up 33 percent in the past five years, and we just can't put up with that kind of thing." This speaker is taking a position with his data. Since anyone who questions the data or the conclusions is going to have to contend with the speaker, there's a good chance that the discussion that follows will not be the most objective.

A second recommendation for insuring objectivity is to solicit all viewpoints on every major issue. Suppose you were discussing the question "Was Eisenhower an effective President?" Suppose that after extensive reading you believed that Eisenhower was not. If in the discussion you spoke only to support your position and you took issue with every bit of contrary material, you would not be responding objectively. Although there is nothing wrong with formulating tentative opinions based upon your research, in the discussion you should present material objectively whether it supports or opposes your tentative claims. If the group draws a conclusion that corresponds to your tentative conclusion, fine. At least all views have had the opportunity to be presented. If the group draws the opposite conclusion, you are not put in a defensive position. By being objective, you may find that during the discussion your views will change many times. Remember, if the best answer to the topic question could be found without discussion, the discussion wouldn't be necessary.

Discussion Is Characterized by Numerous Summaries

Many discussion groups talk for thirty minutes, only to have the leader say, "All right, now that we have discussed, what is your opinion?" at which time each discussant in turn tells what he thought before the discussion started. A discussion group should move in an orderly manner toward intermediate conclusions represented by summary statements seeking group consensus. For instance, on the topic question, "Was Eisenhower an effective President?" the group would have to reach consensus on each of the following questions:

What is one criterion of effectiveness? (Draw intermediate conclusion, ask whether group agrees)

What is another criterion of effectiveness? (Draw conclusion)

What is a third? (Draw conclusion)

Any others? (Draw conclusion)

Did Eisenhower meet the first criterion? (Draw conclusion)

Did he meet the second? (Draw conclusion)

Did he meet others? (Draw conclusion)

Did Eisenhower meet enough of the criteria to be labeled an effective President? (Final conclusion)

This group might draw six, eight, or even ten conclusions before it is able to arrive at the answer to the topic question. A group cannot arrive at the tenth and final conclusion until each of the subordinate questions is answered.

It is up to you as a leader to point up these conclusions by summarizing what has been said and seeking consensus on a conclusion. You must always be conscious of when the group has really arrived at some decision. If left to its own devices, a group will discuss a point for a while, then move on to another before a conclusion is drawn. You must sense when enough has been said to reach a consensus. Then you must phrase the conclusion, subject it to testing, and move on to another area. You should become familiar with phrases that can be used during the discussion:

"I think most of us are stating the same points. Are we really in agreement that ..." (State conclusion)

"We've been discussing this for a while and I think I sense an agreement. Let me state it, and then we'll see whether it does summarize group feeling." (State conclusion)

"Now we're getting on to another area. Let's make sure that we are really agreed on the point we've just finished." (State conclusion)

"Are we ready to summarize our feelings on this point?" (State conclusion)

Discussions Should Have an Apparent Organization

Whether the group is to be functioning with a leader or not, someone must be responsible for presenting the panel, stating the question, presenting the agenda, getting the discussion started, and ultimately, concluding the discussion. The following illustrates a typical opening for a public discussion on foreign aid:

Each year the topic of foreign aid is debated vigorously in Congress. From those and similar debates, it seems obvious that most Americans favor some kind of assistance to selected foreign nations. The question that seems to focus on the key issue of foreign aid and the question we are going to discuss tonight is "What should be the criteria used by the United States in determining which countries receive economic aid?" Discussing with me this evening are, from my right to my left, Barbara Mason, Jim Green, Phyllis Merrit, Steve Conway, Art Vlasik, and I'm Harry Stevens. In order to cover the topic, we've decided to ask what are the present criteria for economic aid, what problems have resulted from present policy, what are alternative criteria, and which of these alternative criteria, if any, should be incorporated. Let's begin with our first question, What are the present criteria for determining economic aid?

If the designated leader opened the discussion, he will ask questions, elicit response from all members, help to maintain objectivity, summarize where needed. If the group is leaderless, each member will shoulder a portion of the leadership responsibility. At the end of the discussion, after the group has reached consensus on the discussion question, the leader, or designate, thanks the panel and the audience for their participation.

Group Assignment

Participants select a question of fact, value, or policy for a 20- to 40-minute panel discussion. Determine method of leadership, establish an agenda, and prepare an individual outline. Criteria for evaluation of the discussion will include quality of participation, quality of leadership, and ability to arrive at group decisions.

Analyze the following portion of a classroom discussion.[1] Notice the contrast between the first part in which discussion is very stilted and the second part which exemplifies many of the characteristics noted above.

Analysis	Discussion
Mr. Loder begins this section by asking the question listed on the agenda.	*Loder:* What are the present criteria for economic aid?
	Brown: According to Robert Kennedy, the criteria which the U. S. has used in the past and I quote: "Full stomachs may not save a democracy, but

---

[1] A portion of a discussion presented in Fundamentals of Speech class, University of Cincinnati. Printed by permission of the participants.

empty ones can seal its doom." I think that during the last eight or even ten years this sums up about what we've been doing. I would cite Public Law number 430, the Agriculture and Trade Redevelopment and Assistance Act, as an example. Under this act which was passed in 1965, underdeveloped countries such as Egypt, India, Pakistan, to cite a few, can receive food from the U. S. government at about one eighth of its wholesale market value.

Loder: Do you have anything to add to this, Mrs. Wynne?

Wynne: Yes, we also offer assistance under our foreign aid program, both directly and through international organizations, to those less developed countries that show a determination to master their own resources toward self-development.

Loder: Mr. Baker, what do you have to say about this?

Baker: Well, I think military reasons are probably one of our major reasons governing our economic aid, and I mean by this securing military bases, in exchange for economic aid. Mutual defense treaties— again a lot of them are connected with our economic aid program. And I think many of our military bases are more or less on the you-scratch-my-back-and-I'll-scratch-yours.

Loder: Miss Leigh, do you have anything to add?

Leigh: Only that economic aid has been given for many reasons.

Loder: Then I assume that economic aid is given on the criteria of making friends with foreign countries both at the economic level and the military. Let's go on to the second problem here. What problems have resulted from our present policy of economic aid?

Baker: I think one of the major problems is that we are embarked on a program of endless bidding between ourselves and Russia to gain favors with other countries. It seems like the smaller countries are in an enviable position where they can sit there and see which big power offers them the most before they make up their mind which way they are going.

Notice that here and throughout this section Mr. Loder asks these stilted, "Yes or No" questions that don't stimulate very much discussion. At this point, a better observation and follow-up question would have been "Mr. Brown says that a major criterion for determining foreign aid is the country's ability to support itself. How much data do we have to support this position?"

Notice that even though each individual presents interesting and important information there is no real discussion of that information.

This example shows that phrasing of the question can yield a rather uncomfortable response.

Mr. Loder needs to test his assumption. He could ask "Is the group agreed that our major criterion for giving aid has been to make economic and military aid?" Actually the group was not ready to draw a conclusion yet. It needed to explore the data in more detail.

The responses to this second question are more representative of effective discussion.

Notice that instead of the leader breaking in and asking whether anyone has anything to add, Miss Wynne carries the point being made a little further.

Here Mr. Loder exemplifies excellent leadership. Notice how he summarizes the point, getting at the essence of what Miss Wynne had to say.

Because of the way the idea was summarized, Mr. Baker has had a chance to reflect on the point and now is able to offer additional data.

Here Mr. Brown picks up the South America allusion and carries it further. In each of these last four contributions, we can sense the discussants thinking *with* each other.

Now Mr. Baker distills much of the last contribution down to the one word "waste." Although he is not the designated leader, this summary exemplifies leadership. Notice, this second part of the discussion incorporates interaction, good data, some good reasoning, and more effective leadership. Conclusions drawn from this section of the discussion will be truly group decisions.

Wynne: And I also think that with our aid to other countries many times instead of giving assistance, we become the doers. Instead of letting the people of the country develop and work with us, we actually go in and take over. And they have no say in what should be done or what should be developed. As a result, I think we create chaos in countries.

Loder: In other words, what we're saying here is, because we are advancing economic aid, we want to manage the economic aid that we are giving to other countries. And this creates problems of ill will and ill feelings.

Baker: I think this is evident in South America, where a lot of American capital has been spent; and, for a great part, we control the industries of these countries. And we've seen where some of the South American countries have gone so far as to take over the industries.

Brown: As far as the aid to South America and the no-strings-attached type of gift, it has seemed that in the past, whenever U. S. money has gone with no strings attached, graft has gone with it. For example, in Vietnam, in 1967, there was 578 and four tenths million dollars given to Vietnam for their reconstruction and their rural program. It has been estimated by our own government and our representatives in Saigon, that only about one eighth to one ninth of this huge sum ever reached the people. The rest of it has been doled out between the elite of the country. I think that that has been our big problem, not only managing the smaller dependent countries, but we tend to make the rich richer.

Baker: I think we could summarize that and say that it is a waste in the administration both at home and abroad in the foreign countries themselves that is a big problem.

Appendix

Four
Contemporary
Speeches

Appendix

The following speeches, all delivered in 1971, illustrate how four men and women in responsible positions met their challenge of effective speaking. In order to get the greatest value from your analysis, examine each of the speeches in terms of the questions asked on pages 16–17 of this textbook.

A Woman Could Be President

A speech by Jayne Baker Spain,[1] Director of Litton Industries, delivered before the Public Affairs Forum, United States Air Force Academy, February 25, 1971.

Members of the Cadet Forum on Public Affairs: My number two son, Kim, has his sights set on one day being a cadet at this Air Force Academy. He is fifteen, and I have been instructed as only a fifteen-year old can instruct his mother. Whatever you do, he said, do it so it won't be held against *me!*

So, may I begin by asking—even entreating—with your superintendent, General Clark, that all my faux pas be credited to me, and not make them cumulative to await my number two son, so that he has to do those punishment tours in addition to those which he earns by himself?

This concern was all caused when he heard what my topic was going to be—that "A woman might one day be president!"

It's not necessary to look back on 1970, and something called the Women's Liberation Movement to say that this might happen. Far-flung and in the future? It would be almost incredible if in the span of your

---

[1] Reprinted from *Vital Speeches*, April 1, 1971, pp. 357–359. By permission.

projected professional life in the Air Force, which will see most of you still active into the Twenty-first Century, if one or even more women do not run for the highest office in this country—and perhaps, win it.

There will be eight presidential elections between November 1972 and November 2000.

One of those elections is almost sure to swing on the ticket which includes a woman as either president or vice president. If it is vice president, vice presidents are known to succeed into the White House oval office with frequency.

In the 1968 election, there were 4,750,000 more women eligible to vote for the presidential candidates than there were men.

The working woman either maintains herself, shares in the maintenance of her family, or in the case of those divorced with children, is often the sole support of her family. More than 30 million women are in this category, and the number increases every year. These women see the tax deductions on their own paychecks. They tend to view politics less emotionally, and more practically with each passing day. They truly want the political field to work for them, and they are getting better at making it do so. When women first got the right to vote, they knew it gave them a say in the make-up of the government which served them: Now that women have a significant margin in the voting, they will be even more demanding and powerful shapers of the future.

Let's just pose for ourselves ten questions. When each is asked, each of you answer yourself honestly as to whether a woman would be more at home, more sympathetic to the cries of the electorate regarding the issue in question than would a man. And then think, too, of that woman in the White House responding to those issues.

Question one: Everything an individual does depends in great measure on his health. Who is it in the family who is most intimately concerned with health from a baby's first cry? A man or a woman?

Question two: Everything an individual will achieve in his lifetime tends to depend on the quality of his education. Who is it in the family who gets its young to school, checks on their well-being, helps with the homework, participates most in the affairs of schools and schooling? A man or a woman?

Question three: If there is need for appeal for charity support, or welfare support, or to raise the moneys for such causes, who are present in the greatest numbers? Men or women?

Question four: When it comes to actual selection of household needs, from food to furniture, what is the sex of the most active selector and consumer pattern setter, and the one who makes the most quality demands? Male or female?

Question five: When it comes to which is the weaker or the stronger, what do the vital statistics show in terms of life span—and therefore, who must take the longer looks and plan farther ahead because of living longer? A man or a woman?

Question six: When it comes to the ownership of America's wealth, in whose hands is it? Men or women?

Question seven: Pollution. That's a good one to get on. Let's take water, for example. If there is anything wrong with it, and anyone apt to get upset about it, who is it who goes to the tap more often in a household? A man or a woman? If the garbage piles up, who is closest to it as it stands there uncollected, and who is most aware of it? A man or a woman? If there is a choking smog blanketing the area, whose hair and whose windows collect most of its worst aspects? That of a man or a woman? (If men's present long hair fashions continue, I may have to consider this a draw.)

Question eight: When it comes to commercial or military operation of jet aircraft, with all their noises, who makes most of the calls to airports and air bases complaining that the house shakes and the kids have been awakened from their naps? A man or a woman?

Question nine: When it comes to safety, we kill more people and seriously handicap more people on highways every year than we have in all of the Viet Nam war. That one aspect alone is colossal. But we are handicapping people in America at the rate of more than 300,000 a year, and have 22 million physically handicapped among us today. So when junior gets his first automobile, who is it who usually accompanies him to the door when he leaves the house, and asks him to drive carefully? A man or a woman? And who is it who never falls asleep until his safe return? A man or a woman?

Question ten: And if you were to explain something as complex as national security in terms of its protection to home, property and family rather than in terms of the size of the defense budget, who would give you the most prompt and urgent constructive response? A man or a woman?

What I have done here is touch on practically every major concern of people today, and it is amazing how more and more of the issues which are becoming uppermost in debates of our time are either equally the concerns of men and women, or more often than not, weighed in the direction of women.

All the stereotypes have been shaken to their very foundations. No matter what Hugh Hefner may have done to make girl watching a national and international past-time, he has consistently avoided or sidestepped the possibility that girl creatures, whatever their physical dimensions, often have astronomical cerebral dimensions as well. Imagine what might have happened if Mr. Hefner had gone one step farther and said, in essence: "All this, and a *brain,* too!"

Women have been creeping slowly but steadily up on this tendency of men to cast them into the oversight department. And the ones who have been doing so have been doing it with something difficult to deny —something called *competence.* This is hard to say *nay* to, when brains, no matter what configuration encloses them, are much in demand.

My reason for developing this thought really leads to something which you should be considering, and most seriously. Perhaps the four classes now here in the Air Force Academy contain a future chairman of the Joint Chiefs of Staff. Perhaps as many as two Chiefs of Staff of that aerospace force which lies in the not too distant future, and perhaps as many as fifty or more highly-placed staff officers in the two and three star categories. If you do not do that well, or even better, then the promise and the hope of professionalism you represent will be unfulfilled, and the taxpayers will have a right to complain about the return they got on their money. Here, right now, you are on the first ladder rung which leads to that special something called competence. On it lives will depend, the principles by which we have lived and prospered will be defended, our country will stand and survive. Without competence, men and women are poorly armed: with competence, they are ready for anything.

If you will accept what I have been saying as possible, what are some of the important ramifications for you of having a woman president of the United States?

For one thing, she will be your Commander-in-Chief!

For one thing, laws remaining the same, she and she alone can give the commands relative to the use of nuclear weapons.

For one thing, she will be sending the budget to the Congress, she will make major determinations in how it will be allocated, and she will defend those allocations.

For one thing, she will want, will expect, will need and will depend on the very best professional advice she can get, and she must trust that advice. Once she trusts such advice, she will go down swinging with it, and will uphold it tenaciously. One of the quarters from which she will get the most vital advice will be from the leaders of our armed forces, and the explanatory contingency briefings she will get from lesser staff officers. Women hope for honesty, and when they get it, they appreciate and respect it even more than men do. And women who believe you, have absolute faith in you and will back you against all odds—all the way. But conversely, once you attempt to lead them down the garden path, chances are they will never walk that way with you again.

In an all male environment such as the Air Force Academy, you can be forgiven for the tendency to think of the girl part of the species as a charming week-end respite—and a pleasant one—much better than looking at these confining walls—or as someone with whom to make haste to the chapel at June week time. But it is taking the short range and limited view of women and what their influence may be on you and your career field. There are all kinds of books for military wives which deal with how to get along with the Colonel's Lady, how to outwit the quartermaster, and what the protocol is for this or that circumstance—but times are changing rapidly. There is practically no meaningful literature which pertains to what we are considering now, but this doesn't mean that there should be no thinking about it.

Consider this: Ours is the same century in which man made not only his *first* flight—120 feet—but he also landed on the moon just a short time ago. We now accept this feat as matter of fact, yet I believe it is not nearly as matter of fact as a woman becoming president. The woman leadership factor is hardly new. England made her greatest moves under Elizabeth I, and consolidated her greatest empire under Queen Victoria. If there had been no Queen Isabella willing to gamble because she believed a man's conviction, and willing to hock her royal jewels for three pint-size boats, who knows how long it might have been before the known world would have included North and South America. In modern times, with India in terms of geographic spread being the most populous nation on earth, how fortunate it may be that it has a woman for Prime Minister. In a country ruled by men for ages past, cursed with a free running, burgeoning population which must somehow be brought into check, it is high time for a woman Prime Minister who can talk to other women about these problems and what to do about them. And one could hardly ask for a country with more spirit and daring and confidence than Israel headed by Golda Meir— and at a time when it is faced with every form of threat and intimidation, and is being tested as never before.

This leads me to state what I believe most sincerely—that it will be the time and the special events of the time, coupled with competence to deal with them, which will make a woman in the presidency possible—and I would be the first to abhor having a woman for president for the simple reason that she is female, the presidency having come to her as some manifestation of a fairness doctrine on the basis that things have been out of balance against women for ages.

And let me tell you this, if you think of women as being frightened of a mouse and therefore paralyzed with inactivity when faced with a great danger such as war, you are wrong. You may be sure she would do everything possible to settle international disputes short of war, but she would not shrink from her responsibilities. As far as you in the Air Force are concerned, I assure you that no woman has to be sold on the absolute necessity of air supremacy, or our cover for invading forces. This is something she innately knows. *Why.* Because as mother of the race she is by nature protective. She wants every mother's son to have everything he needs to provide him with the best chance to survive and be victorious where life is concerned. She could never think politically, for biologically every cell of her being is structured to be protective.

Therefore, I ask you not to be amused, or outraged, at the thought of a female chief executive, but to add that one more eventuality to all the others for which you are being prepared. The one thing for which a military leader can never be forgiven is that of being surprised. People may not pay attention to the advice he gives in time for it to be most effective, and they may call upon him much too late and expect unreasonable, giant-size heroics to save them, but if he is surprised they will punish him with varying degrees of disgrace, perhaps even making him a kind of political leper or scapegoat. Every so often then, conjure up situations short of war which can be saved from war, or deterring war, in preparing strength requirements and justifying them, and yes, even the conduct of war itself, which would involve a woman as Commander-in-Chief—the President of the United States of America. It is not as unreasonable as it may sound—and it's getting more reasonable every day.

A Black-Operated Firm

A speech by Joseph W. Goodloe,[2] *President, North Carolina Mutual Life Insurance Co., Durham, North Carolina, delivered to Afro-American Student Union, Harvard University School of Business Administration, Cambridge, Massachusetts, May 12, 1971.*

---

[2] Reprinted from *Vital Speeches*, September 15, 1971, pp. 709–715. By permission.

Master of ceremonies, distinguished guests and friends.... It's truly a pleasure to be here as the guest of the Afro-American Student Union ... to get to meet and know men who are preparing themselves for work and service in the business world ... to have an opportunity to be on this campus where so many minds have been developed and nutured for work and service in both the public and private sectors.

Your organization, the Afro-American Student Union, intrigues me. I am convinced it can and will provide a meaningful service to its members and to the university. Your list of seven objectives has unusual significance. The day the list was received from Ed Martin, I took it home to show my wife. We read them, and re-read them. We were reminded of the letters we received from our daughter during the two years she was enrolled at Vassar. She had good grades. She liked the school. And, from the letters we received, her teachers and classmates liked her. But, she complained of the isolation and irrelevancy. After two years she insisted (and we agreed) that she transfer to a more relevant environment, Howard University.

We could not help but think that if there had been a student union at Vassar, like yours here at Harvard, conceivably she would have found those two years just a bit happier and a bit more relevant.

The Afro-American Student Union is but one manifestation of the black revolution ... a positive outgrowth that, I predict in the years ahead will be recognized by historians. They will cite the development of student organizations like yours as one of the means of saving the university ... a means of liberating the university and fortifying it for continued growth, prosperity and progress.

Since Ed Martin has been here at Harvard, I have talked with him over the telephone several times. He has really changed. As I talked with him I thought of a frequently quoted statement made by a former chief justice of the Supreme Court: *"A mind stretched by a new idea can never return to the same place."*

After less than a year's stay here at Harvard, it does appear that Ed Martin's mind has really been stretched. And, while his mind can never return to its old place, it is my sincere hope that after 12 or 14 more months of mind-stretching, he will return to our company—The North Carolina Mutual—after he gets his M.B.A.

Now, it is in this "mind-stretching" context that I understand the Afro-American Student Union invited me to talk to you this afternoon. Ed tells me that in spite of your graduate study in the field of business, not many of you are familiar with any black-operated business. Further, that some of your recent speakers have made mention of what, they feel, black-operated insurance companies are *not* doing. Now, quite frankly, I do not propose to offer any especially *new* ideas; I do plan to share some thoughts with you. And, hopefully, these thoughts will provide you with new information, new insights and new ways that a black M.B.A. might be helpful ... no matter where he works—for a black-operated company or for big business.

As you know from Mr. Martin's introduction ... by education, by training, by interest and by work experience ... I am a businessman. It is reasonable then to assume that you, too, have both an interest in and concern for business. Likewise, I suspect, as black M.B.A. candidates, you are raising one of the BIG and unanswered questions in many minds today: And, that is, *"JUST WHAT IS THE FUTURE OF NEGRO BUSINESS?"*

Some twenty-odd years ago, since the end of World War II, the officers of North Carolina Mutual have been wrestling with this question. We have devoted considerable time, thought and manpower to developing our own answers to it.

We have worked out some fairly definitive answers for our company. Since these might not necessarily apply to other companies, I do not propose to discuss other Negro businesses. Rather, I plan to share some thoughts with you in a sort of case study, detailing certain concepts. These thoughts have a general theme-title:

It is not remarkable that any American business operating in the affluent society of the past twenty years can become successful. After all, as several of the more intrepid analysts have pointed out, we *are* living in a business culture.

Our structure is business and industry with an elaborate system of service functions. And, the remarkable thing about black-operated business institutions that survived has been that they became successful and self-sustaining enterprises in a marginal, cultural setting set against the very idea of success in the traditional American manner. Black business then has been described by certain scholars as the "third dimension of American business."

The "third dimension" is said to be the combination quality with dimensions that can create its own favorable climate out of the very problems encountered in the normal universe of both our economic and social systems.

It is really the ability to operate in a cultural setting that is changing, and in turn, to contribute to that change. Social scientists have a term for this phenomena. They call it a "moving equilibrium" . . . in brief, it is the ability to take the limited area of operation of a Jim Crow enterprise out of its constricted economy, catch up with the larger American economy and then become competitive in this larger economy.

Nearly twenty years ago, the American Institute of Management started making annual audits and evaluations of our nation's more outstanding enterprises. Out of this practice of in-depth business analysis they have developed a set of rather positive indices of successful management. Not the least of these is the character of the personal leadership. True, this is an extremely elusive quality. But, repeatedly, in virtually all of their studies the question of leadership tends to bind all the others together.

For example, in the case study evaluation for General Motors, the Institute asked, "What enabled General Motors to attain size, dominate the market while others marked time or died?" The answer, said the appraisers, lies in a "body of men conscientiously following a leader, but doing it out of love for him, not merely out of self-interest." The study pointed out they found the corporation is the "perfect expression of unity within, as it is within an inspired army. Given that spirit, no ordinary obstacles can prevent the group from advancing its purpose."

Generally, in our black-operated institutions, it has been the foresight of the founders and the men of management they selected that provided the unity and vision to penetrate the veil beyond the racially permissible limits of performance. To this we must add the spark of daring, tempered by judgment and industry, needed for success.

If you list the beginnings of enterprises within the constricted Negro economy, you will find a terrifying mortality after only a few years. And, even those who "make it" can seldom be called really BIG business. Theodore Cross suggests in his book that the: "Black Life Insurance Industry is the only significant element of black capitalism in America today." And, he points out that they enjoyed "dramatic growth before 1950 when the low life expectancy of Negroes insulated the black life companies from white competition. Since 1963, black life insurance companies' assets in the aggregate have grown at an average annual rate of 3 percent compared to 9.5 percent for the industry as a whole."

The roots of the nation's most significant black industry go back nearly 200 years to the Free African Society organized in Philadelphia in 1787 for social uplift and self-help.

The trail blazers of Negro business were the fraternal and mutual benefit societies. As McCants Andrews says in his book about John Merrick, one of the founders of our company: "—they furnished the laboratories. They were the business schools in which our leading businessmen have been trained. The Royal Knights of King David trained John Merrick . . . it pioneered the way for the North Carolina Mutual . . ."

But as Dr. Dubois mentioned in his book, *Economic Cooperation*, "The woods are full of the graves of these earlier companies." And, with almost no exception, these fraternal and benefit societies and even a number of bonafide insurance companies suffered from inexperience and poor management. The small black insurance society unwittingly manufactured its own destruction. Without reliable data on Negro mortality and thus no actuarial tables, most groups simply guessed at what adequate rates ought to be. Moreover, they generally made no effort to control their mortality experience by selecting risks according to age or health. Inevitably the group found itself forced to assess each member an extra amount to meet death claims. These assessments on top of the regular dues compelled many members, especially the young and fit, to leave the society. Thus, the membership grew older and the death rate mounted. This required even higher assessments. After another exodus of the fittest members, the societies collapsed.

At this period, there were so many failures that the Department of Commerce published a pamphlet dealing with the failures of black benefit societies. It did point out that they had inadequate reserves. And, the black leadership seized on this to demand that the fraternals, mutual aid and benefit societies qualify as real insurance firms. At this very time, a number of the white-operated insurance companies followed the lead of Metropolitan Life and Prudential in refusing to insure Negroes.

(Incidentally, if any of you desire more details about the early development of black insurance companies, you should ask your librarian to secure copies of Lawrence Brown's unpublished master's thesis, "Insurance of American Negro Lives," and Winfred Octavus Bryson's unpublished doctoral dissertation, "Negro Life Companies."

Both can be obtained from the Wharton School of the University of Pennsylvania.)

A few minutes ago, I made a distinction and suggested that there is a difference between a Jim Crow enterprise ... one operating in a constricted economy and ... a Negro business that makes the break into the larger economy.

I also noted that the remarkable thing about such business was not so much that they succeeded in their operations within the American free enterprise system, but that they had *conquered the elemental barriers up to the level of free competition.*

Traditionally, we have placed *ALL* Negro-operated enterprises under the banner of "Negro Business".... Over the years, the black press, the black clergy and others have been proud of the gallant efforts of Negroes to set up their own enterprises. Nearly seventy years ago, Booker T. Washington urged blacks to establish businesses as a way to break out of the caste system. He said: "... more and more students of the race problem are beginning to see that business and industry constitute what we may call the strategic point of its solution. It is in business and industry that I see the brightest and most hopeful phases of the race situation."

Any critical analysis of Booker T. Washington's statement must be made in terms of his time. Business generally was smaller than it is now. Black business was in its infancy. It functioned without outside competition since there was racial isolation not only from the cultural mainstream but the economic as well. Thus, business opportunity in certain fields was offered by this condition on a small and very elemental scale *without outside* competition.

The seventies provide vastly different times and opportunities. Even in the enclosed caste system period of the past, only a few types of personal service industries or businesses were able to achieve substantial success.

The mortality among black businesses has been exceedingly high from the very marginal relationship of the Negro to the larger population. With increased competition the hazards have increased for Negro business. Any enterprise that moves from the constricted economy of the ghetto to the free economy of the total market place has the hazards of free and open competition. But, a black-operated firm has to meet and beat the standard racial hazards on both levels.

Looking back, we can readily see a close and significant parallel between the development of Negro business with that of American business in relation to England and sóme of the other European countries. As late as 1850, American business was in about the same relationship to European business as black-operated business in Booker T. Washington's day, was to American business and industry. Americans in the mid-nineteenth century had a low industrial technique, inadequate finance, limited markets, inefficient labor and high unit labor costs. Europe and England had an open market, a well established industry and low production costs. American business of the time was at a tremendous disadvantage.

Over the years the relationship has been exactly reversed. American industry, in its fledgling stage, had to seek protection behind high tariff walls.

This was just as many fledgling black businesses today have sought protection within the walls of the ghetto. Or, failing that, to insist on patronage because of ethnic identity. American business and industry originally worked first the domestic market, just as Negro business at the outset must depend upon race loyalty to build a large enough base for later expansion. But, in both instances, the immediate domestic market improved through education, job opportunity and increased earnings which brought greater needs and, subsequently, larger markets. Today's black market is estimated at in excess of thirty billion dollars and is frequently compared to the market of Canada by way of dramatizing the Negro Market potential.

All alert businessmen are aware of the revolution raging in the market place. They know it is not only dangerous but suicidal not to be aware of this fact. Most now know this is no ordinary revolution. For, it rages in supermarkets, in department stores, appliance outlets, banks, specialty shops and even across the desks of insurance agents. It is expressed in unpredictable purchase patterns, in shifting moods, new desires and ever clearer aspirations.

This assessment of the revolt in the market place is not restricted to businessmen of any particular race or color. But, it is particularly severe for the Negro businessman, who has, until fairly recent days, enjoyed the protection of the ghetto tariff wall and the non-competitive environment of certain neighborhoods.

The Black Revolution has sharpened the distinction and the difference between the Negro entrepreneur and the Jim Crow operator. At North Carolina Mutual we define Negro business as simply American business that is owned or operated by Negroes. In contrast, Jim Crow operations are those operated by blacks or whites that probably cannot survive in a competitive environment outside of the ghetto.

Periodically, in the past few years, we have heard a lot about so-called black capitalism . . . Theodore L. Cross, in his book by the same name, defines it as the "strategy which urges creation of new jobs and profit centers inside ghetto areas. The program also seeks to transfer the ownership of ghetto business from white to black control, at the same time building in the ghetto new banks, insurance companies, production, and service facilities."

While I, personally, believe such a "strategy" or program is not only desirable but necessary . . . the selection of the term—black capitalism—is, I feel, unfortunate. First, capitalism is an economic system in which the means of production and distribution are not only privately owned but are *dependent upon free enterprise.* While it is true that we need more black representation throughout the distribution system, we cannot—by implication—think in terms of economic self-sufficiency.

This is the one point on which virtually all economists agree. Complete economic independence in today's world is impossible. No nation, no state, no city nor any community can produce everything it needs. For, dynamic capitalism depends upon the freedom of the owners to engage in mutually profitable activities. The key word is freedom. Thus, capitalism in its pure sense must be multi-colored. It cannot be black and it dare not be white.

It is my personal feeling that the urgent need for the rejection of the term "black capitalism" *as a misnomer* and the acceptance of the distinctions between the Jim Crow operation and Negro enterprise lies not so much with the consumer as it does with black managers. After all, in our society, men fulfill themselves and validate themselves by free choices with political and economic ballots. This means that every social revolution has immediate impact on the market, increasing the power and the profit of the men who command and service the market. Thus, many consumers are already expressing their approval or disapproval of black-operated businesses. Many managers just have not recognized this daily *vote count against them*. Let's hope they will not discover too late that they have been counted out of the game.

It should be clear by now to almost everyone that the revolution of rising expectations in the black communities throughout America has created a new urban economic environment which challenges our realism as well as our profits.

Some men have tried to ignore the implications of the challenge. They insist it was intended for others. But, what men deny in words cannot always be denied in reality. Especially if their goal is the mastering of reality for the purpose of profit and fulfillment.

Businessmen are primarily interested in mastering reality for the purpose of selling goods and services. We want to know—we must know—what exists, why it exists, and how its existence affects our balance sheets.

After all, we are in the business of reality ... We know that it is socially and economically suicidal to ignore real needs ... real forces ... and real demands in the market place.

It is against this background of realism and enlightened self-interest, as well as in the spirit of basic sound marketing principles, that I approach the subject of black power and Negro enterprise. And, I am pleased to approach it in this setting, for the problems we face today are largely marketing problems which cannot be resolved without the help and support of educational institutions. Or, of the involvement and participation of M.B.A.'s like yourselves.

Students of marketing know that over the past forty years we have grappled with fundamental social changes in the life styles of several segments of the population.

We have learned to cope with the teenaged and retired or "golden-aged" markets. And, now, after a long period of incubation, we are confronted with a total *crisis of* identity in the Negro market. Possibly the most dramatic manifestations of that crisis are embodied, of course, in the black power cry. It is a mere surface manifestation of the stirring of a new consciousness which has profound implications for the American businessman—black or white.

I need not remind you of the public controversy over terms like "black capitalism" or "black power." The subject of both has been discussed at length by scholars, the clergy, educators and politicians. But, too few businessmen have discussed the subject in terms of the impact on their balance sheets.

No little part of the disagreement over the meaning of either term is that each of them, like the word freedom, means different things to different people. But, it should be noted that the overwhelming majority of Afro-Americans define the terms in the positive sense of self-development, self-determination and self-control in the political, cultural and economic spheres. And, I depend upon this middle consensus when I say that in my own personal definition of Black Power, it is neither anti-white, separatist nor violent. In its positive and constructive dimensions black power involves an increased interest in the Negro heritage, a deeper appreciation of the possibilities of the Negro community, and a heightened desire for recognition and attention.

If this middle consensus of the overwhelming majority of Afro-Americans is correct, Black Power falls into the traditional pattern of ethnic pride and ethnic solidarity. Over the years, our country has successfully dealt with German pride, Irish pride, Italian pride and Polish pride. Viewed in the context of the reality of history, there is no reason why we should upset the phenomena of black pride.

The study of Black business embraces an inter-disciplinary area where economics, psychology and the social sciences meet. And, the term "Black Power" or even "Black Capitalism" must be examined in terms of the total, Afro-American experience. When we do this, we find that conceptually these terms are not new at all. As early as 1903, John Merrick, one of the founders of North Carolina Mutual, reminded Negroes that a policy "purchased with North Carolina Mutual bought double protection—life protection and Negro employment." This concept was later developed into a slogan for "double duty dollars." And, in the sense of an expression of a doctrine of self-help, racial solidarity and racial loyalty, this term served as an expression of Afro-American thought which anticipated "Black Capitalism" by nearly seventy years.

Now, when we look at a business from its history, it is necessary to view the managers of that business as *actors in a system*. Thus, *the system* becomes an object of study . . . no less important than the behavior of the entrepreneurs themselves.

From this perspective, the North Carolina Mutual Life Insurance Company was an inevitable development. . . . Not its success. . . . But, its origins, as an expression of a century-old evolution in Afro-American institutions. . . . The legacy of a study strand of Negro thinking, exalted by Booker T. Washington through black counterpart of the U. S. Chamber of Commerce, the National Negro Business League. The ideology espoused by Washington and North Carolina Mutual embodied the evolution of uplift as well as the evolution of enterprise. Thus, when our company began operating seventy-two years ago in April of 1899, its motto, *The Company with a Soul and a Service*, was not just a catchy slogan. . . . It was an expression of the ambivalent heritage of Negro business.

North Carolina folklore argues that the state's race relations, in contrast to the rest of the South, have always been amicable, particularly in Durham. One hears a great deal, even today, about the "Durham Spirit." . . . A feeling of pride among the town fathers . . . black and white. They are quick to recall the highlights of inter-racial cooperation and minimize the harsh points of racial friction. There is even a white version of the origins of North Carolina Mutual which cites the friendliness between the races as the explanation for both the inception and the success of our company. . . . This benign version perpetuated by the city historian of an earlier generation, William K. Boyd, offers a contrived dialogue in his book "The Story of Durham."

Boyd's outline of a conversation between John Merrick, a founder of our company, and Washington Duke, the founder of the American Tobacco Company, has Duke suggesting the *insurance company idea*

to Merrick and offering to loan him money until the company could
get on its feet. (Merrick was Duke's barber and often accompanied
him on trips as his valet.) But, by all standards, Merrick was a very
successful small businessman.... He owned six barber shops and substantial real estate. (Three of the barber shops catered to whites. The
other three to blacks.) Thus, Merrick made an important breakthrough
even in his day. For, it is to be noted, there is no record before or since
his time of a barber shop chain in Durham County. Thus, in spite of
this white mythology, there is no documentary evidence of such loans
or the need for them. To credit Washington Duke with the creation of
North Carolina Mutual is, in the words of Walter Weare in his doctoral
dissertation "Black Business in the New South," like having the "tail
wagging the dog."

In analyzing the origins of North Carolina Mutual it is tempting
to magnify Booker T. Washington's influence. While it is true that both
the founders—John Merrick and Dr. Aaron McDuffie Moore—and the
third president and early builder, Charles Clinton Spaulding, were
personal friends of Washington, and he was a frequent visitor to their
homes. Booker T. Washington made his first Durham visit in 1896. He
addressed a large and excited crowd.

He praised business...decried politics and advised his black
listeners..."when it comes to business, pure and simple, the black
man is put on the same footing with the white man and here it seems
is our great opportunity."

Nearly twenty years later, Charles Clinton Spaulding, North Carolina Mutual's general manager, declared in a speech that an address
by Washington had inspired the company.

Mr. Spaulding said: "Some years ago, Dr. Washington visited Durham and made a stirring address.... Dr. Washington emphasized the
value of business...and during that speech there were some good
seed sown in our town, the result of which can be seen today in the
North Carolina Mutual & Provident Association."

Spaulding's tribute to Washington, delivered from the platform of
the National Negro Business League with Washington present, would
seem in large part to have been a "public salute to the king." For, to
suggest that Merrick and Moore were in 1898 acting out a two-year-old
suggestion from Washington would, once again, deny Merrick's prior
business experience and long-standing interest.

The black myths about the formation of North Carolina Mutual
are more pragmatic. The oral tradition in the black community suggests Merrick was negatively inspired by the bothersome, black beg-
gars that plagued him at his white shops. It was the custom of the
times to "pass the hat" at church, fraternal or other functions for a
collection to cover burial expenses of a large part of the population.

And, when these collections proved inadequate, a platoon of self-
appointed collectors would fan out through the business section. Several old-timers, interviewed by Walter Weare for his book, suggest that
organization of an insurance company was John Merrick's answer to
those who expected the town's richest black man and his white customers to assume the burden of Negro welfare. Why not begin a responsible Negro insurance company and end the harassment, make a profit
and contribute to the uplift of the unfortunate at the same time?

It is a curious paradox that Negro enterprises, like John Merrick's barber shops, thrived in a period of racial hostility. This does not mean that Duke and others did not encourage and advise black businessmen. The later history of the North Carolina Mutual bears this out. The fact remains, however, in the wake of the fusion politics of the late 1890's that this was a tragic period in North Carolina, and in our nation's history. A white supremacy campaign swept the state in the off-year election of 1898. "Red Shirts" rode by the hundreds in an effort to intimidate Negro voters. And, as a climax to the bitter campaign, a race riot engulfed the city of Wilmington located 146 miles from Durham. The white dailies spread hysteria over the state, printing every report of racial unrest and feeding a rumor that if the Republicans won the election, that black brigands would besiege North Carolina and form a Negro Republic.

Durham was not immune from this hysteria. *The Daily Sun,* throughout the summer of 1898, vilified Negroes and Republicans without regard to the most modest of journalistic restraints. Passions became so heated that a black man, rumored to have been living with a white woman, was lynched and his body left hanging along the roadside between Durham and Chapel Hill to serve as a ghastly lesson in white supremacy... a lesson which Durhamites proved they could teach as well as anyone.

The general response of the Negro leadership in Durham, when confronted with the nadir of race relations, was nothing short of sublimation into the world of business and education as a substitute for politics and protest.

John Merrick, in his only known public speech, lamented shortly after the Wilmington race riot that "... whites in the New South had turned their attention to making money, and we have turned ours to holding office and paying debts of gratitude."

Of the six men who joined John Merrick in organizing North Carolina Mutual, five had been active in politics. But, they saw little reason to continue in the face of the disfranchisement campaign.... All redirected their energies into business and education, into separate black institutions.

Now, in all of this overt white hostility, there was a massive, covert attack by the scientific racists and their popularizers. Many of them predicted that blacks were destined to die out within fifty years. These prophets of doom portrayed the Negro as child-like. They pointed to rising mortality rates as proof that blacks could not survive without the parental supervision and care enjoyed by slavery. Negro leaders closed ranks. Out of their response emerged a gospel of progress which occupied a prominent position in Afro-American thought until World War I.

Negro schools conducted essay contests on progress and scheduled forums in which whites and blacks debated the question: "Resolved that the Negro of the South is in worse condition than before the Civil War." Self-adulation abounded in black newspapers. The *New York Age* headlined "Afro-Americans own millions." *The Amsterdam News* featured an article series under the heading: "Not a Child Race." *The Detroit Informer* reviewed Negro progress in two issues and concluded "Business Is King."

Caught between two cultures, Afro-American thought is a composite. Constantly creating its own mood, while assimilating that of the larger society. So it was with the gospel of progress and the gospel of the New South. From this perspective the North Carolina Mutual was inevitable.... Not its success.... But its origins, as an expression of a century-old evolution in Afro-American institutions.

The touchstone of any company's growth and strength is the character of its managerial leadership. Good management is something more than a man interested in "not rocking the boat"... the status quo. Good management has the capacity to be innovative and creative ... without the kind of regimentation that has made employment miserable and an uninspiring chore for so many in today's Society.... A successful business, like today's technology, does *not* just happen. And, once it is born, the management must grow with it and be prepared to perpetuate itself.

There are many things that could be said in tribute to our company's founders, as well as those they surrounded themselves with, to carry on their traditions. Possibly, the greatest tribute I could make is to outline the legacy we have in the largest financial institution ... operated by blacks in the world today. (At least this is what the people in the State Department say in their broadcasts over the Voice of America).... Now all of this looms as an even greater achievement when you think of our home base. The city of Durham has less than 1,000,000 in total population, with less than 30,000 blacks. This is not the setting in which you would feel that such an accomplishment could or should be made.

Someone has said that any business institution is but the lengthening shadow of the man or men who established it. North Carolina Mutual is more than the shadow of Merrick and Moore. It is a reflection of the character of these men. Each member of the North Carolina Mutual management family can be said to have inherited the character of the founders and added to it. As Charles Clinton Spaulding, our third president, pointed out in an article in the company magazine in 1924: "Our fallen leaders made sure the company would have a soul in it ... the best we can do is perpetuate the company in their memory ... and hope each one will catch the spirit."

Even though each of these men, Merrick, Moore and Spaulding, had a distinctly different personality, we can recognize certain elements of character shared by all. They were deeply religious men.... Of high personal integrity.... And dedication. Each of them had an over-riding social consciousness and they were dedicated to a philosophy of self-help and racial solidarity. With North Carolina Mutual Life Insurance Company as a central economic base ... Our management has been most active in the development of eleven other institutions: a local hospital, the public library in the black community, a college, three newspapers, a bank, two other insurance companies and a savings and loan association.

Today, three separate financial institutions ... North Carolina Mutual Life Insurance Company ... Mechanics and Farmers Bank ... and Mutual Savings & Loan Association together have a total of over $150 million in assets as their legacy of leadership.

Our founders, and those who followed them, formed the eleven other institutions from the base at North Carolina Mutual. Thus, this company is at once a symbol of Negro Enterprise itself and a vehicle for group self-improvement beyond the limits of its basic charter. Today, with an annual income of thirty million dollars, a payroll for 1,517 employees in 50 job categories, located in thirteen states and the District of Columbia, serving 856,000 policyholders, we see an institution that is a far cry from a day in 1899. According to company history, it was in that year that a forty dollar death claim created such a crisis that a meeting of the officers was required to raise the money to pay it. Now, claims for many thousand times that amount can be paid without notice or knowledge of our officers.

When I speak of the integrity of our founders, three forceful examples of this concept readily come to mind. In the beginning years the 'North Carolina Mutual and Provident Association" ... as it was then known ... was an "assessment company." (This means that the policyholders could be "assessed" for additional amounts if the funds fell short of required needs.)

It is highly significant that no assessments were ever levied on North Carolina Mutual policyowners. And, although the company was under the supervision of the State of North Carolina, it operated ten years before the firm's books were ever examined by the State Insurance Department. When it did, everything was found to be in order.

Finally, although North Carolina Mutual's executives have dealt in millions of dollars ... there are not now, nor have there ever been any millionaires. ... True, they have lived comfortably. But, the fact remains that they have not sought personal fortunes at the expense of the people they served. Emphasis now and always has been on service ... providing a direct, primary benefit coupled with ancillary, reactive benefits. ... The direct benefit, as suggested in John Merrick's "double duty dollar concept" was insurance protection, and the reactive benefits ... the double duty for the dollar's worth of protection ... has been and is today the 50 categories of employment opportunity as well as the funds for investment that, until comparatively recently, were just not available elsewhere.

Now that you have a fairly comprehensive picture of the setting in which our company was formed, the character of the company's management, the philosophy of their operations ... what about North Carolina Mutual today? How are we tooled up to perform in this age of change? How are we meeting the challenges of change?

In my annual report to policyholders last January I was able to report: "In spite of the recessionary downturn, 1970 marked the best year in twenty years and among the best in North Carolina Mutual's seventy-two year history."

Our assets increased by more than 16 percent to $118 million.

The year's income increased by nearly ten and a half percent—to $30 million.

Increase in insurance in force was just under forty-five percent—to nearly three-fourths of a billion dollars.

All of these operational gains are a direct result of our company's long-range plan for sound and accelerated growth. We have one central, operative objective: "To strive for Optimum Growth by utilizing simultaneous means."

As you M.B.A. students know, profitable growth is a universal business goal. Every management has its own hopes and its own desires for achieving this goal. At the same time, there are only a limited number of ways for a company to grow. From your study here at Harvard, I know, you are familiar with them. But, for the sake of our discussion today, let's review them. They are:

By maintaining a company's *share of the business*

By *joint efforts* with other companies

Through *mergers and acquisitions*

By the development of *new markets*

Through the provision of *additional services*

Our 1970 report reflects our simultaneous use of each of these means of corporate growth. The effective date of our merger with the Great Lakes Mutual Life Insurance Co. was January 1, 1970. Considerable time and attention was devoted to consolidating the Great Lakes organization into our agency and home office operations during the year. By eliminating duplication of effort, reducing operational costs and increasing efficiency in the merged operations, we were able to provide dividends to Great Lakes Mutual policyowners for the *first time in four years.*

Possibly the most dramatic area of growth was in the one hundred and thirty percent increase in group insurance coverage. The big increase in this area was accomplished by the "joint ventures" or reinsurance contracts we effected with some of the nation's largest insurance companies. These group contracts, jointly held, include some of the country's most prestigious firms: Sperry Rand, S. S. Kresge, Michigan Bell and P. Lorillard. (Our group coverage now totals thirty-one groups on an individual company basis.)

In the midst of all this we have carried on a program of social consciousness, social uplift and community leadership. Two brief examples:

A number of black, multi-family developers experienced difficulty in securing funds in their local areas. (Good projects with sound economic feasibility.... But, they encountered hostile investment officers.)

We helped finance Durham's Unity Village at a sacrifice in yield because our management felt we have a stake in the future developments that afford human as well as monetary yields.

Finally, three of our officers were in the forefront of United Fund efforts.... One became the first black president of a United Fund in the South. (The fund reached its goal for the first time in 8 years without resolicitation.) The other became the first black vice president of the state organization. Another, held three important chairmanships of the Recreation Board, Board of Social Services and the Durham Air Pollution Committee. (These are but examples of service our managers render on a continuing basis.)

In each of these efforts, our officers have been able to provide black representation on policy-making levels which not only provided black representation but community leadership for meaningful change.

In 1966, our home office building was dedicated by Vice President Humphrey with national publicity. This marked the first time that a member of the Executive arm of government participated in the dedication of a commercial building in the history of our country.

The fact that we built for our future growth and expansion for the year 2000 provided office space for five and ten year leases. This was one means of bringing the Air Pollution Control Office of our country's Environmental Protection Agency to Durham. Since this government agency has nearly 1,500 employees with 320 of them in our building, not only provided our company with rental revenue but, at the same time, helped the city.

Our home office has been described as the "first, integrated, high rise building owned by a black-operated company and located in the South." Today, we have a building population of 740 . . . 419 whites and 321 blacks. . . . We're outnumbered again . . . but, we "own the building" hence have control.

Now, what does all this mean to you?

What does a black-operated business mean to talented, intelligent, highly-trained and well-qualified black M.B.A.'s in 1971?

How can this have any meaning to a black M.B.A. who seeks employment in a predominantly white business institution?

Well, as a black insurance executive, myself, it has several meanings. When I finished Hampton Institute in 1926, I had fewer choices. I was faced with either starting out with North Carolina Mutual or *not* having employment in business at all. Today, you have several choices. As a black M.B.A. you can either bring your talents, skills and knowledge to a black-operated institution and assure its survival or, you can work in the larger, white institutions and contribute to social advancement. In either case, you are in an enviable position to make a long-standing contribution to your race group. Like a Merrick . . . a Moore . . . or a Spaulding. . . . You can work toward the common goal by bringing into focus the resources of business enterprise for group self-help, self-advancement and development of a greater America. The climate, the attitude and the nature of the times are more in your favor than it was in their day.

Make no mistake about it, the black revolution has awakened the conscience of America. Through your experience and exposure here at Harvard and your work in the Afro-American Student Union you have both a perspective and a sensitivity that is needed in black and white institutions. Through you, both kinds of organizations are fortified for survival . . . for growth . . . for prosperity and progress. In the early days of North Carolina Mutual, many blacks thought the "white man's ice was colder" and many whites were convinced that blacks were inferior. Now, while some whites still hold racist attitudes the fact that blacks have, for the most part, undergone their "crisis of identity," most of us now know that "ice is ice" and act accordingly.

Let me give you one quick example of the type of opportunities open to you. In two cities, Greensboro, North Carolina and Palm Beach, Florida, blacks have secured bank charters and launched a stock sale program. In both states the banking department told the organizers to hold off on stock sales almost without exception, pending the employment of a trained and experienced manager. In addition the twenty-three black-owned banks are in need of trained personnel to replace their aging officers.

It has been a pleasure and a privilege to be able to share some thoughts with you this afternoon. In closing, I would like to urge you to carefully evaluate the opportunities for service in our business culture. No matter whether you elect to seek employment with the predominantly white business institutions, with the established, or with the newly-formed black-operated firms, always remember your opportunity, responsibility and assure your commitment. True, the name of the game in the market place is profit. But, the means of optimum dollar return, in keeping with the statesmanlike business approach of the seventies, is that management must concern itself with long-term, indirect or psychic profit as well as the dollar return. Today's management realizes it must, along with "business as usual" help shape the environment. An integral part of that environment is the black population. Afro-American managers with the kind of training you have attained are in a unique position to project up into the economy. *Best of luck and God bless you.*

The Educational Process

A speech by Milton J. Shapp,[3] *Governor of Pennsylvania, delivered before the Delegates to the 50th Pennsylvania Education Congress, Harrisburg, Pennsylvania, September 23, 1971.*

Dr. Kurtzman, your distinguished predecessors and delegates to the 50th Pennsylvania Education Congress. This is, as others have said, an historic occasion. I welcome the opportunity to share it with you, in whose hands rests the fate of our educational system. But before I plunge into my formal remarks, I want to say a few words about a man who for four years has been the leader of education in Pennsylvania— Dave Kurtzman.

Last December, when I was putting a Cabinet together, I asked Dave Kurtzman to remain in a position to which he had already brought great distinction. It was my judgment that his wisdom and experience were crucial to the hopes of a new, and in many ways "green," administration. My confidence was not misplaced.

I need not rehearse for you the full record of his achievement— school district reorganization carried to a successful conclusion; the school subsidy twice revised; intermediate units, a reality since July 1 of this year; the beginnings of a genuine system of state-supported higher education in Pennsylvania; reorganization of the Department of Education; an elaborate program of pupil testing and evaluation, and many others as well.

---

[3] Reprinted from *Vital Speeches*, November 1, 1971, pp. 49–51. By permission.

It is appropriate therefore, that we pause for a moment, and pay tribute to Pennsylvania's first secretary of education—Dr. David H. Kurtzman—for his many services to the people of this state.

The past decade in Pennsylvania education was characterized by major physical and organizational achievements. In higher education, I think of the vast expansion of the campuses at our three great universities and our state colleges, and the birth of a system of community colleges. In basic education, I think primarily of school district reorganization, in which Pennsylvania pioneered.

But these movements are reaching a climax. In part, they are ending because they have accomplished what they set out to do. In part, they are ending because their very success, while opening new opportunities, has created new problems as well.

The need for building and rebuilding our campuses is no longer there. Some experts are actually predicting a declining campus population in the 1980's. But the bricks and mortar phase is also ending because we cannot afford the mounting costs which further construction would entail.

School reorganization is likewise over. It has reduced more than 2,000 districts into just over 500, with resulting economies of scale and richer curricula than were possible in the smaller districts. But reorganization has also created serious human problems as our young people have been herded into larger and larger schools, run by bureaucracies which seem more and more remote, with less and less opportunity for meaningful human relationships.

The task of the 1970's, as I see it, is to humanize education in Pennsylvania—building on the physical and reorganizational achievements of the 1960's, to make our schools and colleges increasingly lively and responsible places, exercising a maturing influence on the young people who pass through them.

What I want to suggest today is a philosophy, rather than a program—preferences rather than solutions. The philosophy springs from my basic assumption, one which lies behind everything I am trying to do, that governments exist to serve the people, not to serve the needs of the people who run them. And we must never forget that public schools and colleges are part of government.

With this in mind, let me describe some preferences, spelling out in each case exactly what I mean, and why.

We should prefer people to buildings; we should prefer education to schooling; and we should be at least as interested in the educational process as we are in the educational product itself.

Let me explain each of these in turn.

It is no secret that I am unalterably opposed to the construction of unnecessarily large and expensive school buildings, whether in the public school system, or on college campuses. What I think is less well understood—and for this I am perhaps partly to blame—are the grounds for my opposition to educational "Taj Mahals."

My opposition is only partly financial. It is true that we have been building, at all levels of the system, monuments which neither the Commonwealth nor the local school districts could afford. But that is only part of the problem.

A building represents not only a financial commitment, but an educational commitment as well. Only certain kinds of learning can take place in certain kinds of buildings. An elementary school building with fixed classroom walls cannot easily be used for "open classrooms"; and a new medical school building with a heavy investment in laboratories and classrooms may be incompatible with some of the changes that are now being advocated in medical education.

So big buildings are not only expensive—they are quite likely to prove obsolete.

They may even be counter-productive (to use the current jargon) from an educational point of view.

I cannot help being depressed at the prospect of some lively youngsters of sixteen or seventeen learning to cope with life in a high school designed for three thousand pupils. A computer schedules their classes; a squawk box organizes their free time. Who in this system nourishes the human spirit? Surviving three or four years at Bigtown High may be good practice for surviving a lifetime in the clutches of General Motors, or the multiversity, or even the Commonwealth of Pennsylvania; but is survival the goal?

What I'm arguing is an approach to education which emphasizes people over buildings; which says, let's spend as little of the available revenue as possible on bricks and mortar, and as much as possible on the people who are the real secret of success. After all, people can learn in a tent and can fail to learn in a palace.

Let me now turn to my expressed preference for education over schooling.

Education is whatever prepares the mind, the spirit and the body for a life of competence and joy. Education can, and does take place in homes, on streets and playgrounds and at work; it also takes place —sometimes—in schools. Schooling on the other hand is what takes place only within the walls of a school.

It is probably true that, "the more education, the better"; it is clearly not true that, "the more schooling, the better."

Nearly every technical and scientific development of the past fifty years has had the effect of increasing the length of schooling—with dubious results for education. This trend must be reversed.

The first reason is a moral one. As schooling becomes the key to positions of power and influence, access to these positions is necessarily limited to those who can afford to spend between 15 and 25 years in school. In spite of our best efforts to foster equality of educational opportunity, there will always be a bias, in such a system, in favor of young people from families with wealth and education. Thus, a heavily "schooled" society is always to some degree undemocratic.

Moreover, the demand for long and arduous schooling tends to create unhealthy social divisions. If you believe "the more schooling, the better," then you can easily be led to believe that people with schooling are somehow superior to those who are unschooled. From this follows the contempt for manual labor which is one of the ugliest features of an affluent society.

A long drawn-out period of schooling is also psychologically dangerous. Our graduate schools today are full of young people in their late twenties, who reached biological maturity ten years ago—but who are not yet, in the quaint language of the common law, fully "emancipated." This is damaging, both to their own self-esteem, and to the regard in which they are held by others; and surely accounts for the destructiveness of some campus activity in recent years.

Finally, a long drawn-out period of schooling is something we can't afford. It already costs an average of $750 annually to educate a child in the public schools. The real cost of educating someone at the undergraduate level runs from $2,000 to $5,000 a year. And it may well cost $25,000 per person per year to train a pediatrician or a psychiatrist. Most of this money has to come from the taxpayers. And they are rebelling.

For all these reasons, then, we must look for ways of reducing the demands of schooling—but not, let me remind you, the demands of education. Here are some suggestions:

1. We ought to begin by making schooling unnecessary for many purposes. Our society is full of requirements—for degrees, diplomas, certificates—blocking entrance to jobs and education. Some of these requirements are reasonable; others are not. Many have been invented for the specific purpose of limiting entry into a particular trade or profession. It ought to be a first order of business to root out every such requirement which is not strictly necessary—and the world of education, where such requirements abound, is a good place to begin.

2. We ought to shorten school wherever possible. With that goal in mind, we ought to explore the year-round school; early graduation; early admission; the three-year college; the combination of liberal arts and professional training; and every other device that promises to shorten the period of time which young people spend without experiencing the full responsibility of adult life.

3. We should do everything in our power to break down the barriers, both physical and psychological, between school and the real world. This will not only decrease the adverse effects of a prolonged period of schooling; it will also turn some schooling into education. The best education unites theory and practice. The more real experiences we can make available to our young people—through part-time employment, internships and a wide variety of other devices—the better the "grist" which they will bring to the academic "mill."

4. Finally, we ought not to forget that education—as opposed to schooling—is something which goes on all during our lives. What we need is a system of schools which is more adapted to that fact than our present one, which tends to assume that everyone under 21 is filled with a lust for learning, and everyone over 21 is dead from the neck up.

So much for my reasons for preferring education to schooling, and the outline of a strategy for implementing that preference.

My third preference is for talking and thinking about the educational process rather than the educational product. Or, to put the matter somewhat differently, *how* children learn is just as important as *what* they learn.

You may think this strange, in view of my background as businessman and engineer; and it certainly isn't a popular view, at a time when everybody is talking about educational "productivity."

But it's precisely my background and training which tells me that there are important—indeed, crucial—differences between the manufacture of TV cable and the "manufacture," if you will, of college graduates. To cite only one of them: the cable doesn't care what you do to

it, and what matters is only that it have the necessary strength and con-
ductivity; but the student has strong feelings about the whole process,
feelings which cannot be ignored.

Knowledge and expertise—the ability to focus knowledge on a particular problem—are important in a society based on technology.

But if we look at education simply as the business of "manufacturing" so many doctors and lawyers, so many teachers and accountants,
so many carpenters and plumbers—and much of the current talk about
"productivity" is in these terms—we are going to make our schools
even less human institutions than they are now.

What are the consequences of agreeing, as I hope you do, that the
process is at least as important as the *product?*

One consequence is to minimize the importance of formal curricu-
lar requirements. Certain skills can't be dispensed with. But beyond
the ability to communicate with words, and to reckon with numbers,
it's not easy to label any body of knowledge as "indispensable."
Shouldn't we therefore allow our schools and colleges a wide latitude
so that teachers and students can explore together what really interests
them?

A related consequence has to do with what I will call the need for
a "democracy of competence." What students need upon graduation is
not the possession of large chunks of knowledge, which will be largely
obsolete by the time they are thirty anyway, but certain qualities—self-
confidence, integrity, the ability to work with others and the ability to
analyze problems, and these qualities can be developed in a wide variety of ways.

For example, if athletics are an important part of education—and I
firmly believe that they are—then we should develop physical education
programs which aim at two things: the nurture of physical health and
vigor on the one hand, and the development of confidence through competence on the other.

Judged by these standards, our present athletic programs fall short
in several ways. For one thing, they tend to emphasize the needs and
interests of men over those of women. And they focus on the athleti-
cally talented at the expense of the uncoordinated. We all rejoice that
Penn State is ranked among the top ten football teams in the country;
but we ought to be equally concerned about the health and self-confi-
dence of the youngster who may never get beyond tenth grade.

Another consequence of emphasizing process rather than product
is that the internal procedures of the school or college become crucial.
The student council faces a decision: whether to allocate funds to one
activity or another. There is usually no *right* decision; the key question is, by what process is it reached? By reasoned discourse among the
students? Or heavy-handed hints from dean or principal about "the
best interests of the school?"

I am, as you know, in the process of putting students on the boards
of trustees of our state colleges and universities. I am under no illusion
that their presence will result in better decisions; my hope is simply
that the legitimacy of those decisions will be more widely accepted.

There is more to say—but time is running out, and so, perhaps, is
your patience.

I have stuck to principles, rather than programs, in the hopes of il-
luminating some of the assumptions which will govern educational

policy in a Shapp Administration. Some of you will disagree with all or part of what I have said. I hope you will articulate those disagreements, so that we may have a lively discussion of the principles which ought to guide the development of our educational system.

If you are in fundamental agreement—and I hope many of you are —you must address yourselves to the tough questions involved in basing particular programs and policies on these principles.

The decade ahead will not be an easy one for the men and women who aspire to lead our schools and colleges, our Board of Education and the Department itself. You know that already. But it can be an exciting one. We must create and sustain schools and colleges in which young people can grow to maturity, prepared, not just to take their places in the community, but to work to change that community in accordance with some conception of the common good. That will require vision rather than expertise.

What Did You Say?

A speech by William A. Nail,[4] *Director, Public Relations, Zenith Radio Corporation, delivered to the Seventh Indiana University Broadcasting Institute, Bloomington, Indiana, July 17, 1971.*

I am very happy to be here, and it was very *flattering* of Prof. Bannerman to invite me to visit with you for a few minutes today at your Institute banquet, and share some thoughts about broadcasting.

Although I was pleased by the invitation, I asked Professor Bannerman if he had thought of inviting Dr. Frank Stanton, Chairman of CBS. He told me he had asked but Frank Stanton was occupied with some business with the Congress and "Selling of the Pentagon" documentary, and Dr. Stanton declined.

Well, I said, if Dr. Stanton is tied up, what about Nicholas Johnson, the outstanding young FCC Commissioner, who has a great deal to say to this new "electronic generation." He really turns young people on.

Prof. Bannerman said that he agreed that Nick Johnson does turn young people on, he had *tried* to get Nick Johnson to come down to speak, but Nick Johnson was on a hiking tour in Northern Canada and couldn't get back.

And Nick Johnson had declined.

Being modest—and believe me, I have a great deal to be modest about—I still felt that there must be somebody else who would fill the bill better than I could.

I asked Prof. Bannerman if he had thought of inviting the most celebrated media personality of recent weeks, Dr. Daniel Ellsberg who got the *New York Times* interested in the Pentagon papers. He said he had thought about it but that Dr. Ellsberg had a prior commitment on the Dick Cavett Show and then had to keep some dates with his lawyers. Dr. Ellsberg couldn't spare the time, and he *declined.*

---

[4] Reprinted from *Vital Speeches*, September 15, 1971, pp. 723–726. By permission.

Then—although I was less flattered—I got to thinking perhaps I did have *some* qualifications for talking about communications. Actually, I had *several* qualifications. And since these other three gentlemen were otherwise engaged, perhaps you *would* consider listening to me after all, since Prof. Bannerman had extended the invitation to come to Indiana.

Probably my *best* qualification is two sons on your side of the generation gap—one preparing to enter Williams College this fall, and another just going into his sophomore year at Oak Park–River Forest High School. We *do* communicate without a translator—although it is difficult at times. But we have kept the gap from becoming a *chasm*.

Another qualification that comes to mind is the fact that I have a four-year-old Collie dog named Angus I can communicate with.

When I say "sit" he usually sits. And when I say "ball" he usually can find a tennis ball somewhere in the house. He will chase a stick when I throw it. Sometimes he will bring me the paper. He does bark back sometimes. But despite the garbling of the messages I give him, I haven't been bitten yet.

Maybe a *third qualification* is the fact that as a seventeen-year-old in Central Texas, a few years back, I was asked by a girl friend one day if I wanted to fill in on a radio program they were producing. This was during a summer institute, by the way, for high school seniors and recent graduates. I said, Yes, I had done some speech work and debate and what we used to call 'declamation'—in high school.

She said, Well, I didn't even have to talk, all I had to do was read from a script.

I had four lines on the show—*LIVE*. My four lines were part of a "special" for the Fourth of July on a 250-watt station called W-A-C-O in Waco, Texas. It wasn't transcribed or taped. Did you ever think a microphone—a LIVE MIKE—looked like a fire-breathing monster?

Each of my four lines was for a *different* character, and—that brings me to my real qualification to be here. The one thing that qualifies me more to stand up here and talk about communications today was the fact that I portrayed, in one line, Henry Luce, the founder of the *Time–Life–Fortune–Sports Illustrated* empire. They told me I was "best" with my one line for Luce; and worst in my portrayal of Heywood Broun.

That just about sums up my *major* qualifications. While they are a little thin, it does outline a period of the fairly recent past in broadcasting, with which I have been identified since 1943.

While I know it's not very popular, or smart, to say today that things haven't changed very much since WACO, 1460 on your dial, 250 powerful watts, in 1943—the fact of the matter is that the real objective in getting your ideas across *hasn't changed* much—except for the hardware—microphones, cameras, and all the paraphernalia that is necessary to broadcast or somehow or another get a message from your brain to another person's brain.

The one thing that hasn't really. changed is the condition of the man or woman on the *receiving end*. What I mean by this is summed up by the title of these remarks, *"What Did You Say?"*

It was a much simpler world in 1943 and 1953, and 1963, than it is today. To those of us who have been part of communications in this period and have sort of grown up (*and begun to grow old with it*) it doesn't seem nearly as complicated as it really is. Most of us can almost say the same thing my old friend Jules Herbuveaux, a former vice president of NBC, says when somebody asks him—"Where *were* you when broadcasting was begun?" We can almost say with Jules, "Well, I was standing there when it was invented." Of course, Jules *was* standing there—I wasn't, and Professor Bannerman wasn't, but we have been at this trade long enough to feel like we were. (*Maybe that's one of the troubles with us.*)

But if you will lend me your credibility for a few more minutes, I will try to explain what I mean by my earlier remark—That . . . despite all of the additional electronics and hardware, the millions of television and radio sets, thousands of newspapers and radio stations, millions of records, record players, tape machines—plus all the complex, complicated gear that it takes to produce programs—the thing that has changed the *least* in the business of getting our ideas across to another person—whether it's one person or hundreds of millions—*the thing that has changed the least is on the receiving end.*

No communication ever takes place without two things happening. Somebody has to say something and somebody has to hear it, or see it, and understand it—and *respond.* Broadcasting alone is not communication.

A transmitter is no good without a receiver. The TV receiver or radio receiver is no good without the listener—and is still no good unless the listener turns it on. Even if he turns the machine on, the whole complex chain is still no good unless the viewer listens to the sound, watches the picture, *understands what he is seeing or hearing,* and *responds.*

"What Did You Say?"

Let's take a look at two or three examples from the history of communications.

First, let's go back several million years. When the first caveman got up off his all-fours, cupped his hand to his mouth and yelled to his partner down the trail that there was a lion on the cliff that was ready to jump down and kill him, *the message was sent.*

If his partner under the cliff, in danger of being eaten up by the lion, cupped his hand behind his ear and picked up the message, *and ran, effective* communication took place.

It wasn't mass communication, but if there were three people under the cliff, in danger of being eaten by the lion, and the three of them cupped their hands behind their ears, got the message and *ran*— then *mass communication* was born.

I don't know that it happened exactly that way, but it could have. The *cupped hand behind the ear is the twin of the cupped hand around the mouth.* You cup your hand around your mouth to make your voice travel farther. You cup your hand around your ear to pick up sounds in the distance more clearly, or if you are hard of hearing, to make up for poor hearing.

Now, skip a few million years to the North American continent, find a group of Indians on a hill. They want to tell a group of friendly Indians on a hill some miles away that the buffalo are headed in their direction, and that they should get together and head them off at the pass.

It was too far for the cupped hand to help the voice carry that far, but they did have a fire that could make smoke and a blanket that could do things with that smoke—*new technology*.

The Indians on the *far* hill *saw* the puffs of smoke; they *could read* the puffs of smoke; they *understood* them; and they *got* on their horses. They met the smoke-signal-sending Indians, and *headed the buffalo off at the pass*. The results of that communication were meat for the winter, buffalo robes—a successful hunt.

Let's jump now to more modern times—you may recall an old movie on TV in recent years called "Lloyds of London." A man on one side of the channel peers through a telescope and sees on the blades of a windmill across the channel, lighted letters going around which spell out a message in abbreviated form. This was the beginning of what is now a "wire service" for news, which now uses high speed teletype machines. The guy on our side of the English Channel, looking through a telescope, had to *see* those letters and had to *understand* what they meant and get back to the people of Lloyds of London and *warn them* to protect investment in insurance worth millions and millions of dollars.

What would have happened in this story, which has been played over and over again on the late show, if the guy on our side of the English Channel had turned the telescope around and looked through the wrong end.

The windmill sending the message is too far away to hear the question *"What did you say?"* The same thing is true for the smoke-signal-sending Indians on one mountain. The same is true of our early caveman friend with the cupped hand shouting to his friend in danger of being eaten by a lion.

Each of these communicators, or, if you will, early broadcasters, had the same problem: they were sending the message—but *was anybody looking or listening?* If they were looking and listening, did they understand? *Did they really hear, understand and respond?*

From the windmill communicating to the man with the telescope in the late 18th century, very little happened in communications, except pony express and railroad mail delivery, until the invention of the telegraph. Sending messages by dots and dashes over wires would eventually span this continent and ultimately, the world. This was followed by the telephone (although with Ma Bell's strike situation across the country, we may all go back to windmills, telescopes, smoke signals and cupped hands!)

On the heels of the telephone a number of scientists around the world, culminating with Marconi, were trying to send these dots and dashes through the air. They finally succeeded, and began this century's first communications revolution. Everything that has happened in radio and television has flowed from that brief message that Marconi tapped on his machine and somebody picked up a short distance away.

What was first the "toy" of high school students, whose parents were convinced that it was only a "fad," has now become a multi-billion dollar industry and changed the course of history. Today, we not only have dots and dashes, but voices are picked up out of the air, pictures can be sent all the way around the world via satellite, and we can watch a man *planting the American flag on the moon*, in *real* time.

I wonder if the man on the receiving end of that first message of Marconi's had to tap back, *"What did you say?"* All of us know from our own experience, when the American Astronauts first stepped on the moon—if we were watching our television receivers or listening to our radios—nobody had to ask the question, *"What did you say?"*

John F. Kennedy, in his inaugural address said, "Ask not what your country can do for you, ask what you can do for your country." Those listening to the radio or watching television didn't have to ask the question, *"What did you say?"*

When Harry Truman said the presidency *means* the "Buck stops here"—nobody asked "What did you say?"

But today, when a student is sitting in a class and a distinguished professor of some complex subject lectures, very often every man and woman in the class quickly has the question in their minds *"What did you say?"*

Stockholders receiving annual reports from corporations will read the message from the president about what's gone on during the past year and when they're finished, have the question, *"What did you say?"*

From my experience as a teacher a number of years ago, I often would read an examination paper or listen to a speech in class and my first question would be, *"What did you say?"*

In these complex and perilous times, very often we *don't have the time or the means* to get the message the *second time.* We don't have the means or the time to ask the question, *"What did you say?"* If we want to get a message from one person to another *it has to come through clear the first time.*

That is the reason I feel certain in my judgment that things haven't changed very much since that hot Fourth of July in 1943 in Waco, Texas when we did that Fourth of July documentary on the 250-watt radio station.

The problem then was the same one we all have today. I don't know how we got across that hot 4th, but we were trying to get a message across about the meaning of independence and freedom. We were in a studio; our listeners were scattered across hundreds of miles. We had no way of hearing their question, *"What did you say?"*

As director of public relations of a large corporation, I approve a press release, an annual report, a report to stockholders. We try to state facts about our industry or company to radio, TV or the press. My basic problem is still the same as it was on that hot Fourth of July —to get the message across so the guy on the receiving end doesn't have to ask *"What did you say?"*

Unfortunately, we don't always succeed. I suppose you don't either. But that's the reason you are here this summer at the Broadcasting Institute here on the beautiful Indiana University campus.

The role of the broadcaster, the communicator, the advertising copy writer, the public relations man, the public speaker, the guy who writes the business letter, the guy who writes the love letter, the guy who writes the letter home—is to get ideas and information across simply, in an easy to understand and attractive way. Elizabeth Barrett Browning, in one of her Sonnets from the Portuguese, "How Do I Love Thee" said more in a very few lines about love than many of us could say in our broken prose if we filled up as many pages as are in a *Sears Roebuck catalog.*

What it all boils down to is this: Anybody who has anything to say in words or in pictures to be transmitted from one mind to another—regardless of all the modern electronic paraphernalia and hard work you go through to reach that reader, viewer or listener—has to ask *himself* the question *"What did you say?" before* he begins to transmit. The only way we can be sure that our ideas achieve their objective is to be *clear* about what we want to say and *who* we are trying to reach. That means *understanding* the guy on the *other* end, whether you are using the cupped hand, the television receiver, or the windmill.

There's really not so much of a generation gap today—there is a *listening and understanding gap*—whether it's between generations, races, countries, political parties, manufacturers, consumers or the government.

Millions of people today are *hearing* messages and asking *"What did you say?"* The principal reason so many people are asking that simple question is that the people who are doing the writing, the talking, the speaking, the producing, the broadcasting, the printing, the publishing should be doing more *listening* themselves—should become more sensitive, should learn more about the people they are trying to reach, before they cup their hands around their mouth and transmit the message or turn on the television camera and start broadcasting.

I have never really understood Marshall McLuhan—and doubt he understands himself—when he says, "The medium is the message," but I think I know what he means. Whether the medium is the message or not, the thing that those of us on its side of the camera, the microphone or the printing press have to understand is the *simple fact* that there is a medium *and* a message. And after all, whether the medium becomes part of the message or the message is transmitted by the medium—the *message* is the *important* thing.

That means that paragraphs, commas, semicolons, periods and colons are still important. It means that an understanding of the language is still important. Clear speech is still important. The ability to write clearly is still important. To get an understanding of ideas and the facts is important. Without the ability to speak clearly, a broadcaster—regardless of the kind of electronic paraphernalia he has to work with—isn't a broadcaster unless somebody *listens* to him, *understands* and *responds*.

Today's complex and expensive commercial television messages that cost 40 or 50 thousand dollars a minute to produce, and 60 to 100 thousand dollars to telecast on a national network, have the same objective as the legendary first radio commercial broadcast in New York in the early '20's.

As you know, broadcasting started as a service by manufacturers to sell radio receivers. Then someone got the bright idea that if people did listen and understand, they would *respond*. The story that Johny Johnstone, an early radio newsman, told me about the first radio commercial in New York was that there was a Long Island real estate man who had an interesting development of new houses. But nobody was coming out to see them, and nobody was *buying* the houses. He got a friend of his who was working on WEAF in New York to broadcast several times that on the *following Sunday* there would be *watermelons hidden* in many of the houses in this housing development. The prospective customers who found them would get the watermelons *free.* As it turned out, according to Johnstone, the real estate man got rid of a good many watermelons—and they also sold some houses.

"What did you say?"

There are a vast number of messages competing for our attention— newspapers, magazines, signboards, radio and television—limiting the messages to those that are intended for mass audiences.

If we have an ambition to get a message across to a mass audience we must not only *understand* but absolutely *feel* in our *bones* and our *viscera* that this so-called "mass audience" is made up of individuals— people like you and me. We are talking to *one person at a time.*

In talking to that one person at a time, our messages—whether they are sales messages, information, education or entertainment— must keep the *individual,* his needs, his wants, and his *interests* foremost when we are putting together that message—whether it is pictures, sound or print.

If I'm trying to sell television receivers, I not only want them to remember the name "Zenith," I want that person to *believe* my messages after he has used the set so that when he does buy that receiver and installs it in his home its performance is as high in quality, is as reliable and easy to service as my original sales message said that it was.

If, in selling the television receiver, or the automobile, the washer, the dryer, the box of cereal, we say things about the product that the potential customer does not understand, or make claims for that product that it doesn't live up to, then we have contributed to what has now become a national cliché—a *credibility* gap.

Our customers, with good reason will say, sarcastically, *"What did you say?"*

It is easy to let your enthusiasm run away with you if you are sold on your company's product, but it's not as easy to put that message into a form that makes claims that are *thoroughly backed up,* so that when the television receiver is switched on, the customer can say, "Yes, it's as good as they said it was."

"What did you say?"

There are all kinds of messages coming to us from many different sources. There are messages coming from young people. Messages from old people. Messages from white people, black people, and many of the people that all of us are trying to talk to and communicate with are saying, *"What did you say?"*

There is a lot of talk about our environment and a lot of people are asking, *"What did you say?"*

People talking about civil rights, and a lot of other people are listening and asking, *"What did you say?"*

There are other people buying products that disappoint them and they are writing the manufacturer or their congressmen and asking, *"What did you say?"*

To have *too many people* ask that question when we are trying to communicate with them *means we didn't ask the question, "What did you say?" first before* we cupped the hand or sent the smoke signal. We need to *listen*—try to put ourselves on the *receiving end* of the message, *before* we try to transmit to that listener, viewer or reader.

A lot of people are saying a lot of things about a lot of subjects.

Dr. Charles Keller, retired director of the John Hay Fellows program and retired professor of history at Williams College, goes around the country talking with teachers and young people in high schools. He has devoted the last years of his career in *education* to *listening* and *sharing* experiences with others—to try to demonstrate what you *learn*, when you *listen* to others.

Dr. Keller listens continually to young people and their ideas. In a talk that he made to a meeting of librarians last year, he used a poem by a high school student that he had met in Portland, Oregon. I would like to share with you a part of this poem, which illustrates in a way the *answer* to the question—*"What did you say?"*

I found beer cans floating under dead fish,
and a forest converted to a chemical factory—
an image on the boob-tube
informed me of '100 percent chance precipitation'
and spoiled the surprise.
I looked for the moon and found Apollo 8, Telstar, Halley's Comet
    and a Boeing 707.
Beauty is neither electronic nor man-made.
Stars are more silver than aluminum, and
wax fruit are blasphemous. Beauty is
that which is natural, original, and unexpected.
I am waiting for the day when computers
program themselves,
and *leave us to ourselves*, and
I am watching for the day that
the last blade of grass is removed
to make room for a missile factory.
I am waiting for a machine that can
fall in love, and
I am watching for an IBM card for God.

For a postscript, I'd like to borrow another idea from Dr. Keller ... in seeking out an answer to this question—"What Did You Say?"

He believes that to be able to answer that question before you begin talking, or broadcasting will be easier if we concentrate on an "Inner Space" program—that is a program concerned with our own inner resources—To quote Dr. Keller—"a feeling of identification with the past and with one's neighbors; an acquaintance with the decisions people have made in the past and are making now; a knowledge of the basis on which decisions have been and are being made; the development of the attributes of judgment, sensitivity, taste, compassion, wisdom, imagination, wonder, and delight ... a variety of interests ... and a desire to be creative ..."

"What did you say?"

Index